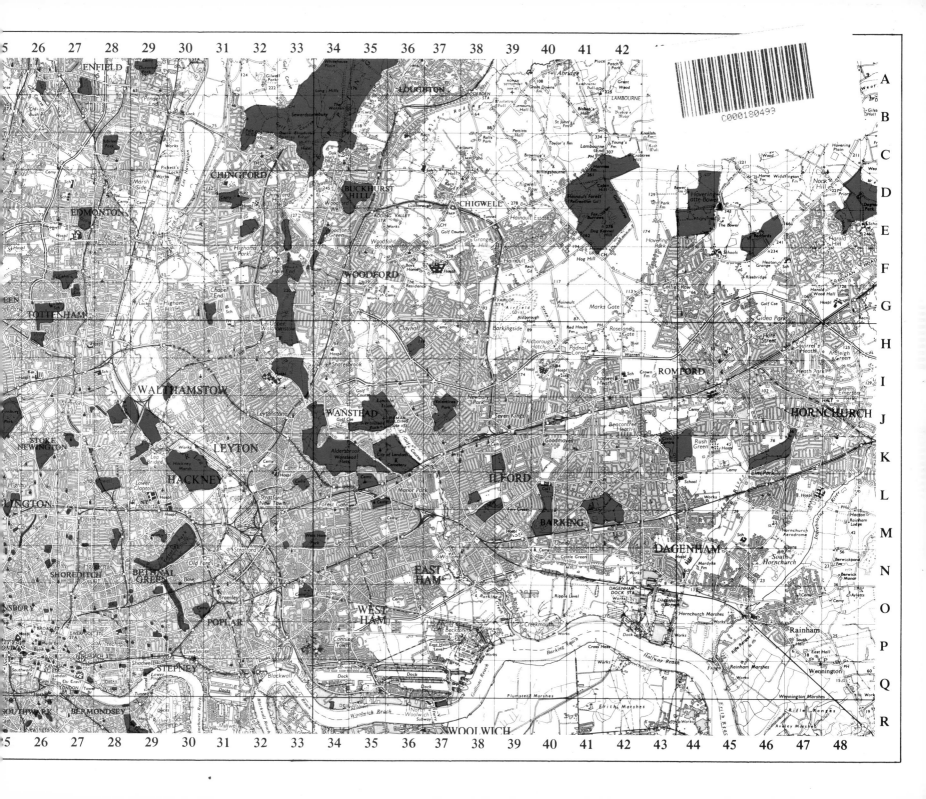

THE OPEN SPACES OF LONDON

THE OPEN SPACES OF LONDON

ALEC FORSHAW · THEO BERGSTRÖM

ALLISON & BUSBY
LONDON NEW YORK

First published in Great Britain 1986 by
Allison and Busby Limited
6a Noel Street, London W1V 3RB
and distributed in the USA by
Schocken Books Inc.
62 Cooper Square, New York 10003

British Library Cataloguing in Publication Data

Forshaw, Alec
    The open spaces of London.
    1. London (England)—Description—1981-
    —Guide-books
    I. Title   II. Bergström, Theo
    914.21'04858   DA679

    ISBN 0-85031-662-6

Book design: John Latimer Smith

Set in 10/11pt Palatino by
All Print Services
Printed and bound in Great Britain by
Jolly & Barber Ltd, Rugby.

Foreword

Since this book was written the Greater London Council has been abolished. The ownership and management of the forty-one GLC parks have been handed on to the individual control of the separate London boroughs, even though this means dividing some parks between more than one authority. It remains to be seen whether the different boroughs will be capable of showing the consistent care and concern for the recreational needs of the whole of London.

CONTENTS

INTRODUCTION AND HISTORY

CHAPTER ONE

PAGE 9

CHAPTER TWO

HEATHS, COMMONS AND WOODS

PAGE 15

CHAPTER THREE

THE ROYAL PARKS

PAGE 43

CHAPTER FOUR

MUNICIPAL PARKS

PAGE 67

This book is intended as an introduction to the full variety of London's open spaces, their history and their character today. Whatever your needs — whether it's a day out for the kids, a walk for the dog, a bash with a bat and ball, a sunny spot to munch a sandwich or a secluded seat to rest weary legs and thoughts — there is somewhere near you in London. Open spaces offer to young and old freedom for the spirit and enrichment of the memory.

> Such, such were the joys
> When we all, girls and boys,
> In our youth-time were seen
> On the Echoing Green.
> WILLIAM BLAKE

CHAPTER 1
Introduction and History

London's open spaces are one of its finest and most appreciated assets. Of all the world's capital cities none can rival London for the number or variety of its outdoor pleasures and green spaces. New York has Central Park, Paris has the Bois de Boulogne, in themselves larger than almost any park London can offer, and those New Yorkers or Parisians who live nearby are lucky indeed. Yet Londoners are more fortunate, for they are never far from a park or garden.

Even in the heart of the City, nestling among huge office blocks and financial institutions, there are dozens of small sheltered gardens, often relics of medieval churchyards. In London's West End the Georgian property speculators built their grand houses around elegant garden squares. In the poorer residential districts Victorian philanthropists and twentieth-century local authorities provided municipal parks for public recreation.

The vagaries of English law ensured that ancient heaths and common lands, where villagers once grazed cattle remote from London, were not engulfed by the urban sprawl of the nineteenth century. Throughout the suburbs old village greens escaped the builder's spade, protected by feudal rights and customs. The extraordinary and continuous power of the monarchy preserved the large royal hunting parks near their palaces, long after they were used for hunting. Today Hyde Park, Green Park and St James's Park form a glorious green swathe through central London from Kensington Palace to Parliament Square and Westminster Bridge.

Many of the private mansions and estates of London's wealthiest aristocrats and businessmen from Tudor to Victorian times have not only survived, miraculously, but are now open to the public. Chiswick, Kenwood and Osterley rank among the nation's most precious treasures. Nor do the delights of modern London end with the famous royal parks and stately homes. Hundreds of lesser-known squares, small community gardens, hidden churchyards, sequestered courts and forgotten cemeteries offer unex-pected tranquillity in the busiest areas and unsuspected beauty in the drabbest.

The bare facts and figures of London's open space are remarkable in themselves. Greater London, the area made up by the thirty-two London boroughs, contains 42,494 acres of public open space, equal to sixty-six square miles. This is spread among over a thousand different parks and gardens, from the broad vistas of Richmond Park to tiny pocket-handkerchiefs. Lumped together they would form a block eight miles square. In addition there are 3,000 acres of cemeteries. Twelve per cent of the total area of Greater London is open space, not including the river.

Ownership and maintenance is a complex business, divided among numerous separate authorities and bodies. The government, through the Department of the Environment, controls the royal parks, some 6,000 acres. Next largest is the Greater London Council, who own 5,500 acres within London and a further 12,600 outside in the Green Belt. Within their forty-one parks the GLC provide a staggering range of facilities — two cycle tracks, four athletics tracks, sixteen fishing lakes, forty-one cricket pitches, 116 tennis courts and 291 football pitches, even a ski slope. Running costs are currently £14 million per annum. In addition the GLC owns and manages eight piers on the river from Greenwich to Kew which handle four million passengers each year on boat trips.

Surprisingly the City Corporation owns 3,000 acres of open space in London and 7,000 acres altogether, mainly in Epping Forest. This is ten times as big as the City itself! The London boroughs are responsible for the majority of the rest but the National Trust, Church Commissioners and National Playing Fields and Allotments Association take care of a significant number. Individual private estates and organizations such as the Wimbledon Common Conservators complete the mosaic, a typically English muddle of history and tradition.

The English love parks more than any book about them. As Voltaire noted: "That is well said, but we must cultivate our garden." This peculiarly nationalistic horticultural obsession goes back a long way. In literature the garden has been revered as a paradigm of beauty and perfection. "There is a garden in her face, where roses and white lilies grow," mused Thomas Campion. "A garden is a lovesome thing, the purest of human pleasures," wrote Francis

Bacon. The roots, of course, are biblical: "God the first garden made, and the first city Cain" (Abraham Cowley). Here was a religious justification for urban parks and garden suburbs, if it was needed.

Recreation and sport is an even older human passion than the adoration of lilies and roses. Roman Londonium almost certainly possessed an amphitheatre and hippodrome for chariot racing, although their specific sites are unknown. The Romans were not keen on ball games but the average citizen who might be content with a spectator's seat at the gladiator fights probably also enjoyed field sports in the forests and woods outside Londinium or fishing for salmon in the Thames.

Hunting of wild boar and deer continued to be a popular pursuit in Saxon and early medieval times. The low-lying land beside the river was often rather too marshy or swampy but the higher ground further afield afforded excellent terrain for killing game. Most of what is now north London was covered until the Norman conquest by the forest of Middlesex, described by William Fitzstephen, clerk to Thomas à Becket, as "a great forest with wooded glades and lairs of wild beasts, deer both red and fallow, wild bulls and boars". St John's Wood, as its name implies, belonged to the Knights of St John. The district we call Soho today, in the heart of modern London, was named after the hunting cry, "so-ho". Beyond the River Lea the dense forest of Waltham stretched eastwards to merge with the forest of Essex.

Within the thick greenwoods of Middlesex, Essex and Kent tiny hamlets evolved from clearings and brakes — Hamestede, Cambrewelle, Ilefort and Enefelde. According to the Domesday Book, large tracts of forest had become apportioned to the manors of these villages for use as common land. The lord of the manor might be a nobleman, bishop or abbot but the serf had rights of estovers (collecting timber and firewood), pannage (grazing pigs), turvery (cutting turf and peat) and piscary (fishing) on the common. Only in the royal hunting forests such as Enfield Chase and Greenwich Park was the common man disbarred, on pain of death.

Gradually the forest margins were pushed back for agriculture or reduced by excessive lumbering and grazing to rough and barren heathlands. Often their leached soils and impoverished vegetation prohibited arable farming and ensured that they remained as commons. It took Henry VIII to reverse this trend by seizing monastic lands in the Dissolution and designating new royal hunting parks close to his London palaces (see Chapter 3).

Today Epping Forest and perhaps the spinneys of Highgate Woods and Holland Park are the only remnants of the vast impenetrable forest which once flourished on the clays and alluviums of the London basin. Theydon Bois is one of the few surviving woodland villages still with the feel of a forest clearing. Gone are the timbered glades which supplied the charcoal burners of Collier's Wood, and the mighty oaks which hemmed in Wood Green. The forest of Middlesex has disappeared, as has the administrative entity. But for the County Cricket team, the Boat Race and anachronistic postal addresses, Middlesex is virtually a forgotten name; even the MCC stands for Marylebone, not Middlesex.

Medieval Londoners revelled in a wide variety of sports and outdoor pleasures as well as hunting and hawking. Fitzstephen pictures London as "a merry and pleasant place", with frequent holidays for religious festivals. Immediately outside the strait-jacket of the City walls, rebuilt but not expanded since Roman days, Londoners flocked to favoured patches of flat dry ground to amuse themselves, away from the labyrinth of narrow alleys and cramped houses within the City. The smooth field beyond Newgate, now known as Smithfield, was popular for jousting, tournaments, miracle plays and all the fun of Bartholomew Fair. To the north, outside Cripplegate and Bishopsgate the uncultivated wasteland called The Moor attracted less organized pastimes.

Fitzstephen records how on Shrove Tuesday "after dinner all the youths go into the fields to play at ball, some in Hand-Ball, Foot-Ball, Bandy-Ball and in Cambuck and Cockfighting; and some also apply themselves to other dishonest games, less profitable and useful, whereby the said Realm is likely in a short time to become destitute of archers". In winter "when the great fen or moor is frozen, many young men play upon the ice; some tie bones to their feet and under their heels and shoving themselves by a little picked staff do slide as swiftly as a bird flieth in the air". Perhaps Torvill and Dean could learn something yet! In 1373 a group of apprentice tailors and skinners were arrested for carrying knives while playing football (present-day Jeremiahs, take note).

Archery was officially encouraged rather than wrestling and ball games for blatant military reasons — "no small assistance in our warlike acts", was Fitzstephen's enthusiastic summary. Part of The Moor, known as the Artillery Fields, was cordoned off for archery practice. Similar ranges were set up at Westminster (Artillery Row) and at Newington Butts on the south bank. Smithfield meanwhile had fostered a cattle market, and a rash of extramural taverns, boarding and bawdy houses. Elizabethan London began to expand rapidly, to include Holborn, Clerkenwell and Whitechapel, and south of the river Southwark and Bermondsey. The octagenarian John Stow, who died in 1605, lamented the loss of the green meadows where he had played as a boy. Moorfields, ill-drained, boggy and for the time-being unsuitable for building, became firmly established as London's playground, providing space to walk, to dry clothes, to exercise horses and to pull the long-bow. It covered a wide area, from Whitecross Street to Bishopsgate and Shoreditch High Street, and included the plague pit cemetery of Bunhill and Finsbury Fields. Gradually the swampiest parts were filled with refuse and drained. A new gate, Moorgate, was cut into the City walls to improve access.

During Stuart times the fashions of leisure changed. The medieval pleasures of bear-baiting and football were now regarded as savage or unseemly by intellectuals and the more civilized pastimes of walking in ornamental gardens or playing bowls found favour. Moorfields was properly levelled and planted with neat avenues of trees for the *beau monde* to promenade. High society frequented the new theatres at Hoxton and the Globe at the South Bank, the bowling greens of Clerkenwell, or strolled in the open country of Goodmans Fields near Whitechapel and St George's Fields in Lambeth.

Hunting remained popular with some of the nobility but no longer *de rigueur*. The Stuart kings had generally more genteel natures and frailer constitutions than the rumbustious Tudors. Charles I even abandoned the royal Hyde Park for hunting and opened it for public recreation. Here the smartest citizens could parade on Sundays in their best clothes. The archery butts were kept and protected as artillery ranges; the rougher sports of wrestling and cock-fighting continued in less salubrious districts. Nevertheless

a fresh attitude to public recreation had been ushered in.

London was spreading westwards apace, offering exciting opportunities and demanding new facilities. Inigo Jones's Piazza at Covent Garden and Lincoln's Inn Fields both adopted Renaissance concepts of open-space planning, transforming old market gardens and grazing land. They produced a blueprint for the development of London's West End (see Chapter 6); squares became universally accepted as the best form of building.

The Restoration of Charles II instilled a renewed sense of jollity and gaiety into London life which sought novel outlets. As a complement to the formality and exclusiveness of the posh garden squares, the second half of the seventeenth century saw a rapid growth in spas and pleasure gardens on the outskirts of London. These more than compensated for the loss of traditional recreation grounds such as Goodman's Fields and Moorfields in the general spate of new building.

Competition was intense in wooing the custom of London's leisured and well-to-do, and by the end of the century a wide choice existed. Outlying villages such as Islington, Hampstead and Streatham suddenly became attractive resorts for the idle rich. Medicinal spring waters were the rage, tapped and bottled for their recuperative gifts. Tea-gardens offering cheesecake and syllabub accompanied by a selection of oriental and herbal teas, and rustic taverns selling choice ale and wines sprang up to cash in on the boom. Those with money to burn could fritter away their time at the Spaniards Inn or Wells Tavern in Hampstead, Canonbury Tavern, Highbury Barn or White Conduit House in Islington, Bagnigge Wells in Clerkenwell, the Dog and Duck or Finch's Grotto in Southwark. Old village fairs at Greenwich, Hampstead and Battersea expanded into cosmopolitan carnivals, complete with stuntmen, tricksters and pickpockets. Race meetings at Epsom and Kensington drew every section of the community and fuelled the widespread addiction to betting and gambling.

By 1690 there were over sixty pleasure gardens dotted around London, but among all these a handful emerged to dominate the social scene. Cuper's Gardens on the South Bank occupied the ground where Waterloo Station and the National Theatre stand now and was noted for its fireworks, performing dwarfs and circus. Marylebone

Gardens were the height of refined fashion, a venue for sophisticated music and conversation. Most famous were Vauxhall Gardens, opened in 1661. In June 1666 Samuel Pepys wrote in his diary how he went "to the Spring Garden at Fox-Hall and there stayed, pleasantly walking and spending but sixpence till nine at night". Its twelve acres were ingeniously landscaped to form avenues of elm and cherry, glades and arbours concealing classical statues and secret grottoes, florid temples and pavilions. Beyond the boundary hedges, fields of hay and wild poppies stretched as far as the eye could see.

In 1730 Vauxhall Gardens were upgraded and reopened. Frederick Prince of Wales became a patron, Handel was master of the music, anyone who was anybody had to make an appearance; "even bishops have been seen in this recess without injuring their character." Masked balls, or masquerades, became regular and extremely popular events, held *al fresco* on summer evenings with illuminations at dusk. All you needed was money — a bottle of burgundy might cost five shillings (say £25 today). Pimps and racketeers flourished.

Vauxhall's profits inspired a rival venture at Chelsea. Ranelagh Gardens, which opened in April 1742, offered entertainment and refreshment to cream off the wealthiest clientele from Vauxhall. Hefty admission charges kept out the *hoi polloi*. Centrally placed among lavish and exquisite Chinese gardens stood the great Rotunda, designed to resemble a Roman amphitheatre, and the catalyst for Ranelagh's success. It was a safe place to wander alone and horse patrols were provided for the journey home to Mayfair or St James's. A constant flood of balls, galas, masques and pantomimes at Ranelagh graced the London calendar. "Nothing in a fairy tale ever surpassed it," remarked Walpole.

For the well-heeled, of whom London had more than its fair share, this was a golden age of political stability and prosperity, stimulating a building bonanza which spawned the majestic squares of the Grosvenor and Harley Estates, and sustaining extravagantly opulent and luxurious pleasure gardens. Gainsborough's ethereal portrayal of the Mall in St James's Park, adorned by ladies of breeding and beauty and dancing lapdogs beneath a sylvan canopy of feathery leaves summarizes this non-industrialized paradise. By contrast, the wild heaths and commons around London were infested with highwaymen and robbers, definitely not the place to go for a Sunday afternoon walk. Constable's paintings of Hampstead Heath, however, reflect a new romantic spirit, the awakening appreciation of untamed nature. Times and opinions were shifting.

The nineteenth century witnessed dramatic changes as the industrial and railway age shook and transformed London. The promiscuous and tolerant ways of Georgian society were replaced by stricter moral codes based on strong religious and work ethics. Recreational habits altered rapidly. Ranelagh Gardens shut in 1803, soon after Marylebone and Cuper's Gardens. Vauxhall struggled on until 1859. By then it was no longer in the country and residents of adjacent houses complained of noise and rowdiness. The licence was withheld and the land auctioned for building. The mineral springs and flower gardens of Sadler's Wells disappeared, leaving only the theatre. The resplendent Spa Fields Pantheon in Clerkenwell and decadent Highbury Barn were replaced by churches. Today the eighteenth-century gardens are remembered mainly by pubs and street names — only Ranelagh survives as public open space.

The opening of Cremorne Gardens in 1843 off the King's Road, Chelsea, was a rare exception to the trend. The patronage of high-living Edward Prince of Wales ensured its popularity for *fêtes-champêtres*, dancing and balloon ascents. Whistler's *Falling Rocket*, painted in 1874, depicts a dazzling fireworks display at Cremorne Gardens. Most of the other Victorian resorts were teetotal tea-gardens, like Copenhagen Fields, or shady dives and skittle alleys such as Merlin's Cave and the Rosemary Branch in Islington and Montpelier Gardens, Walworth. Reformers did their utmost to suppress these profligate evils. The Salvation Army acquired the Eagle Tavern Gardens in City Road in 1882; nearly every fairground was closed.

In their place the Victorians created new parks where healthy outdoor exercise could be enjoyed. Walking, gentle rowing or sedate horse-riding were acceptably sober and spiritually uplifting activities. Bathing pools were provided for hygienic reasons in the poor districts, drinking fountains for refreshment, bandstands for public entertainment. By now all the royal parks were open to the public. On the other hand the railway companies and cheap house builders, encouraged by the General Enclosure Act of 1845, smashed ruthlessly across London's commons and market gardens. The Commons Preservation Society fought valiantly to oppose their destruction and in the nick of time legislation was passed which prevented the annihilation of every last field and village green. In 1866 an Act of Parliament introduced powers to protect existing commons and to lay out new parks for the public. Hampstead Heath and Epping Forest were saved after long and arduous battles in the courts. Disused burial grounds were levelled and landscaped to provide small gardens in the heart of the city.

Energetic sports acquired a new respectability. Every schoolboy and active adult was encouraged to participate in organized team games, all played in the best amateur spirit, but seeking high standards of excellence. National and international competition required new stadia for special pitches and to hold large enthusiastic crowds of spectators. Kennington Oval, originally part of Kennington Common, was the main arena, venue for the FA Cup Final in 1871, the first rugby international in 1872 between England and Scotland, and the first Test Match between England and Australia in 1880. The pavilion was built at Lord's Cricket Ground in 1889; the Wimbledon All-England Lawn Tennis and Croquet Club held their inaugural championship in 1877. For the individualist there was sculling on the river, or the latest fad of cycling.

After the severity of the 1850s, when temperance and prohibition put an end to many amusements, the inception of Bank Holidays in 1871 was a fillip to outdoor recreation and heralded a more relaxed attitude to play and leisure.

By the end of the nineteenth century the configuration and management of central London's public parks was much as we know it today. Various Acts of Parliament, such as the London Squares Preservation Act 1931, ensured that privately owned open spaces could not be developed without official permission. Between the First and Second World Wars the tentacles of the London Underground sparked a massive boom in building, particularly to the north, a tidal wave of suburbia which swept far out into quiet countryside, ruining the very rural charm which the estate agents' enticing advertisements had so extolled.

At Edgware the 400-acre Canons Park, where the Duke of Chandos had resided in his sumptuous palace, was broken up and sold off in job lots to speculative builders, leaving only a small pocket as playing fields. The Empire Exhibition at Wembley in 1923 obliterated the gardens of Sir Edward Watkin's leisure park where he had started and aborted the construction of a larger version of the Eiffel Tower. 140,000 people crammed into the Wembley Stadium for the 1923 Cup Final; the rest of the area was smothered with factories and houses.

The new suburbs were provided with their own public recreation grounds, but often extremely functional and unimaginative spaces. Golf courses, cemeteries, sports grounds and allotment gardens were the main takers for any open space which was on offer. The horticultural tradition of the English upper classes came to mass fruition in the neat rear gardens and allotments of London's suburbia. Here at last was a chance for everyone to participate, to play at being a gentleman farmer, or to help the war effort; there was no lack of motivation. Allotments, often squeezed into unlikely spots beside railway lines or gasworks, remain an extraordinary sight for foreigners — rows of shacks and sheds, beanpoles and raspberry canes, ugly winter stumps of brussels sprouts and all the untidy paraphernalia of vegetable gardening. London's lead pollution hardly seems to dampen the fervour.

Many of London's parks suffered badly in the Second World War. Air-raid shelters and anti-aircraft batteries were dug, turf was ploughed up for potatoes, railings torn down for munitions. Indiscriminate bombs blasted craters and wrecked monuments; no doubt many unexploded bombs and shells still lie snugly in the mud of London's lakes and ponds and in the ooze of the river to surprise future generations of archaeologists. After the war several open spaces were commandeered for "prefabs", prefabricated temporary housing for the homeless.

Even before the war the importance of containing the outward growth of London had been recognized by instigating Green Belt controls to limit the extent of the built-up area and stop London merging with other nearby towns. The post-war plan for London, produced by Patrick Abercrombie, reaffirmed and tightened the Green Belt. Sadly it did little to maintain farmland in good agricultural condition or prevent the marginal fields and orchards being

13

taken over by golf courses and gymkhanas, or squatted by gypsies. All too frequently such scrubland degenerated into rubbish dumps, car breakers' yards or caravan sites.

Within London new criteria were laid down for the provision of public open space, based on a crude overall goal of four acres per one thousand people and a hierarchy of parks of different sizes. It was intended that local parks of five acres, district parks of fifty acres and metropolitan parks of 150 acres should interlock to cover all requirements for outdoor recreation, equally accessible to all Londoners. It has proved to be a rather academic exercise. Parts of London, such as Richmond or Kensington, enjoy a surfeit of riches; other boroughs are hopelessly deficient. Jargonistic talk of catchment areas and theoretical acreages in wordy planning documents are well intentioned but impractical.

New parks have been created, Burgess Park in Walworth, for example, much to the amazement of civic authorities in other countries, and against great odds. Some spaces such as St Paul's Playing Fields in Hammersmith have been lost. Overall, the amount of open space continues to increase, slowly. At present the regional parks of the Lea and Colne valleys look better on paper than on the ground but time will help. The naked gravel pits of the M4 and Dagenham corridors will one day appear to be natural lakes.

The variety of activities within London's parks and open spaces has also multiplied. Over the last thirty years parks have lost their stuffiness — they are there to be used, by CND marches, rock concerts, fun-runs or sponsored walks. There are summer evening concerts of classical music at Kenwood and Crystal Palace, orienteering exercises in Epping Forest, frisbee-throwing competitions in Hyde Park. Joggers, windsurfers and rollerskaters have all become new converts to London's parks. Adventure playgrounds, special facilities for the handicapped, nature trails and ecology centres are as numerous today as Victorian bandstands and drinking-fountains were a century ago.

Wildlife is being increasingly regarded as a vital aspect of London's heritage. Within the harshness of our concrete urban jungle thousands of plants and animals survive in the sanctuaries offered by parks and open spaces. Botanically the municipal parks are artificial man-made environments.

In the nineteenth century, planes were the most widely planted trees and replaced the more traditional species of lime, elm and chestnut in the older royal parks and squares. In the 1960s and 1970s Dutch Elm disease accounted for the rest of London's elms; only a few injected specimens were kept alive in Kew Gardens. Although the plane is not a native tree it does remarkably well in smoky and polluted air, hence its popularity.

The Victorians liked to adorn their parks with exotic plants and introduced many new trees such as evergreen oaks, copper beech, false acacia, arbutus and trees of heaven. Even the heaths and commons were carefully regulated by planting and thinning. Any naturalness is deceptive.

Probably the wildest and most unadulterated habitats are to be found in the large neglected cemeteries where a succession of weeds, undergrowth and indigenous trees have colonized and choked the abandoned graves. These places provide the best cover for a huge variety of insects, birds and mammals, even snakes, frogs and toads. Hedgehogs, weasels and foxes have resettled in corners of London where one might have thought they would never return. Despite the profusion of sycamore saplings wild flowers and fungi can flourish here, unthreatened by the gardener's trowel.

Ornithologists enthuse over sightings of redstarts nesting on patches of derelict land, kestrels hovering above railway embankments, or herons raiding the Barbican ponds for fish. Pigeons, sparrows and seagulls no longer rule the roost.

The protection of wilderness is now seen to be essential for the more unusual flora and fauna, least adapted to urban life. Ecology parks have been set up on small areas of waste ground, near Tower Bridge and beside the Regent's Canal in Camden, shielded from unwanted human intrusion and allowed to regenerate naturally. Given time these may mature to become London's most treasured open spaces, and the rarer plants and animals may evolve to cope with strange surroundings.

CHAPTER 2: Heaths, Commons and Woods

London's commons, heathlands and greens are perhaps the most remarkable and in some cases the least appreciated of its open spaces. Unlike the formal parks, royal, aristocratic or municipal which every capital city possess, or the London squares, cemeteries and churchyards, the commons, heaths and woods have not been created by urban dwellers. Instead they are relics of an ancient landscape, all that is left from the engulfing wave of bricks and mortar which even now threatens to roll over yet more acres of countryside, joining town with town, industrial estate with hypermarket.

As with many things that seemingly have always been there and always will be there, too many Londoners take their common lands for granted. Frequently they are unspectacular spaces, barren and windswept, lacking the bright flowers, exotic trees, ornamental shrubs, artificial lakes and tidy paths which characterize London's parks and gardens. But to the educated eye they provide evidence of the geology and natural history of the London region, a living testimony to the great forests, wild heathlands and intricate network of villages and hamlets which once surrounded the tiny medieval city.

Often their survival has been more by luck than judgement, but in some instances it is the result of fiercely contested legal battles waged in the last century between would-be developers and conservationists. Without these champions of civil liberty and the vagaries of English law London might now be a much duller and more tightly packed place.

It doesn't require a degree in geomorphology to comprehend that London lies in a river valley. The navigability of the Thames from the sea as far up as the lowest feasible bridging point was the primary reason for London becoming established as a trading and military post. The river and its numerous tributaries wind through a low-lying alluvial plain on a base of heavy clay, fertile for farming but liable to flooding and difficult to drain. Terraces of gravels and silts provided safe ground for settlement on the valley floor but on the edge of the valley high spurs of tertiary sands and glacial deposits produced inhospitable terrain of heath and forest, unrewarding for the farmer, brick-maker or potter. This topographical variety not only means that London's present-day suburbs are frequently pleasantly hilly but are also blessed with

areas of heath and wood of unusual natural beauty and freedom.

The closest outlier of sandstone to the Thames in London is at Greenwich, where almost from the river bank the land rises steeply through royal Greenwich park to the flat high plateau known as **Blackheath**. Ecologically Blackheath was no different from many of London's other commons and heaths, black acidic peat soils prohibiting cultivation and the wild gorse and bracken deterring grazing. What marked out Blackheath as one of London's most celebrated open spaces was the fact that the Romans built their Watling Street from London to Dover across it. Perhaps it followed a more ancient routeway, for neolithic tumuli were found on the heath and inexpertly plundered in 1784. The heights of Blackheath afforded clear views of London, north to the river and south back into Kent. It was the last great look-out point before London, high and dry, the natural place for any approaching army to camp.

Wat Tyler's Kentish mob assembled on Blackheath before descending on a complacent London in June 1381 to join forces with Jack Straw's Essex rabble. Jack Cade's army camped overnight in 1450, and Lord Audley's Cornish rebels were rounded up here in 1497. Their corpses were buried in mass graves such as Whitfield's Mound. Blackheath was the chosen place for the Lord Mayor and court to meet the gallant Henry and his small brigade of mercenaries after his victory at Agincourt, and where similar civic dignitaries welcomed Charles II's return to London in 1660, a magnificent occasion marked with flags, bells, music, wine and ale. Blackheath's proximity to the royal palace at Greenwich facilitated other rendezvous. Henry VIII met the shy Anne of Cleves on the Dover Road at Blackheath before leading her down to Greenwich. On this wild heath James I introduced to England the Scottish penchant for thwacking a little ball with cumbersome wooden clubs; Royal Blackheath Golf Club is the oldest in the world, now moved to Eltham.

Greenwich Park and its Ranger's House was carefully divided from Blackheath by a high wall. The heath was common land, the meeting point of the four manors of Greenwich, West Coombe, Lewisham and Old Court. For centuries, during the long gaps between military parades and encampments it was a happy hunting ground for robbers and highwaymen. The gibbet on Shooter's Hill

Page 15:
Hampstead Heath,
near Kenwood.

probably scared tremulous passengers in the Dover coach more than their potential assailants. The burning of the gorse, to amuse George IV's wife, removed some of their cover, but more discouragingly in the 1800s houses began to be built around the periphery, such as the Paragon on the south-east side. Inexorably the expanding village of Blackheath, by now a London suburb, marched up the hill towards the heath. In 1871 the surviving 267 acres were acquired as public open space, putting a stop to the excavations of gravel, some of which filled with water to form ponds. All Saints Church was the last encroachment. The following year the old fair held on the south-east corner of the heath every May and October was suppressed.

Today Blackheath is excessively civilized, an unremitting tract of grass, criss-crossed by busy roads. Yet it remains a thrill to climb up out of Deptford and to emerge on the heath high above the smoke and dirt of south-east London. Fear of muggers and rapists has discouraged restocking with gorse, which at least makes life easier for the kite flyers who revel in Blackheath's sweeping winds. The prettiest part is down near the Paragon by the round pond and elegant willows where a few of the roads have thankfully been closed. On the north the bushy trees of Greenwich Park form a cosy backcloth, and from the gate the 20,000 runners emerge for what has become the traditional start of the annual London marathon.

North London's most celebrated heath had a more perilous battle for survival. Apart from the royal parks **Hampstead Heath** is probably London's most popular open space and one of the most varied and extensive. It was certainly the most fought-over.

Until the seventeenth century Hampstead was a remote insalubrious village, inhabited by pig farmers and washerwomen who dried their clothes and linen on the windy heights. The small village was surrounded by a wild and inhospitable heath, thick with thorn and gorse, which stretched south to Chalk Farm, east to Highgate, north to Finchley and west to Kilburn. It was common land, owned by the lord of the manor, available to all parishioners to graze their animals in proportion to their station.

During the Great Plague Hampstead became attractive as a refuge from the horrors of infection and disease. Judge's Walk and King's Bench Walk recall the evacuation

Hampstead Heath, looking south to Parliament Hill.

Left:
Hampstead West
Heath, from The
Hill.

Right:
The ladies' bathing
pool, Hampstead
Heath.

of lawyers from the Inns of Court. The Vale of Health, however, is not what it sounds — more probably a corruption of "heath". This enclave of Victorian houses on one side of the Heath was previously an unhealthy swamp, infested with mosquitoes, chronically bad for asthma and rheumatism. The "discovery" of recuperative spring waters during the eighteenth century boosted Hampstead's position as a spa. Well and Flask Walks, and their taverns, became popular resorts for the medically infirm; respectable houses appeared in the village for well-to-do Londoners who favoured rustic surroundings. The newly awakened appreciation of natural beauty attracted artists and writers, notably Shelley and Keats whose museum in Keats Grove is where he wrote his "Ode to a Nightingale". Hampstead was Constable's favourite residence, and the Heath the subject of several paintings. Though not exactly the Montmartre of London, Hampstead acquired a reputation for bohemian and intellectual residents which it still maintains today.

The battle for the Heath started in 1829 and was waged for over forty years. Thomas Maryon Wilson was lord of Hampstead manor but lived in Charlton House ten miles away. As absentee landlord he made repeated attempts to sell off the Heath for profitable development, in so doing stirring up a hornets' nest of protest. Wilson began by clearing much of the gorse scrub from the heath and digging for sand and gravel. Ornamental trees were planted to prepare the way for residential streets. In 1845 East Heath Road and the viaduct and pond were built as a prelude to a rash of large villas covering the Heath. All Wilson needed was a private Act of Parliament to enclose and build. Throughout London's suburbs such acts had been a formality; Hampstead proved different. Between 1853 and 1866 Wilson promoted ten bills in Parliament. Each one was ferociously opposed and defeated. The fight was led by Samuel Gurney Hoare, a Quaker banker who lived near Whitestone pond, and a committee of distinguished local residents, including four MPs. In 1866 Wilson ignored the law and began building at Squires Mount. Gurney Hoare took out a lawsuit and halted the incursion. The case was never heard, for in 1870 Thomas Maryon Wilson died. His benevolent son capitulated to the preservationists and in 1871 sold 240 acres of heath to the Metropolitan Board of Works for a mere £45,000.

Since that first victory the Heath has expanded fourfold. In 1886 Parliament Hill Fields were bought for £300,000; Golders Hill Park in 1899 for £38,000, Wildwood in 1904 for £43,000, and, finest of all, 200 acres of Kenwood in 1927, the Iveagh Bequest. Not every battle was won. One of Wilson's last acts was to sell off the manorial land down to Swiss Cottage. "How fresh the air blew over these fields," wrote a helpless protester, where now Fitzjohns Avenue and Arkwright Road are lined with gigantically forbidding red-brick mansions. No doubt many of the

Opposite:
The open fields
near Highgate
Ponds, Hampstead
Heath.

18

influential Hampstead gentry who campaigned against Maryon Wilson did so out of self-interest. They could see only too well what had happened to pleasant villages like Tottenham, Clapham and Hackney, smothered with Victorian housing. If so, what matter; without the Heath neither Hampstead nor Highgate would be what they are, and all London would be the poorer.

It would take a small book to do justice to the joys of Hampstead Heath and its 825 acres. Whitestone Pond, 443 feet above sea level, is arguably the focal pivot, the highest point in London, one of the chain of beacons which harnessed England during the Armada. The pond, named after the milestone 4½ miles to Holborn Bars, is a haven for model boats and dogs and horses on hot days. From behind Jack Straw's Castle and the steep sides of North End Way, where Jackson hanged on Gibbet Tree, lovely sunset views stretch across West Heath over the canopy of birch and alder away to the distant cone of Harrow-on-the-Hill, the next outcrop of Bagshot Sand. These views are most dramatic from the overgrown ramparts of The Hill, encircling Manor House Hospital; these elevated arcades of redbrick and pergolas of decaying wood are a fairyland fantasy of Edwardian grandeur, perched above the wild woods. Beyond West Heath **Golders Hill** is a delightful municipal park, just 36 acres, but good for tennis, flowers and bandstands, a few grand oaks but un-heathlike.

Northwards the Sandy Heath is pitted by Wilson's gravel extractions, now picturesque dips and dells. South-east the main heath slopes down to Hampstead Ponds and **Parliament Hill** which though only 320 feet high offers the best view of London. From here the gunpowder plot traitors supposedly assembled to watch the blowing-up of Parliament in 1605 and were arrested. It was a good spot to watch the Royal Wedding fireworks in 1981. Parliament Hill is north London's answer to Blackheath for kite enthusiasts, and the best toboggan run for those rare days of snow.

Between Parliament Hill and Kenwood ancient barrows and tumuli are covered with clumps of trees, standing among wide rolling meadows, heavy with summer pollen. **Kenwood** is protected by a ring of woods, but the view of the house from the south-west gate is as splendid as Blenheim or Burleigh. This is one of London's great houses (see Chapter 5) and a remarkable adjunct to the Heath.

From within the muddy mulch of these woods tiny rivulets trickle south in search of the Thames, the head waters of the Kilburn and the Fleet river, on their way feeding the six Highgate ponds.

Each pond has its own function and character — toy boats, mixed and segregated bathing, a stock pool and a bird sanctuary. In one you may spy the Great Crested Grebe, in the next the deafening racket of petrol engines controlled by fifty-year-old boys. Some leathery athletes claim to swim every day of the year in the murky depths of the men's pond. Treacherous winter ice has taken its toll of foolhardy daredevils. Maryon Wilson's viaduct still spans the artificial lily pond. As an impressionable youth I saw these arches through the eager eyes of a railway fanatic, not as a greedy man's folly.

People come to Hampstead Heath for a hundred different things — dogs and joggers, fishing rods and toddlers, lovers and codgers. 'Appy 'Ampstead Fair at the Vale of Health and by Downshire Hill is the Bank Holiday draw. The pubs are always packed — the Bull and Bush, Jack Straw's Castle, the Wells Tavern, the Spaniards and the Flask. Kenwood must even thank the one-time landlord of the Spaniards Inn for entertaining the angry Gordon rioters with free beer in time for the troops to save the then Lord Chief Justice's house from arson.

On Hampstead Heath you will find beauty in all seasons, the limes of Boundary Path, the rippling water through reeds and willow, slender copses of silver birch. Ignore the clumsy blot of the Royal Free Hospital, for this is the depth of London's countryside, a leafy skyline broken by the spires of Christchurch and St Michael's and the dome of Holy Jo's.

London's largest open space was also saved in remarkable circumstances at a similar time to the preservation of Hampstead Heath. **Epping Forest** is enormous, as big as all the Royal Parks put together. From the fragments of wood and common in Newham Epping Forest extends nearly fourteen miles north into rural Essex, a long thin tongue only two miles across at its widest covering the high ground between the Lea and Roding valleys. These nine square miles of woodland, scrub and grass are the best reason for living in the suburbs of Walthamstow, Chingford or Loughton, so readily derided by West Londoners.

Opposite:
The Hill,
Hampstead West
Heath.

21

Yet Epping Forest is just a tiny remnant of the great forest of Waltham on the heavy clay of Inner Essex, the jealously guarded hunting-ground of English kings and their courtiers from the seventh to the eighteenth centuries. For a thousand years Norman, Plantagenet, Tudor and Stuart monarchs controlled the use and abuse of the forest. Charters were continually renewed throughout the Middle Ages; Rex was lex. Terrible penalties, including death, were exacted for poaching. Dogs were muzzled and even had their claws removed to protect game. Henry VIII, obsessed with hunting, tried to extend the Crown's interest; Charles I attempted to exploit the forest for revenue, to the constant irritation of the local manors and commoners.

After the Civil War the monarchy lost interest in hunting and sought more refined pleasures. The Crown gradually relaxed and abandoned its stranglehold on the forest, whereupon new threats to its survival appeared. Pepys, who worked in the naval ministry, recorded how thousands of oaks were felled and floated down the River Roding to Barking Creek and thence to the Woolwich and Deptford shipyards. In the eighteenth century large quantities of sand, gravel and turf were removed, and deforested land ploughed up for farming. The forest glades became increasingly lawless, sheltering gangs of robbers and discharged soldiers. The notorious "Waltham Blacks" charcoaled their faces at night before plundering nearby villages and farms. "Through the wild brakes of Epping Forest lay a dreary landscape, bushy and forlorn, where rogues start up like mushrooms in a morn."

In the nineteenth century, house-building at Leyton, Walthamstow, Chingford and Woodford encroached ruthlessly on the forest. What had been a forest of 60,000 acres in 1640 had shrunk to a tenth of its size. By 1865 deforestation was accelerating at such a pace that within a decade it would have vanished. The Commons Preservation Society was founded and in 1871 an important legal case upheld the commoner's rights of Tom Willingale, a local woodman. Moreover in 1854 the City Corporation had acquired 200 acres of Aldersbrook Farm for the City of London cemetery, and with it commoner's rights. They took on the battle to save the forest through the courts. A board of commissioners was established to prevent further encroachment and under the 1878 Epping

Forest Act the Corporation of London bought the remaining 5,600 acres. In 1882 Epping Forest was declared open by Queen Victoria to the public for ever.

Today the ancient court of verderers meet with elected members of the City's Common Council to manage the forest. Rights of pannage and grazing cattle still survive for the forest parishes of Chingford, Walthamstow, Leyton, Woodford, Wanstead, Ilford and West Ham. Cattle grids on the roads prevent the animals wandering out of the forest, but these days few commoners exercise their rights.

Epping is unlike any other London open space in being so natural. Nothing here has been planted: every oak has grown from an acorn fallen from another oak, every beech from a beech nut. Not to say that people have had no impact. Tree-felling in the past has left areas of open grassland and scrub, and even in the wooded glades few of the grand beeches are more than 200 years old. Several of the meres and ponds occupy former gravel pits. Human intervention in fact has contributed to Epping's variety. Birch, holly, hornbeam, hawthorn, chestnut and alder flourish here, as well as the giant kings of the forest. On the forest floor wild spring flowers push through the sea of last year's leaves; exotic mushrooms and toadstools materialize overnight among the moist autumnal debris of decaying fallen branches.

Epping harbours a rich wildlife. Boars and wild cats were hunted out of existence, and the famous pure breed of black fallow deer is now confined to a small area, but badgers, foxes, stoats, rabbits, hares, hedgehogs and squirrels abound. Mute and feral swans share the meres with thousands of migratory geese and ducks. Connaught Water is the biggest of the dozen ponds in the forest. Broken up by several islands and surrounded by trees, this lake is lovely in early morning or evening sun, patrolled by swans and mallards. Wood pigeons flap noisily in the trees and magpies make sorties for food, their long tails extended like Bleriot's primitive aeroplane.

From Connaught Water the River Ching meanders south through the forest to Highams Park and the Lea valley. This and several other lakes are popular with fishermen. Warren Pond is often squalid with their litter, the banks chewed by their waders and stools. One or two meres are harder to find, deep in the thickest thickets of the forest. Blackweir Pond, known as the Lost Pond, is worth

Opposite:
The Rookery, Streatham Common; giant Cedars and tame squirrels.

22

the search, an undisturbed sanctuary for contemplation. Throughout the forest small streams dribble out of marshy bogs and cut steep little glens which twist through the woodland glades in search of the sea.

Ambersbury Banks and Loughton Camp are further reminders of man's meddling over thousands of years. These unspectacular earthworks are probably pre-Roman British. Local tradition claims that Ambersbury Banks was the site of Boadicea's final and fatal showdown with Suetonius. In reality it is unlikely that either side would have chosen a dense wood as a battle ground — as insubstantial a myth as Battlebridge Basin at King's Cross.

The oldest building in the forest is Queen Elizabeth's Hunting Lodge, a half-mile west of Connaught Water on Rangers Road. The queen was an expert markswoman and used this splendid lodge to shoot deer from the galleries. The massive oak beams were built to last till the crack of doom, but now house an excellent museum, open from Wednesday to Sunday, 2 p.m. to 6 p.m., packed with forest exhibits to fire any fertile imagination. What should be a delightful setting is spoilt by the awful mock-Tudor Royal Forest Berni Inn next door, in the worst "Scottish and Newcastle" style. The mundane keeper's cottage is an equally poor companion. The old Epping hunt, when a beribboned stag was released and pursued by a jovial throng of local lads, was disbanded in 1882. The ancient Essex fairs continue, now fun-fairs confined to Leyton and Wanstead Flats and Havering Green.

For over a hundred years Epping Forest has been the playground of the East End. At weekends thousands of Londoners picnic, ride horses, orienteer, fish and walk their dogs there. It has always had an abnormally and unjustifiably bad reputation for rape, murder and skulduggery — enough to scare away many south or west Londoners. Perhaps this is a blessing. The staff at the High Beach Conservation Centre are only too aware of the problems of overcrowding, litter and car-parking, and the threat to wildlife. Traffic through the forest, including the main A11, is an annoyance, though sometimes a reassuring lifeline for navigation! The M11 has helped to reduce the traffic, but the greatest concern has centred on the new M25. After a lengthy public inquiry this has been built partly in tunnel to minimize its impact on the north end of the forest. We shall see.

The forest's southern outposts, cut off from the rest by the mean Victorian houses of Leytonstone, have their own peculiar character. **Wanstead Flats** is a broad heathland, as flat as its name suggests, but with a bleak beauty. Apart from trees at the edges, some gravelly ponds and a few scraps of thorn hedge, the Flats are a fawny haze of wild grasses where the wind blows keenly and the horizon stretches way to distant tower blocks and pylons. In Capel Road the timeless oak hedge contrasts with grotesquely pollarded limes in front of suburban terraces, and the veranda of the Golden Fleece.

Wanstead Park, north of Aldersbrook Road and the City of London cemetery, is also owned by the City Corporation. The east side slopes naturally down to the River Roding which fills the heronry and perch ponds dotted with attractively wooded islands. Despite its semi-wild state, this park used to be the grounds of Wanstead House, a magnificent Palladian mansion built in 1715 but demolished in 1824. Soon after, the tessellated pavement of a Romano-British farmstead was found here. Today a curiously colonnaded colonial-style house stands in the middle. With its white flagpole it resembles something on a Ceylonese tea plantation, except for the two drab park-keepers' houses behind. The quiet serenity of Wanstead Park seems far removed from the deep forest glades of Epping.

Further east **Hainault Forest** was, like Epping, part of the great forest of Essex. "Forest" is now a misnomer for Hainault; the trees were felled in the mid-nineteenth century and the area farmed. The most famous feature was the Fairlop Oak, a massive tree with a girth of thirty-six feet. Lightning and gales destroyed the original oak in 1820, but a replacement was planted in 1909 on a playing-field. The Fairlop fair, held from 1683 under the spreading canopy of the oak, ended in 1851. The Greater London Council now own 1,000 acres of Hainault Forest, one of their largest but most disappointing parks. A golf course and motorbike scrambling circuit are the main features. Apparently the GLC have ambitious plans but it will be hard to recreate any feel of the forest.

The saving of Epping and Hampstead were highlights of Victorian endeavour, but just two examples of numerous tussles between builders developers and preservationists. Every rural parish had its common land, owned by the lord

Opposite:
Highgate Wood; an idyllic setting for the cricket club.

Left and right:
The ornate gardens
of The Rookery,
Streatham
Common.

of the manor and used under feudal law by the commoners. The disastrous Statute of Merton enacted during the Wars of the Roses enabled enclosure of common-land throughout England simply by a private Act of Parliament, without the consent of the commoners. In the nineteenth century the temptation was too great for many squires to resist. By selling common land for housing, enormous profits were there for the taking. Railway companies relentlessly pushed bills through Parliament in order to lay their tracks across the cheapest land.

In the first half of the nineteenth century dozens of London's fine open spaces were lost, particularly north of the river where common land in Notting Hill, Chelsea, Kensington and Islington was enclosed. Brompton Heath, for example, was completely built over, remembered now only by Thistle Grove off Brompton Road. The newly established Metropolitan Board of Works desperately instigated legislation to prevent the total demise of London's commons. A select committee set up in 1865 introduced the Metropolitan Commons Act 1866, which forbade the enclosure of common land within a fourteen-mile radius of Charing Cross. It came only just in time, and was to involve the taxpayer in thousands of pounds' worth of expensive compensation.

Most of London's famous commons are south of the river, places that are familiar to all Londoners if only as underground or bus destinations. **Clapham Common** is as well known as its top-deck omnibus passenger, a vast and anonymous expanse of grass, criss-crossed by paths and surrounded by hustling traffic. The thick cover of gorse and broom, which once hid polecats and hedgehogs, disappeared soon after the Metropolitan Board of Works acquired it in 1877 from Clapham manor. Swamps were drained into neat ponds, swine and cattle were banished, and now even the grand elms have gone, diseased and felled. In the late seventeenth century the common was fronted by fine houses as Clapham became a fashionable suburb for city merchants. Pepys first visited Clapham in 1663 and lodged in "the wonderfully well furnished house" of Dr Dennis Gauden beside the common. Here Pepys collected his library, which he later bequeathed to Magdalene College, Cambridge. Zachary Macaulay had a house in The Pavement and his son Tom (later Lord) had the common as a playground — "that delightful wilderness of gorse bushes, poplar groves, gravel pits and ponds, great and small, a region of inexhaustible romance and mystery". Clapham Common lacks mystery today. The ponds where little boys used to fish for sticklebacks are now the domain of model-boat fetishists. The monotonous grass is good for football and whippets, but short on poetic inspiration, even after a few pints of Winter Warmer in the capacious Windmill public house.

Wandsworth Common, a half-mile west, is similarly flat, once part of a huge tract of common pasture in the manors of Battersea and Wandsworth. Total extinction was averted in 1871, but not before the railway had been built slap across the middle, ruining the peace and quiet of gypsies who had camped regularly on the common. To the north the Royal Victoria Patriotic Asylum was opened in 1854, intended for dependants of victims in the Crimea, later to become Emmanuel School, and not to be muddled with the Surrey House of Correction nearby, now Wandsworth Prison.

The commons of the two parishes of **Tooting Bec** and **Tooting Graveney** were also intersected by the railway but less savagely than at Wandsworth. Tooting Bec Common is the larger and more interesting. Oak and sycamore spinneys, clumps of brambles and hawthorn scrub engender a wildness quite lacking at Clapham. Naturally-worn paths, rather than tarmac, and the rough gravel banks of the ponds are mercifully unmunicipal, and even the lido is carefully screened by trees. As usual, villagers had rights of pasture, cutting fern and turf and digging gravel. Furzedown, the district to the south, recalls the impenetrable heathland, subsequently denuded by overgrazing and then built on.

Tooting Graveney Common, much smaller, lies west of Dr Johnson Avenue. Tooting was Dr Johnson's second home, where he spent his summers with the Thrales at Thrale Place. Mr Thrale owned Southwark's Anchor Brewery, later bought by Barclay and Perkins and now closed down by Courage. Mrs Thrale provided a sympathetic ear for the doctor's lengthy discourses when his inherent laziness reverted to talk and tea.

After the levels of Tooting, Clapham and Wandsworth, **Streatham Common** is refreshing, rising steeply from Streatham High Road, the old Brighton road, up to Norwood. The Common was welcome pasture for cattle drovers on their way to Smithfield, and the taverns of Streatham village were a well-deserved refuge after the forbidding gloom of Norwood. By 1700 Streatham had become more than a drovers' stop-off point and was famous for its mineral springs, not exactly on the scale of Bath but a draw for hypochondriac Londoners. John Aubrey believed Streatham water to be good for the sight, a worthy complement to Epsom's salts. Although

Streatham's heyday was short-lived, the biggest surprise on Streatham Common, the Rookery, harks back to those fashionable times. This formal garden, with giant cedars, yorkstone terraces, and steps and lawns hopping with tame squirrels, is a total contrast with the oak scrub and wild grass of the Common which looks out over the amorphous oblivion of south-west London. In the walled garden stands one of the three wells of Streatham spa, dating from 1659, brimming with cool water beneath dank ferns, and the source of a tiny stream which gurgles forth bound for the River Graveney. Dr Johnson, though no lover of Nature, used to walk here from Tooting. How ridiculous that Dr Johnson's thatched summer house, his favourite resort in his dotage, was moved to Kenwood, when the Rookery would make a perfect home.

Further south, **Mitcham Common** is a sprawling 480 acres of breezy grassland, dissected by roads and railway, merging with a public golf course, sewage farms, sports grounds and power stations. This is not a cosy space but provides a lung for the dreary suburbs of Hackbridge, Mitcham and Wallington. In 1848 the Chartists assembled here before their shambolic march to Parliament. The French composer Hector Berlioz, who happened to be in London at the time, lamented: "My poor friends, you know as much about starting a riot as the Italians about writing a symphony." He had a point, though French symphonists are hardly thick on the ground. None the less Mitcham Common does not evoke revolutionary fervour.

Wimbledon Common is a different story, for this is one of London's finest open spaces. Unlike the commons acquired by the Metropolitan Board of Works, Wimbledon Common retains its common rights and is owned and maintained by the Commoners Association, comprising local residents. No danger here of municipal neatness. Half as big again as Hampstead Heath, though lacking Hampstead's hills and views, Wimbledon Common is a varied landscape of silver birch woods, heather and sandy grassland, marshy ponds and meres. In the middle is the famous landmark of the windmill, white and dramatic. The present one was built in 1817, but there have been many more before on this site. Another notable feature is Caesar's Camp, a circular and probably Stone Age earthwork. The name is entirely spurious — the Romans and Caesar in particular never had any dealing in the place.

Until 1875 it was a highly impressive monument, with steep ramparts and deep ditches like Maiden Castle in Dorset. The lord of the manor began flattening the ground for building until a High Court order stopped him. Sadly, the damage was irredeemable.

South of Caesar's Camp the Common becomes a golf course and adjoins **Cannizaro Park,** which includes Lady Jane's Wood. The rest of the Common is easy to get lost in, full of delightful clearings and glades, home of the Wombles. The shallow King's Mere and Queen's Mere are especially lovely, freezing over readily in winter and one of the first places in London to skate outdoors during a cold spell. The noise of the A3 spoils the northern fringe; Tibbet's Corner, where convicted highwaymen once swung from the gallows and where disaffected young men resolved their points of honour by duelling, is now a thunderous underpass.

North of the main road, **Putney Heath** is a small extension of the Common, previously much bigger until suburban Putney spread south from Putney Bridge up the hill. Before the mid-nineteenth century, when Roehampton was nothing but a country lane, Putney Heath was joined to **Barnes Common.** This gentle heathland of stunted trees and bushes, its springy grass like soft down, is now fragmented by roads and railway. West of Rocks Lane, small patches of gravel and scrub lead to the serene village pond of **Barnes Green,** quiet and comfortable. North of Lower Richmond Road, tall lines of poplars lead across Beverley Brook into Barn Elms playing-fields, once part of the private estate of Francis Walsingham which from 1884 to 1939 was a fashionable club. Barn Elms is now a public recreation ground and sports centre. The strangest feature of Barnes Common is the disused cemetery, plundered and overgrown — no place for the timid.

South-east London is equally well-endowed with commons, perhaps none so fine as Wimbledon, but important pockets of fresh air in the urban smoke. **Peckham Rye** is among the oldest of recreation grounds, mentioned as far back as 1300 for sport and outdoor pursuits by country folk. Parishoners have continually and successfully resisted enroachment, so that the Common survives intact, not split up by roads. This broad expanse of grass is relieved magically by a solitary tree in the middle. From here the horizon is low and the sky wide and open, so rare in London. Apart from Young's Clock House public house, the backcloth is semi-elegant houses and trees.

Adjoining the Rye to the south is **Peckham Rye Park,** forty-nine acres bought in 1894 as farmland and landscaped with trees, lakes and watercourses. The park is as enclosed and municipal as the Common is exposed and barren, full of mature laurels and ornamental shrubs. **One Tree Hill Park,** half a mile south at Honor Oak, is famous for its oak under which Queen Elizabeth 1 reputedly picnicked on a country outing from Greenwich, the spot now marked by a newer specimen.

Beyond the heights of Greenwich and Blackheath, **Woolwich Common** is the first of a cluster of commons and heaths covering the inhospitable sandy soils of the Shooters Hill ridge. Woolwich is a cold and windswept place in the shadow of the Royal Military Academy, gaunt and imposing. The Common has never recovered from the 1870s when it was requisitioned during the Franco-Prussian war for military training. Despite acquisition by the Metropolitan Board of Works in 1878, the War Office maintained rights of drill, and it remains remarkably bleak.

Eltham Common, virtually contiguous, is by comparison richly wooded. The Common is made up of Oxleas Wood, Castle Wood, Jack Wood and Shepherdleas Wood, mature oak, birch, beech and chestnut. From the ridge there are stunning views to the City, St Paul's and the Post Office Tower. Hidden in the thickets of Castle Wood a weird Gothic folly commemorates the gallant officers in the East Indies and the marines who captured Malabar — truly colonial stuff. A small oasis of lawn makes a pleasant change from the bracken undergrowth, best in autumn when the floor is crunchy with acorns, sweet chestnuts, conkers and beech nuts.

Plumstead Common also enjoys fine views over the Thames, but its hundred acres are fragmented and largely bare. Before being nibbled away for buildings it was much bigger and more continuous. Now tongues of houses lick up towards the gravelly Common and into the nearby Bostall Woods. The east end, known as the Slade, is exceptionally steep, but to the south it slopes away more gently to Shoulder of Mutton Green at East Wickham, originally part of the Common.

Until the South Eastern Railway was built in 1839, most of the boroughs of Bromley and Lewisham were rolling

Opposite:
Queen's Mere,
Wimbledon
Common.

28

woodland growing on gravels and marls, merging with the undulating dip slope of the North Downs. **Petts Wood** and **Chislehurst Common** are large surviving tracts of this beautiful woodland, a sanctuary for suburban dog-owners, joggers and Sunday afternoon strollers. In Tudor and Stuart times the Pett family were shipbuilders and planted oaks among the coppiced birch and sweet chestnut. This is typical Kentish wood, with grand oak trees spreading high above the sturdy chestnut faggots. In spring the carpet of bluebells is a sight not to be missed.

West London has a good sprinkling of commons, vital reservoirs of space among houses and traffic. It is hard to imagine triangular **Shepherd's Bush Common** as a simple village green, surrounded by a few cottages, a pub and a shop, and known as Gagglegoose Green. Today the old pond has been drained and filled and any rural atmosphere has vanished with the maelstrom of traffic and the weight of new buildings. Litter and noise compete for supremacy. Only the war memorial provides a parochial touch on Remembrance Sunday.

North of White City, **Wormwood Scrubs** is a vast open area, better known perhaps for its prison than its recreational delights. When opened in 1874 the prison was proclaimed the finest specimen of penal architecture in England, built entirely by convict labour, even down to the firing of the bricks. Today the grey grime and excessively heavy chimneys of this grim bastion of Victorian punishment are a forbidding backdrop to the bleak and stark Scrubs. The northern side, called Old Oak Common, is flanked by the Great Western Railway. The signal-box bears the name as 125s roar past to Reading but there are few supportive oaks. To the west an appallingly dull council estate, reminiscent of Dagenham or Sunderland, completes the unglamorous neighbourhood. The 193 acres of Wormwood Scrubs is relieved by the running track, home of the Thames Harriers club, and the ranks of goalposts where seagulls perch to digest their scavengings.

Equally large and rather disappointing is **Hounslow Heath**. This used to be bigger than Epping Forest, a wild terrain of 6,000 acres ruled by highwaymen who robbed travellers on the old Roman Road to Salisbury. Hounslow barracks, Heathrow airport and the suburbs of Feltham ensured that only a fragment survived, and no longer the wildest place in London.

Many of west London's most enjoyable commons are small. **Ealing Common,** despite being truncated by the North Circular Road, is a pleasant expanse of turf lined with limes, poplars and horse-chestnuts. The surrounding streets are comfortably Edwardian, flickering memories of Ealing comedies. **Acton Green** and **Chiswick Common,** which straddle the embankment of the District Line, are likewise bordered by the Norman Shaw elegance of Bedford Park, opulent red-brick villas from the turn of the century. **Lammas Park** in South Ealing, with its neat avenue of chestnuts and sturdy park railings, is now far removed from the intentions of the original lammas land common.

With the notable exception of Hampstead Heath, little common land has survived in north London. Finchley Common, where London's defences were shambolically erected against Bonnie Prince Charlie in 1745 and where the notorious escapologist Jack Sheppard was recaptured, had virtually disappeared by 1880. The residents of Finchley lacked the political clout of Hampsteadites; now of course they have Margaret Thatcher! In the north-west, **Stanmore** and **Harrow Weald** Commons are splendid tracts of wood and heathland, a vital part of the green belt between London and Watford. From Old Redding there are fine views south to Harrow Hill's spire, and a pleasantly rural drink to be quaffed in The Case is Altered public house, probably named after the Casa Alta from Wellington's Spanish campaign. The largely untraceable earthwork of Grimsdyke runs nearby, while hidden in the woods behind impenetrable banks of rhododendrons is the neo-Tudor Grimsdyke House. W.S. Gilbert lived here for twenty-one years after the death of Sullivan, as a retiring country squire, sadly to drown in the garden lake rescuing a young swimmer in difficulty.

Surprisingly the majority of Hackney's open space is common land, mainly lammas lands. These were fields owned by the lord of the manor, farmed in strips from Lady Day (1 April) until Lammas tide (1 August) known as "bread mass". From harvest until Lady Day the common serfs could graze their animals. By no stretch of the imagination can Hackney's commons be called picturesque or rural, but they are at least islands in a cold sea of brick and concrete, useful rather than ornamental.

Clapton Common is the most northerly, straggling along

Opposite:
Peckham Rye; bleak and windswept in March.

Clapton Common Road, flanked by some fine Georgian houses on the south side. Sexby whimsically claimed that "early in the morning, before chimneys and factories poison the air with their smoke it is possible to sniff the ozone of the pure sea breeze". The Hasidic Jews and West Indians of Stamford Hill scarcely seem to notice.

Stoke Newington Common has a railway across the middle and the same line was unkind to **Hackney Downs** and **London Fields**. Hackney Downs used to be crossed by Hackney Brook, "a still and rippling spring", now culverted and forgotten beneath a drab stage of tower blocks and busy roads. London Fields is best loved for its summer open-air swimming-pool during those occasional heat waves. **Well Street Common** is too close to Victoria Park to attract more than dog-owners and joggers. It was preserved by Sir John Cass when he built the Cassland estate, replacing rustic hovels with grand brick terraces. Today a "Fun 'n' Fitness" trail has been installed to tempt the energetic. Seagulls wheel overhead looking for debris or fly off to join the companionable ducks in Victoria Park.

Millfields, either side of Lea Bridge Road, are orientated towards active football and cricket. Across the River Lea, a popular route for Danish marauders in King Alfred's time, and past the Jolly Anglers public house, where no doubt the Danes would have stopped for a pint or two of Viking lager given the chance, lies the yawning space of **Hackney Marshes**. These meadows, skirted and intersected by the Lea and its tributaries, were never suitable for building, owing to flooding. After their acquisition by the London County Council in 1893, some flood protection was carried out, whereupon hundreds of football pitches were laid out. Every Sunday since then thousands of pairs of boots have been muddied and shins bruised. How many million goals have been scored? The area's most recent claim to fame was the mysterious bear, an amusing hoax which flummoxed the police in 1982. Hackney Marshes are part of the **Lea Valley Park**, a huge area stretching up into Hertfordshire among a *melange* of reservoirs, filter beds, marshlands, playing-fields and waterways, criss-crossed by pylons, railways and causeways.

Perhaps even more peculiar than London's commons are the medieval village greens which somehow have survived within the all-consuming megalopolis. **Islington Green** was at the centre of Domesday Iseldon, the apex of the triangle formed by Upper Street, Lower Street (boringly renamed Essex Road in 1930) and Cross Street. The trees, cenotaph and battered statue of Hugh Myddelton (purveyor of fresh water to London via the New River from Amwell in Hertfordshire to Sadler's Wells) are a dim reflection of a distant past when geese and pigs wandered on the green and villagers came to collect their water. Even more changed, alas, is **Clerkenwell Green**, smothered in cars, motorbikes and public conveniences. By comparison, **Camberwell Green** remains remarkably verdant and cheery, despite being a traffic roundabout.

In the East End, **Bethnal Green** is a welcome enclave of trees and grass in a grim and gloomy part of town. It is not easy to envisage Bethnal Green as a rural hamlet of wattle, daub and thatch. It was famous for its legend of the blind beggar, supposedly the son of a noble slain at the Battle of Evesham in 1265, and his beautiful daughter. The green, originally part of Stepney Common, was saved in 1690 when the village expanded rapidly to accommodate an influx of Huguenot silk weavers, overspill from Spitalfields. Next to the green stood Bethnal House, where Pepys stowed his diaries and valuables in 1666, which from 1700 was a lunatic asylum. In 1868 the Bethnal Green Museum, exhibiting toys, lace and Rodin sculptures, was built on part of the green, leaving nine acres of pleasant gardens.

Further out on the fringes of east London **Woodford Green**, with its duck ponds and cattle troughs beside the High Road, is more rural, still boasting cows which wander oblivious of the traffic. At Havering-atte-Bower the rural picture is complete; **Havering Green**, once famous for its Ascension Day fair, is complemented by church, pub, vicarage and manor house. **Hadley Green** too has a charming feel of the country. At the junction of Kitts End Road an obelisk marks the bloody Battle of Barnet, fought in 1471 after the mercenaries of Edward IV had sharpened their swords at Whetstone.

Turnham Green beside Chiswick High Road in west London is known for its Civil War skirmish, the battle that never was, when Charles came nearest to capturing London and re-establishing power. No evidence remains today, however, of the trenches and gun emplacements thrown up by London's militia.

The old manor of Fulham, owned for centuries by the

Opposite:
Tooting Bec
Common; a spinney
of oak, sycamore
and bramble.

Bishop of London, still has its village greens. **Brook Green** near Hammersmith Broadway is a five-acre oblong of trees and grass with an excellent pub at the western end. **Eel Brook Common** and **Parson's Green** flank the King's Road. John Stow noted 400 years ago that Parson's Green had "very good houses for the gentry". The same applies today following the invasion of Fulham by the media set in the early 1970s.

Kew Green (see Chapter 7) is genteel and picturesque. However, London's most beautiful village green is undoubtedly **Richmond Green**, one of the largest in England and in a perfect setting, tucked behind the bustle of George Street. On the south-west side, Maids of Honour Row and the Tudor archway into Old Palace Yard recall times when the Green was used for royal jousting tournaments. After the palace was demolished in 1665 and the monarchy had moved elsewhere the green reverted to a more lowly function of grazing sheep and village football. Today it is one of the most idyllic places to play cricket in London.

The commons and greens have been protected through the ages by common law and statute. Yet London also possesses several other natural woods and heaths, saved specifically from development in order to provide Londoners with space to relax and play. **Highgate** and **Queen's Wood**, philanthropically acquired by the City Corporation, are superb examples, high and dramatic beech woods on the north-eastern slopes of Highgate. In 1894 the poet A.E. Housman lived nearby while writing *A Shropshire Lad* and frequently walked in the woods. He complained vehemently when undergrowth was cleared too vigorously to reveal the Archway Road; how aghast he would be today over the Archway motorway proposals, which eat into the west side of the woods. "Is the team ploughing?"

Not far away, south of Falloden Way, **Big** and **Little Woods** were carefully incorporated into the innovative plans for Hampstead Garden Suburb by Raymond Unwin after the land had been bought by Henrietta Barnet. These are fine mature oak woods where dogs can chase squirrels and children play hide-and-seek.

Trent Park, north of Cockfosters, has been preserved by the Greater London Council as a natural terrain of fields, hedgerow and spinney, a country park where one can roam

Right:
The Rookery,
Streatham.

Opposite:
Queen's Wood,
Highgate.

Page 36:
Lesnes Abbey
ruins, looking north
to Thamesmead.

Page 37:
The River Thames,
near the new
barrage at
Woolwich.

34

among cowslips and forget-me-nots. The only blot is the unimpressive architecture of the teacher-training college in the middle. Like Whitewebbs and Forty Hall (see Chapter 5), Trent Park was part of Enfield Chase, a great hunting reserve of the Plantagenet kings, entered from Southgate and Potters Bar.

Twenty miles south on the opposite edge of London, **Addington Hills** and **Bromley Common** are two popular areas of gravelly and hummocky woodland, relieving the suburban sprawl of Croydon, Selsdon and Hayes. Further east, **Bostall Heath** offers the sylvan delights of pine, larch, birch and hazel and undergrowth of gorse, broom and bracken, thriving on the sandy pebbly ridge east of Plumstead. It belonged to Queen's College, Oxford, who owned the manor of Plumstead, until they sold it for £5,000 in 1877. The GLC now manage Bostall Heath together with **Lesnes Abbey Woods** nearby, one of the loveliest and least known parks in London. Sloping down from the heights to the Thames floodplain, Lesnes Abbey Woods overlook the Leggo-like towers of Thamesmead, a brave new world of housing and factories on the Erith marshes. These flood-prone marshes were farmed by thirteenth-century French monks, who built their monastery slightly above danger level, with deep woods rising steeply behind like an amphitheatre. The remains of the abbey have been superbly restored and stand among immaculate lawns. All

components are meticulously labelled, even the serving hatch for local paupers. The woods are a perfect backcloth, ablaze in spring with wild daffodils, bluebells and anemones.

On the western outskirts at Greenford **Horsenden Hill**, 270 feet above sea level, offers long views out to Windsor, the Chilterns, Crystal Palace, Harrow and Westminster, while the Grand Union Canal winds below. This rough grassland, perhaps an ancient hill fort, is set among a strange amalgam of arterial roads, housing estates, golf course and scraps of fields. This is the limit of Betjeman's metroland:

> Out into the outskirt's edges,
> Where a few surviving hedges
> Keep alive our lost Elysium,
> Rural Middlesex again.

The **River Thames** is without doubt London's single most important natural feature, from the genteel banks of Hampton to the wide estuary beyond Erith. This famous strip of water, flowing like an artery through the heart of London, has been a lifeline for trade and transport, and an immense asset for recreation. The strength of the tides, the muddy banks and the disconcerting amount of pollution have discouraged all but the maddest or most inadvertent swimmers. The appalling filth of human sewage and industrial effluence virtually eliminated fish from the lower Thames in Victorian times. "A Stygian pool, reeking with ineffable and intolerable horrors" is how Disraeli described it. In this foul water the celebrated medieval oyster-beds, which once fed London's poor, perished; salmon and sea trout sensibly found other rivers to spawn. Above Teddington Locks, where the Thames is no longer tidal, the fresh water is cleaner, and less full of flotsam and jetsam. Here fishermen crouch patiently under their umbrellas with their transistor radios, maggots and tackle, waiting for minnows. Downstream the Port of London Authority claim that salmon have returned to the lower Thames, together with seventy other types of fish. Not yet, though, the oyster-beds.

Boating for pleasure, as opposed to getting from A to B by ferry or barge, was, like so many sports, a Victorian innovation. Even those who could not afford to row or sail enjoyed walking along the river banks or across the many new bridges. Pleasure boats plied up and downstream between Westminster, Greenwich and Hampton, as they still do. Elderly but elegant paddlesteamers, like the *Waverley*, moored along the Embankment and ran day trips to Margate or even across the Channel.

The Thames is not the easiest of rivers for personal boating. Even now individual boats cannot be hired in Central London. The tidal races through the bridges and the commercial traffic are too dangerous for the inexperienced. Only the dwindling breed of licensed watermen can operate here. Until the Second World War they were a vital part of river life, numbered in thousands. They even had their own padre, the Reverend Black. Alas, no more; the death of the docks was the demise of the waterman also.

Further upstream the public can hire rowing skiffs at Richmond and Kingston. Above Teddington the comfortable waters are plagued with pretentious fibreglass cruisers, oozing with gin and the *nouveau riche*, annoying the ducks, water rats and fishermen with their swish wash. At Walton-on-Thames sailing dinghies tack busily up and down their narrow course.

The Thames is better known for its competitive rowing, the Tidesway Scullers and the Boat Race. All weathers, all seasons from Putney to Richmond the scullers skim, pairs, fours and eights past Chiswick Eyot, schools, colleges and clubs, with little men bawling instructions through megaphones from the cox's berth. The Oxford-Cambridge boatrace, begun in 1856, is the longest-running river event, a marvellous carnival along its $4\frac{3}{4}$-mile course, the riverside pubs at Hammersmith, Chiswick Mall and Barnes packed with partisans, an armada of motor launches in the wake of the straining crews.

In central London the Thames today is not as it appeared to Roman sappers and engineers 2,000 years ago. Then the river was much wider and shallower, even fordable at places. Their first bridge, if not actually a pontoon, stood on flimsy wooden piles. Peter of Colechurch's nineteen-arch stone bridge acted as a sluice through which the tide raced, trapping a lake upstream. This pool was where the Thames froze in the seventeenth and eighteenth centuries, when the mini-Ice Age produced some abnormally severe winters. In 1684 the Thames froze from bank to bank. John Evelyn remarked, "There were divers shops of wares quite

Opposite:
Greenwich; Wren's masterpiece viewed from Island Gardens on the Isle of Dogs

Page 40:
Lyle Park, near the old Woolwich ferry and new Thames barrier.

Page 41:
St. Katharine's Dock; Tower Bridge behind.

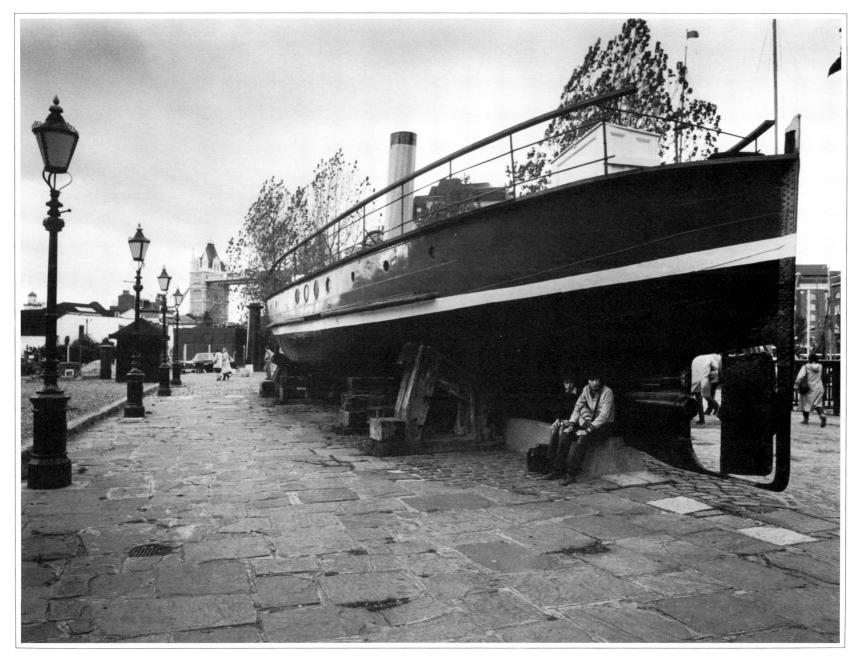

across as in town. Coaches plied from Westminster to the Temple, to and fro as in the streets — it seemed to be a bacchanalian triumph, a carnival on the water." It is theoretically possible that the new Thames barrage could do the same, but only if our winters deteriorate radically. Moreover, the Thames is now much narrower, and hence deeper and faster flowing. The Strand was originally literally a riverside strand. The Adelphi, Albert, Victoria and Chelsea Embankments all encroached into the riverside muds and gravels.

Sadly, in east and central London it is impossible to walk continuously beside the river. Warehouses, factories, power stations and the immense docklands prohibit access to the waterfront for long stretches. In the absence of a towpath or mall, the public must be content with the various parks which abut the river. **Battersea Park**, **Victoria Tower Gardens**, **Edward VII Memorial Gardens** at Shadwell and **Jubilee Gardens** on the South Bank all offer pleasant riverside walks (see Chapter 4). The pavement of Jubilee Gardens is inset with poems and stanzas extolling the Thames. Unfortunately, the **Embankment Gardens** from Temple to Charing Cross are separated from the river by the road. In the City and on the south bank special efforts have been made when redeveloping derelict wharves and warehouses to incorporate new promenades by the river. Perhaps one day it will be possible to walk either bank from the Tower to Parliament, or from Rotherhithe to Vauxhall.

Cutty Sark Gardens at Greenwich, opened in 1957 and extended since, is a fine riverside space, home for the *Cutty Sark* and for *Gipsy Moth IV*, in which Sir Francis Chichester circumnagivated. Enjoy the thrill of the pedestrian tunnel which leads under the river to **Island Gardens** on the opposite bank, unquestionably the best view of Greenwich. Wren's masterpiece was clearly meant to be approached by water. The garden, small but well tended, was laid out in 1895, and the tunnel opened soon after, replacing the old ferry. This is the southern tip of the Isle of Dogs, once the marshy kennels for the king's hounds, but now a depressingly bleak part of London.

Downstream, **Lyle Park** (named after the sugar baron) off North Woolwich Road is a good place to watch river traffic, similar to **Royal Victoria Gardens** a mile east. These lie next to the famous Woolwich ferry, once owned by the Crown who suppressed rivals at Erith and Greenwich. It still operates but suffers in competition with Blackwall and Dartford tunnels. The gardens are unremarkable except for having a view of the Thames barrier.

At Rotherhithe **King's Steps** and **Cherry Garden Pier** are deliberate attempts to open up the bankside for recreation, exceptionally well and cleverly done with plenty of nautical amusement. The maritime attractions of **St Katharine's Dock** have gone even further. This marina/water museum in the shadow of the Tower of London has become a tourist trap *par excellence*, a veritable ant-hill of Americans and Japanese lapping up the sawdust in the absurdly named Dickens Inn and snapping up the Scotch tweeds in the gift shops. A place to avoid if you want peace and quiet.

The upper reaches of the river above Hammersmith are bordered by the grounds of some of London's finest stately homes and palaces — Syon, Ham, Marble Hill, Hampton Court and Kew Gardens. **Dukes Meadows** beside Chiswick Bridge are wide and green, a favourite vantage point for the finish of the boat race where on other days the silent river glides past flowering banks. **Tagg's Island** at Hampton and **Garrick's Ait**, with domed temple and statuette of Shakespeare, are perfect places to watch the gentle flow.

Upstream of Putney Bridge a continuous towpath on the Surrey bank leads ever on to those Thameside delights of Windsor, Cookham, Marlow, Henley, Wallingford, Abingdon and the distant spires of Oxford. But that is a journey of 100 miles, the domain of Jerome K. Jerome, a gross of riverside pubs, and an adventure beyond the bounds of this book.

CHAPTER 3: The Royal Parks

The royal parks are the showpieces of London's open spaces. They are the most visited, the best known to tourists, and the most written about. The vast majority of the copious books and guides on London's parks and gardens deal exclusively with the royal parks. This book attempts to redress the balance; they are after all only 6,000 acres out of a total of 45,000 acres of public open space in Greater London. Nevertheless it is important not to underestimate the contribution which the royal parks make to London. They are probably the finest metropolitan parks in the world, with an unrivalled history and a rare beauty; London should be justifiably proud of them.

Their existence is almost entirely due to the passion of the monarchy in Tudor and Stuart times for hunting, coinciding with the opportunity which the Dissolution of the monasteries gave to Henry VIII for appropriating large tracts of land from the Church to the Crown. Most of the royal parks began as Henry's personal hunting ground on countryside grabbed ruthlessly from abbots, friars and priors. Although the regal disposition towards blood sports faded gradually, the power of the Crown and the recreational demands of its subjects ensured that these parks were never built on.

Their status is peculiar, quite unlike the private palace grounds found on the continent at Versailles, Fontainbleau or Vienna. In London the public acquired rights of access and passage across the royal parks, sometimes maintaining ancient rights of way which existed before the Crown confiscated the land, as on the monastic estate of Hyde Park. In the seventeenth century, foreign visitors were astounded to see commoners strolling freely and casually in Hyde Park or St James's. When Princess Caroline first arrived at Kensington Palace, before marrying George II, she asked Prime Minister Walpole how much it would cost to enclose the royal park with a high brick wall to keep the people out. "Three crowns," replied Walpole. "So cheaply?" questioned Caroline. "Madam, I mean the crowns of England, Scotland and Ireland!" Charles I had found out the hard way that meddling with people's established rights and freedoms was a dangerous and lethal business.

Today the royal parks operate under a typically British compromise. Strictly speaking they remain in the ownership of the Crown, but the Queen herself plays little part in their management or maintenance, which is handled by the State in the guise of the Department of the Environment. They are used by the people.

The four central royal parks, St James's, Green Park, Hyde Park and Kensington Gardens, have been described, rather preciously, as "London Green". Stretching from the south-east tip of St James's Park in the heart of Whitehall to the north-west corner of Kensington Gardens at Notting Hill, this three-mile wedge of open space, interrupted only by the traffic of Hyde Park Corner and Constitution Hill, is an enormous lung in the centre of London. How many property speculators have marvelled at the potential value of this real estate, and shaken their heads at its survival as trees and grass!

St James's Park, closest to the river, was originally swampy ground occasionally inundated by a high Thames tide. Until the Dissolution this worthless land was owned by the abbey of Westminster and supported a small leper colony. Nobody except the afflicted or the samaritan ventured here. Henry VIII took over in 1532, built a new mansion for himself, St James's Palace, and stocked the land with well-fed deer and game. The park was enclosed by fencing, and maintained exclusively for the king and court's pleasure. Here he could amuse himself by killing his supper and exercise his horses and hounds.

James I, more of an intellectual than aggressive hunter, established a small menagerie in the park to house larger animals which were too cramped in the Tower. These included an elephant which was given a gallon of burgundy each day in winter to keep his spirits high! James's son, Charles I, neglected the park and zoo during his traumatic reign. In the Civil War he was hounded out of London, but he returned there defeated to face trial and sentence. In January 1649 he walked bare-headed through a leafless St James's Park on his way to the scaffold at Whitehall, a lonely and diminutive figure, stripped of everything except his pride.

On the Restoration Charles II immediately set about reviving the park and opening it to the public. The Merry Monarch had a refreshingly modern approach to outdoor recreation, being totally uninterested in barbaric pastimes but passionately fond of birds and animals, trees, flowers and lakes. André Le Nôtre, already famous from his exploits at Versailles, was hired to advise on redesigning the layout. The muddy pools and bogs fed by the Tyburn

Page 43:
St. James's Park,
late summer.

Opposite:
The lake, St.
James's Park, from
the footbridge.

44

stream were merged into a thin straight canal running the length of the park and flanked with regimented rows of trees. Grand perspective with long symmetrical vistas was the height of seventeenth-century fashion. South of the canal, formal gardens of neat box hedges and gravel paths were set out, including a fountain triggered by a hidden device when trodden on. To the north The Mall was laid out, a broad avenue with four lines of trees, not as an approach to Buckingham Palace which did not exist then but as a place where the king could play pall-mall, a type of croquet named after the Italian *palla a maglio* (ball to mallet).

Charles adored St James's, walking his spaniels, feeding the ducks, and even swimming in the lake without the slightest qualm at being seen naked by his subjects. He stocked the canal with exotic ducks and formed an aviary on the south side which became known as Birdcage Walk. Everyone was thrilled when in 1666 the Russian Ambassador presented two pelicans. The Baleavian crane with its long wooden leg was an equally popular curiosity. Fencing was removed to allow free public access, and disreputable behaviour such as duelling was forbidden. For the common man, seeing the king was the chief attraction. Nevertheless the snobbish Pepys admitted to lying down on the grass by the canal and sleeping awhile, "it being mighty hot and I weary". Tom Brown's description is more vivid: "The green walk afforded us variety of discourses from persons of both sexes. Here walked a beau bareheaded, here a French fop with both hands in his pockets, carrying all his pleated coat before to shew his silk breeches."

Little changed in the eighteenth century except for the infamous swan, Jack, king of the canal, whose longevity and violent hatred of dogs was renowned. In 1814 John Nash was commissioned to build an oriental bridge supporting a small wooden pagoda across the strip of water. It succumbed to an over-enthusiastic firework display, but in 1827 Nash was called in again to remodel the entire park, as an appendage to Carlton House, home of George IV. Informality was the latest vogue. The straight canal was widened and curved and a large peninsula, known as Duck Island, projected into the lake to form a bird sanctuary. Irregular clumps of trees and individual weeping willows were planted beside the lake to break up the long panorama. A new Chinese bridge, minus pagoda,

completed the willow-pattern, sadly replaced in 1957 by a modern functional footbridge. Elsewhere hillocks and vales were carefully sculptured to give unexpected views of shrubberies and flower-beds. Being so much in the public eye St James's had no choice but to change with the times, keeping up with the latest fashion in landscape design.

Today it vies with Regent's Park as the best kept of the royal parks (howls of protest from all the others!). A platoon of about fifty keepers, gardeners, undergardeners, seedsmen and rangers maintain the superb floral displays, velvet lawns and magnificent trees, and undertake the chores of litter collection. The splendid lake, with its fountain and hundreds of ducks, geese and gulls, dominates the park. The tradition of pelicans survives; feeding time, daily at 4 p.m. at the east end of the lake, is great entertainment. Peckish humans can fill their own beaks and bellies in the Cake House nearby. The most extraordinary avian ritual involves the annual migration of families of mallards with their flightless fluffy youngsters from their tulip-bed nests to the Serpentine, when the police hold up the traffic to let them pass.

St James's Park is surrounded by famous buildings — Buckingham Palace, St James's Palace, Carlton House Terrace, Clarence House, The Admiralty and Horse Guards Parade. The backcloth of domes and spires of Westminster and Whitehall evokes an almost Turkish flavour, an illusion now slightly jolted by the massive concrete Home Office complex which replaced the lofty red brick of Queen Anne's Gate. The Mall is associated in every loyalist's mind with those luxurious State processions — opening Parliament, royal weddings and funerals and Trooping the Colour. Adulatory statues of Captain Cook, Lords Clive and Kitchener, Nelson looking down from Trafalgar Square, the Marine Memorial to the Boer War and the 2,300 tons of Carrara marble in the Queen Victoria memorial outside Buckingham Palace are imperial spectators to these pageants alongside the myriad mortals who queue for hours.

St James's Park tolerates all these and more; the thousands of trippers and tourists and the hordes of lunchtime office workers who fill the summer deckchairs. Yet the park offers more than this, on an early spring morning or at autumn dusk when the mist rises from the lake and the ducks settle down to sleep. Here, in the heart

Opposite:
The entrance to Green Park from the Mall, near Buckingham Palace.

of London, one can find peace and sanctuary. As Disraeli said so eloquently, "In exactly ten minutes it is in the power of every man to free himself from the tumult of the world."

Lying north of St James's, **Green Park** is the second part of the royal bailey around Buckingham Palace. This triangle of fifty-three acres is the smallest and least dramatic of the royal parks. The name refers rather banally to the dominance of trees and grass, and the absence of flowers, apart from spring bulbs, and other adornments. Originally it was rough woodland, next to the "drie ditch bankes of Pikadilla". The Tyburn, now culverted, flows across the park *en route* from Marble Arch to St James's Park lake, and from its course the land rises steadily up Constitution Hill to Hyde Park Corner.

Charles II enclosed Green Park as a place for royal picnics. Trees were planted and paths laid. In the middle an ice box was dug, filled with snow in winter, covered with straw and used to chill summer wines. Queen's Walk, on the east side, was named after Caroline, wife of George II. Now it is lined with fine mansions from Lancaster House to the Ritz, exuding the affluence of club land. In 1749 Green Park was the chosen site for the elaborate Temple of Peace, erected in ornate Doric style to mark the end of the War of Succession. An ambitious firework display celebrated its opening, but the initial reluctance of the fireworks to ignite encouraged excessive use of firebrands, whereupon the entire Temple was engulfed in flames. In the ensuing riot only Handel's specially written *Music for the Royal Fireworks* salvaged any dignity or respectability.

In the first half of the nineteenth century, clearings in the park were popular launching-pads for daring balloon ascents. Rather strangely Green Park continued to suffer a history of violence and disorder, not only from personal duels. Constitution Hill witnessed several assassination attempts, including three on Queen Victoria and one on Edward VII. In 1945 the victory celebrations developed into a mob orgy, at odds with the normally unassuming and undemonstrative nature of the park.

On Sundays the Piccadilly railings are festooned with lurid paintings, etchings, watercolours, mirrors and cheap fancy goods, a smaller version of the trash market along Bayswater Road. It's an uncomfortable clash with the soft turf and stoical tree trunks of the park behind.

Hyde Park is the largest of the four central royal parks,

Green Park.

48

and the nearest thing in London to New York's Central Park. Like St James's it had a monastic past. In the Domesday Book the Manor of Hyde was listed under the estate of Eia, but his successor Geoffrey of Mandeville bequeathed the land to Westminster Abbey for the monks to farm and grow timber. Henry VIII seized their holdings, fenced the wooded areas to prevent poaching or rustling and inflicted savage punishments on trespassers.

In 1637 Hyde Park became the first royal park to be opened to the public, a major innovation. A racecourse, called the Ring, was a popular attraction, but not for long, or so it seemed. In 1642 the Parliamentarians requisitioned the park to dig trench defences against the king's forces who were poised in Oxford to attack London, and after Cromwell's victory it was resolved that Hyde Park be sold for ready money. In 1653 it fetched £17,000, in three lots. John Evelyn complained in his diary: "I went to take the air in Hyde Park and was made to pay a shilling by the sordid fellow who had purchased it." The Puritans were theoretically against public entertainment or recreation but found such dogma hard to enforce; on May Day 1654 the park was packed with revellers, even including the Lord Protector himself. To Evelyn's huge relief, in 1660 on the restoration of Charles II the royal parks were reclaimed without compensation; once again Hyde Park became London's largest public recreation ground.

As at St James's the park provided a venue for displaying social fashion — the show shop of the metropolis, full of fops and dandies. The circus of ostentation was concentrated around a newly built thoroughfare extending from Kensington Palace through the park via Constitution Hill to Whitehall. Rotten Row, possibly a corruption of *route du roi* or (less likely) the gaelic *rattanreigh*, meaning straight path, was lit by 300 lamps at nightfall. It became a parade ground of equestrian skill and elegance, and beaux and belles driving in smart coaches. A tradition was established which continues to this day. In Edwardian times ladies rode side-saddle down Rotten Row and it remains the most popular place in London for horse-riding, not just by the Household Cavalry but also for the horse-minded public and annual rallies of carriage and fours. Outside St George's hospital at Hyde Park Corner, where traffic now roars through the underpass straw used to be laid on the roadway at night to damp the noise of horses' hoofs.

Hyde Park.

49

George II's wife, Caroline, took careful heed of Walpole's advice and adapted quickly to the English system of wooing the public rather than erecting barriers against them. She became the leading figure of fashion among the beau monde, the Lady Di of her day, and was responsible for the single most important alteration to the park, the construction of the Serpentine. At her request, the boggy course of the River Westbourne was excavated in 1730 under William Kent's supervision, to form an enormous curving lake, forty feet deep and a mile long. When the Serpentine was recently drained for cleaning, remains of tree stumps and the monks's timber causeway were found in the mud.

The Serpentine was ideal for aquatic events — the great frosts in the eighteenth century when risky crossings of the ice by horse and carriage attracted huge wagers, or the re-enactment of Trafalgar with model ships and pyrotechnics in 1815 to celebrate victory over Napoleon. More morbidly, it provided a watery grave for frequent suicides, including Harriet Westbrook, first wife of Shelley. It is arguable whether more deaths in the Serpentine were due to the foulness of the water, the Westbourne having become little better than a public sewer.

The Serpentine bridge was built in 1826 by George Rennie, the last bridge still standing in London designed by the Rennie family. Its elegant stone parapets afford one of the finest prospects in London, the tree-lined lake framing the distant towers of Westminster Abbey and Parliament. Only the totem poles of the Hilton Hotel and Knightsbridge Barracks impinge on the periphery of this perfect composition.

The Serpentine is one of the best boating lakes in London, and on a windy day a good test for the occasional oarsman. In summer the south side is roped off to provide a swimming lido. The water is cleaner than it looks — the Westbourne is culverted and smelly no longer, and the Serpentine is now fed from the mains, mildly chlorinated. In those stiflingly hot evenings of 1976 and '77 it was bliss to plunge into the warm brown water. On the banks, reptilian sun-worshippers soaked up the rays from April to October, turning into leathery wrinkled lizards. On colder days the tattered deck chairs flap disconsolately in the wind.

The Victorians could not resist adding statues and monuments. The naked figure of Achilles, cast in gun metal from Waterloo and suitably located near Wellington's Aspley House, had caused a stir at its unveiling in 1822. Prostitution had already brought protests that the lung of London was becoming the lust of London. Achilles's nudity did nothing to quieten the prudes of the day. Decimus Burton's triple arch and screen erected in 1828 at Hyde Park Corner was far more appropriate, and in 1850 Nash's replica of Constantine's triumphal arch was moved from outside Buckingham Palace to Marble Arch, transforming the squalid area where Tyburn gallows had stood from 1571 to 1783. As at Hyde Park Corner, traffic has since taken an unholy hold. The widening of Park Lane in 1960 took twenty-one acres from the park; John Betjeman and others denouced such vandalism, to no avail. Marble Arch with its carpet of crocuses now houses a police station and is isolated by an unceasing whirlpool of vehicles from the park and Speakers' Corner.

This is one of Britain's institutions, a place where any man or woman can stand and say what he likes, with the freedom of speech which is supposedly the envy of the world. The Reform League succeeded in establishing Speakers' Corner in 1866 following clashes between demonstrators and police. In today's media world of television and radio, orange-box oratory is not the powerful voice it used to be. Now most of the Sunday speakers are cranks or humourists, most of the audience amused or bemused tourists. Trafalgar Square and Jubilee Gardens have taken over as more usual places for mass rally addresses, although Hyde Park remains the best assembly point in London for big demonstrations and marches. The great CND rally in October 1983 rivalled the Royal Wedding fireworks in 1981 when hundreds of thousands of people flooded into the park, bringing central London to a grinding halt.

The most spectacular but now least evident addition to Hyde Park was the Great Exhibition of 1851, held inside the famous Crystal Palace which was built specially for the occasion. The idea was Prince Albert's, inspired by the 1849 Paris exhibition, and he chose the site on the south of the park between Rotten Row and the Knightsbridge barracks. Joseph Paxton's novel design was bold and controversial, an enormous cathedral of glass and iron, tall enough to enclose several mature elm trees and with room for over

Opposite:
The CND rally in Hyde Park, October 1983.

100,000 exhibits. 300,000 people attended the opening ceremony on 1 May, and six million others followed during the next six months to see the wonders of the modern world. Profits were staggering, enough to finance the construction of permanent museums in Exhibition Road, South Kensington. By popular demand, the Crystal Palace was carefully dismantled and re-erected in a new park at Sydenham (see page 76). Hyde Park returned to a more normal way of life. Certainly the eye-catching glass hexagons and pyramids of the cafés beside the Serpentine make no attempt to compete with Paxton.

Although the last of the deer were removed to Richmond in 1830 the grass continued to be kept down by sheep until 1939. With its wide expanses of grass, its boating and swimming, its football pitches and Speakers' Corner, Hyde Park maintains an unpretentious versatility. **Kensington Gardens**, though separated from Hyde Park only by West Carriage Drive, has an altogether more refined air; some would even shudder to hear it called a park.

Having been part of Henry's hunting empire it reverted to being the private grounds of the Earl of Nottingham until 1689 when William III, seeking less damp conditions for his asthma, hit on Kensington as a suitable residence. Nottingham House, dismissed by Evelyn as "a patched up building with gardens" (hardly estate agent's propaganda), was duly acquired for £18,000 and transformed by Wren, Hawksmoor, Vanbrugh and Kent in turn into **Kensington Palace**. Wren alone spent £60,000 on the house. Kent's alterations for George I were much criticized — "observe the great inferiority of design and decoration," moaned one of Wren's fans.

Queen Anne expanded the gardens, at the expense of Hyde Park, but it was Queen Caroline who organized the landscape we know today. In addition to the Serpentine, whose western arm, The Long Water, lies within the Gardens, she planted long avenues of trees, created the Round Pond in front of the palace and stocked the gardens with red squirrels and tortoises.

Kensington Palace remained the primary royal residence until 1790 when the court moved to Richmond. William III, Queen Anne and George II all died at the house, the latter just as he was about to take a postprandial stroll in the gardens. Thereafter they were opened to the "well-dressed" public, except soldiers, sailors and servants.

Victoria spent her first eighteen years at Kensington, including the first three weeks of her reign, the last monarch to live there. In 1840 after Victoria had left for Buckingham Palace, the Gardens were opened every day to everyone. The hooped entrance to Kensington Palace Green marks Victoria's height — she was clearly a petite woman. Today those bits of the palace not open to the public provide London flats for the royals — Princess Margaret, the Duke and Duchess of Gloucester, Prince and Princess Michael of Kent.

The Broad Walk in front of the Palace remains the main north-south axis of the gardens. It is uncommonly wide and the little hill at the south end sloping down to Gloucester Road is almost ready-made for rollerskates, despite official notices. In the mid 1950s the avenue of elms was cleared, under the pretext of disease but plausibly for civil defence purposes. Where better in central London for light aircraft to land and evacuate the queen? Similar rumours exist about military installations under Hyde Park between the Park Lane car park and the barracks. Whatever the motives, the tree sprites had their revenge in the 1970s when Dutch elm disease ravaged England. Five hundred elms disappeared from Kensington Gardens and Hyde Park alone. Spindly saplings of lime and plane are scant replacement.

West of Broad Walk Vanbrugh's orangery is delightful, if much restored. Nearby, the sunken garden remains little changed. Sadly, the gates are kept locked and this paradise with carp pool and terraces holds its secret. The Round Pond, about one-third of a mile round, is a perfect little sea for model sailing boats and urban gulls — perhaps not quite what Queen Caroline intended, but no matter. She would have loved the bandstand nearby and the crowds who sit to listen in summer.

The Victorians and Edwardians contributed most of the Garden's statuary. Most dynamic, perhaps, is the leaping horse and muscular figure depicting *Physical Energy* by George Frederick Watts. Most loved by children is the charming sculpture of Peter Pan, erected in 1912 beside the Long Water by George Frampton, immortalizing James Barrie's fairytale; or the quaintly carved stump of the Elfin Oak in the playground, restored with help from Spike Milligan.

Dominating all is the Albert Memorial, unquestionably

Opposite:
Green Park; the arctic freeze of 1985.

Page 54:
Picnicking in Kensington Gardens.

Page 55:
A mounting stone in Kensington Gardens.

the most extravagant monument in London. This indulgently ornate edifice faces the Albert Hall across Kensington Gore and overwhelms the southern part of the Gardens. Gilbert Scott's "masterpiece" was finished in 1876 and cost £120,000. Ever since, critics have fallen over each other in their haste to condemn it. Perhaps the pomposity of the design provoked those rude descriptions of Albert sitting ruminantly on the cosmic lavatory, about to be rocketed into orbit — light touch-paper and retire. The absurd frieze of "famous men", painters, musicians and philosphers — a ridiculous concoction of Bach, Archimedes, Wren, Hereward the Wake, Shakespeare and Newton, all with virtually identical smug faces — doesn't help. But perhaps it is too easy to mock this uncomfortable feat of engineering; undoubtedly the Albert Memorial, if not a work of supreme beauty, is a summation of the Victorian Age.

Running parallel to the southern boundary of the gardens, the Flower Walk epitomizes equally well the gentility of Kensington Gardens. Here, in summer and on warm spring and autumn afternoons, nannies parade their precious cargoes past the herbaceous borders, rich with colour and scent; elderly dowagers gingerly take the air, accompanied by their prim housekeepers, before returning to smart Kensington flats for tea. At one time this might have been sipped in the Serpentine Gallery, now converted into an art gallery which holds special exhibitions. To the north beautiful lawns sweep past Queen Caroline's temple and slope down to The Long Water. This is the perfect place for a romantic picnic before a Promenade concert, a bottle of light chilled wine, an assortment of salami and cheese, bathed in evening sunshine.

Regent's Park is the most northerly of the royal parks and perhaps more than anything else contributes to the refined atmosphere of St John's Wood, Primrose Hill and Marylebone. Without this enormous block of parkland the grubby suburbs of Camden Town and Lisson Grove might have merged, the Eton and Portland estates would have lost their exclusiveness and the whole balance of north and south London might have changed. It could easily have happened but for the endeavours of three men at the beginning of the last century, for unlike the other royal parks Regent's Park has not enjoyed continuous use for recreation.

The thickly forested land between the small hamlets of St Marylebone and St Pancras, within the Manor of Tyburn, had belonged to the Abbey of Barking. Village pigs roamed and rooted among oak and ash for acorns and truffles. The seizure of St James's and Hyde Parks, in addition to the palace grounds at Eltham, Richmond, Nonsuch, Greenwich and Hampton Court, had still not satisfied Henry VIII's greedy appetite for hunting and sport. Marylebone Park was duly enclosed in 1538 and its boundary carefully fenced.

Unlike the others it did not become public in Stuart times. In 1649 Cromwell confiscated the land, which when surveyed was reckoned to contain 16,297 trees, 2,800 of which were immediately felled for the navy. Charles II regained the land, by now virtually deforested, but, being preoccupied with his plans for St James's, leased it off for farming. Marylebone's proximity to town and the rich clay soils enabled profitable production of milk, butter and hay for London's markets. The New Road (Euston/Marylebone Road) was built in 1757, south of which Edward Harley, Earl of Oxford, laid out his Georgian streets and terraces. Beside the New Road, White House Farm became a popular inn, the Jew's Harp Tavern. The small-holdings flourished.

In the 1780s the 125-year leases started to fall in, which is where the story of Regent's Park really begins. Day-to-day estate management was handled by John Fordyce, a civil servant but also a man of unusual energy and vision. He suggested that the Crown should retain and consolidate their Marylebone estate and set up a fund to buy out outstanding leases. In 1793 Fordyce was appointed surveyor-general to a board of commissioners, and with the personal blessing of the Prince Regent, later George IV, instigated a competition for high-class residential development. To the south, London was bursting at the seams; never was an area more ripe for development.

A local man, John White, submitted a scheme in 1809 but was rejected. Instead, John Nash who had been introduced to the Prince Regent by Humphrey Repton was appointed. Nash, "a thick squat dwarf with round head, snub nose and little eyes", was a genius of his time, with a flair for grand design. His plan, though borrowing unashamedly from White, was brilliant, and quickly gained the enthusiastic patronage of the prince — a circular park of 500 acres with two concentric rings girdled by a lake, bordered by terraces

facing inwards, and within the park fifty-six detached villas, each sited to be invisible to any other, appearing to possess the whole. Behind the terraces, which were normal houses disguised as palaces by elaborate pediments and statues, Nash planned service areas, mews and a hay market, while to the north barracks for the Lifeguards were to be separated from the park by the new Regent's Canal. His masterstroke was to link the self-contained parkland estate with Westminster by a new boulevard to rival the arcaded Rue de Rivoli in Paris. Portland Place and Regent Street extended as a triumphal royal mile down to the prince's residence at Carlton House. By sweeping away the poorer property on the west side of Soho it refashioned the West End, dividing Mayfair from Soho. "Once and once only has a great plan for London affecting the capital as a whole been projected and carried to completion," wrote Summerson. Nash succeeded where Wren had failed after the Great Fire.

In Regent's Park Nash rejected the formal squares of the Portman and Grosvenor estates. His plan involved a combination of town and country, which established a new fashion for urban and surburban living. Regent's Park was essentially the first garden city, an idea which spawned Bedford Park, Hampstead, Welwyn and Letchworth Garden Suburbs and Port Sunlight. Good old Nash.

The commissioners requested some amendments — the number of villas was reduced to only eight, the barracks were shunted to the east and the canal was moved to skirt the north edge of the park (bargees and their swearing were considered undesirable elements). Nash was fifty when work began in 1812. The Napoleonic War hampered progress; the canal, linking the Grand Union at Paddington with the Thames at Limehouse, was finished in 1820, the terraces and villas by 1828. Nash's pupil, Decimus Burton, took over in his dotage, firming up the details from Nash's sketchbook.

Sussex, Cornwall, Cambridge and Cumberland Terraces, which front the Outer Circle, remain among the most magnificent and exclusive private residences in London, as Nash intended. The park inside, however, quickly evolved into a public space. By 1841 the private lawns of villas in the park had shrunk; the rest was public. In the same year sixty acres of **Primrose Hill** were acquired by the Crown from Eton College and tacked on to the park.

The hill had long been a popular view-point and regular picnic spot. This helped to compensate for the forty acres cordoned off for the newly established Zoological Gardens (see Chapter 7).

Otherwise Regent's Park survives fairly much intact, but now with its avenues and gardens fully matured, as would delight Nash. The lake dominates the north-west quadrant between the Inner and Outer Circle, and, though much smaller than the Serpentine, is excellent for boating. Birdlife thrives on the six pretty islands — swans, moorhens and lanky herons. Water supply was problematic initially. The canal had only enough to feed itself and, although the Tyburn was tapped, residents soon complained about the smell. Mains water is now pumped in, but some of the backwaters are still rather slimy and stagnant.

In 1867 forty men and boys were drowned, and a hundred rescued, when the January ice gave way. Since then the lake has been lowered and skating forbidden. Seven years later a convoy of barges carrying munitions and gunpowder blew up underneath the Macclesfield Bridge near Avenue Road. A spark from a bargee's pipe was blamed, rather than sabotage. Scars of the explosion are visible on the trunk of a plane tree close by. But this disaster pales beside the horror and savagery of the IRA bomb attack in July 1982 on the bandstand beside the lake. Although the blast rocked north London and outraged society, the bandstand was determinedly re-erected and concerts bravely resumed within a month.

Earth excavated for the lake was piled into a mound in the middle of the Inner Circle. This forms one of the features of Queen Mary's Gardens, which is the loveliest and most secluded part of the park. These gardens were originally laid out in 1838 under the auspices of the Royal Botanical Society of London, a suitable companion for the Zoological Society, who had set up recently next to the canal. Until the society was disbanded in 1932, flower shows were held annually, the forerunner of the Chelsea Flower Show. In 1935 it was re-christened Queen Mary's Gardens and elaborate iron gates were erected. The heavenly rose garden, the azaleas and the iris and flags beside the pond make this an exquisite place of rare tranquillity. Also within the Inner Circle, but discreetly hidden by trees and bushes, is the open-air theatre. It opened in 1932 with Sir Nigel Playfair as Malvolio in *Twelfth*

Opposite:
Toboggans on
Primrose Hill.

Night. Shakespeare, especially *A Midsummer Night's Dream*, is the staple diet, and extremely atmospheric on warm evenings.

Several of Nash's villas have been replaced. St Dunstan Villa was rebuilt in 1937 as Winfield House for Barbara Hutton (of Woolworth fame), a plain brick building but difficult to see through the trees. It is now the residence of the United States Ambassador, and explains why Regent's Park is London's "little America". Gaudy gum-chewing kids of embassy staff sporting outlandish baseball uniforms are a familiar sight and sound, and the tennis courts near the tea pavilion echo with the grunts and groans of would-be McEnroes and Connors's.

South Villa was demolished in 1913 to make way for Bedford College. There were loud protests as functional institutional buildings were put up in its place, encroaching insensitively into the south-west side of the park. North Villa was taken over by the Islamic community in 1948, since when their Central London Mosque has sprung up like a huge copper mushroom next to Hanover Gate. Unlike mundane Bedford College, this magnificent structure would surely have been approved of by Nash, blending superbly as it does with the pointed domes of Sussex Terrace. He did, after all, design the Brighton Pavilion.

The other terraces which were decaying and squatted in the early 1970s are now restored and immaculate. Nash's Broad Walk remains the axis for the east side of the park, ornamented by Nesfield's flower garden at the south end with its urns and herbaceous borders. Baroness Burdett Coutts, Victorian philanthropist *extraordinaire*, donated the gigantic drinking-fountain, and the *Boy with Dolphin* statue was taken from Hyde Park.

The arm of the canal which once extended down to Cumberland Market was filled in 1942 (now partly the Zoo car park). The new animal houses, aviary and terraces for mountain goats dominate the skyline along Prince Albert Road. Apparently Richard Wagner stayed here for a while and wrote some of *Die Walküre*. Perhaps the Zoo was an inspiration — shame it wasn't Saint-Saëns. To the north Primrose Hill slopes gently up to its grassy summit, 219 feet above sea level. At dusk gas lamps flicker into life and the evening call of One Hundred and One Dalmatians drifts across the London countryside in our childhood memories.

London's four other royal parks lie south of or immediately beside the river. **Greenwich** is a glittering jewel in the crown of south-east London, modest in size but an exhilarating park of steep hills and marvellous views. Greenwich's other attractions — the *Cutty Sark*, the National Maritime Museum and the Old Royal Observatory — ensure that the park is one of the most visited by tourists and sightseers.

Greenwich is also the oldest of all the royal parks, with a hundred years' head start over most of the others. In 1433 Humphrey, Duke of Gloucester, uncle and regent to the young frail Henry VI, enclosed 200 acres of pasture and heath next to his manor at "Estgrenewich", and stocked the park with plump deer. After Humphrey had mysteriously been disposed of, Queen Margaret took up residence and established Greenwich as the favourite country seat of the monarchy. Westminster and the court were seven miles away by river. The old fishing village of Greenwich and the wooded slopes of the park rising up to the wild landscape of Blackheath made this one of the prettiest places most easily accessible to London. Evidence of foundations from a Roman villa in the park suggests that others were of the same opinion rather earlier.

Elizabeth I loved Greenwich and spent most of her spare time there, frequently picnicking in the park. It was her Sandringham, Balmoral and Windsor, rolled into one. James I replaced the old wooden fence with a brick wall, two miles long and twelve feet high, most of which survives, and he commissioned Inigo Jones to build a "house of delight" for his wife. The Queen's House (see page 98) was eventually completed for Henrietta Maria, wife of Charles I.

Thereafter, Greenwich Palace fell out of favour and Charles II ordered the demolition of the medieval buildings. However, he kept the park, and as at St James's looked to the great French designer Le Nôtre to add style and grandeur. Le Nôtre's intention was to plant majestic avenues of chestnuts and elms which would focus on the perfect architecture of the Queen's House. Alas, he committed the cardinal sin of failing to make a site inspection. His two-dimensional plans looked fine on paper but showed complete ignorance of the contours — the Queen's House is 100 feet lower than the crest of Blackheath Avenue! This blunder, not surprisingly, rather

Opposite:
The Queen's House, Greenwich, with the Royal Naval College behind.

tarnished his reputation. Blackheath Avenue is instead terminated by the much later statue of General Wolfe who conquered Quebec in 1759. He had lived at Macartney House, on Croom's Hill overlooking the park, and is buried in St Alphege's church.

Charles II's other contribution to Greenwich was the construction in 1675 of the Royal Observatory on the top of the hill. Named after the first Astronomer Royal, John Flamsteed, this is now a museum of ancient astronomical instruments, but is most famous for its meridian line, the key point of reference for longitudinal measurement. Here you can stand astride the brass strip set into the paving, one foot in the west, one in the east. 1984 marked the centenary of the international acceptance of the Greenwich meridian and Greenwich Mean Time. A white chalk line was extended down across the turf towards the Queen's House, bisecting rose beds, a grand idea which should be kept.

The park became public domain in 1705. At the same time Wren was appointed to build a new Royal Naval Hospital, similar to the one for soldiers at Chelsea. The Queen's House was incorporated into the symmetrical design, though it is now once again functionally separate, accommodating part of the National Maritime Museum. The park hosted the much-fêted Greenwich Fair, which twice a year provided riotous entertainment for enormous crowds that flocked from far and wide. Dickens described it as "a three-day fever which cools the blood for six months after". No wonder the Victorian prohibitionists suppressed it in 1857.

For a park of 200 acres Greenwich contains remarkable variety and always seems bigger than it is. Perhaps it is the hills — a skateboarder's paradise — which disguise the rectangular shape, or the uncultivated deer sanctuary, known as the Wilderness, in the south-east corner. There are dozens of interesting bits and pieces — Queen Caroline's sunken bath, now rather tamely filled to save dogs from jumping in and trapping themselves, the hollowed-out stump of Queen Elizabeth's oak, or the horticultural charms of the Flower Garden and the Dell. To the west are the fine eighteenth-century houses of the genteel middle classes on Croom's Hill and the splendour of the Ranger's house and its rose garden. On the east side, the quirky turrets of Vanbrugh Castle rise dramatically above the walls of Maze Hill.

The start of the London Marathon has replaced Greenwich Fair as the biggest carnival of the year, and provides the greatest headache for public conveniences (imagine 20,000 runners jostling for a last-minute pee!). Throughout the rest of the year a sprinkling of joggers test their legs against the steep inclines, struggling to resist the temptation to stop and admire the wondrous views over the twin-domed Royal Naval College to the idle cranes and gantries of dockland. Such superiority is worth the tarrying.

Richmond Park, on the other side of south London, could scarcely be more different from Greenwich, more than ten times larger and as wild and uncultivated as Greenwich is neat and ordered. Unlike all the other royal parks, Richmond has not been civilized with flower beds, rockeries, avenues of trees and tarmac paths. It has survived as all the others began, as a deer park, an open woodland where a person could ride for miles without having to clear a fence and where deer could roam freely.

Charles I established Richmond Park in 1637 as a replacement for Hyde Park, which he had opened to the public. By then the old medieval palace beside the river at Sheen, renamed Richmond by Henry VII, had been abandoned. Charles enclosed his deer park up on the high plateau to the south, well away from Richmond village, and surrounded the 2,500 acres with a ten-mile-long wall. The locals were not amused but were allowed limited access for collecting firewood. In 1751 Princess Amelia, daughter of George II, tried to prevent even this by blocking all public access. John Lewis, a local brewer, sued for entry and won his case. The judge ordered ladders to be placed where the boundary wall crossed ancient rights of way; Ladderstile Gate on the Kingston side marks this remarkable victory for the common man. Princess Amelia resigned her rangership in high dudgeon.

Unimpeded access for the public regrettably also means free access today for the motorcar. As well as killing about thirty of the deer each year, cars — particularly the huge weekend jams — ruin the peace and quiet of large chunks of the park and spoil what could be the finest cycling in London. Fortunately the park is big enough for the walker and the deer to escape the worst of the fumes and exhaust.

Unquestionably the seven hundred red and fallow deer are the masters of Richmond Park, never out of sight. With

Richmond Park.

Left:
Open Savannah
near the Pen Ponds.
Right:
Beside Isobella
Plantation.

no predators except the lunatic driver, their numbers have to be carefully culled. This conveniently supplies venison for royalty and the Cabinet, with any surplus exported to Germany. At rutting the grunts of the bay stags have to be heard to be believed; in spring the sensitive hinds will attack uncontrolled dogs who threaten their fawns. The deer preserve and enhance the savannah-like quality of Richmond, a beautiful undulating plain of wild grass and scrub. A herd of giraffe or antelope would not look out of place.

The forested plantations require protective fencing. Finest of these is the Isobella Plantation, dating from 1823, which now comprises the most luxurious woodland garden, a rich canopy of trees sheltering azaleas, rhododendrons, fern and heather. These woods are the daytime lair for the foxes, stoats, badgers and weasels who hunt abroad at night. The bleak Pen Ponds are similarly a refuge for the water fowl — coots, grebes and divers — and the skeins of honking Canada geese who flock here in winter.

The only formal part of the park is the garden of Pembroke Lodge on the north-west side near Richmond Gate. This whitewashed house was originally the mole-catcher's lodge, now a restaurant and flats for park-keepers. More famously it was the boyhood home of Bertrand Russell. The gardens are neatly arranged and

include an ancient barrow known as King Henry VIII's Mound. From this vantage point most people look west down to Ham village and the river and often miss the less obvious gap through the trees which frames a narrow view of London. From here Henry supposedly watched for the firing of the rocket which announced the execution of Anne Boleyn at the Tower, and his freedom to marry Jane Seymour.

White Lodge, on the other side of the Pen Ponds and near the golf course, is the largest building in the park. Rather confusingly, it was built by the Earl of Pembroke for George II as a shooting-box. His wife Caroline liked it more as a house, and even Queen Victoria used it occasionally. Edward VIII was born in White Lodge and Queen Elizabeth the Queen Mother lived there after her marriage to the Duke of York before the abdication. The Royal Ballet School occupy it now, as nice a place as one could wish in which to learn to dance. Who needs aerobics when the vast openness of Richmond Park provides the best breathing space in London?

If it were not for the barrier of the A3 road, Richmond would run directly and naturally into Wimbledon Common from Robin Hood Gate. Beyond Wimbledon and Worcester Park, between the suburbs of Cheam and Ewell, lie the remnants of what was once another great royal hunting park, **Nonsuch**. The very name smacks of Tudor England, conjuring up the spendthrift frivolity and unrivalled frippery of the king. At Nonsuch Henry VIII built a palace to outshine all his other palaces, finished just before his death in 1547. It was annexed by Cromwell, but Charles II on regaining possession showed no interest and gave it away. Rambling ramshackle Nonsuch was demolished in 1688 for its building materials. Today the estate is a large suburban park, full of fine trees, owned by the local council. Until the archaeological dig in 1959 the exact site of the palace had been forgotten; stones mark the outlines of the foundations. Henry's other little-remembered palace was Eltham (see page 112), where some of the buildings remain but little of the park.

Those who want a clearer picture of how the Tudor brick of Nonsuch might have looked need travel no further than **Hampton Court**, beside the river six miles upstream from Richmond. Hampton Court Palace, with its expansive formal gardens and parkland of Bushy and Home Parks, is one of the great stately houses of England, the match of Blenheim or Castle Howard, a rival even to the grandeur of Versailles.

The palace itself is, quite simply, vast. St James's, Kensington and Buckingham Palaces seem parsimonious in comparison. Its size is the more incredible considering it was not built by the king but by a commoner. Cardinal Thomas Wolsey was a self-made man, not even an aristocrat; he rose to become, for a while, the second most powerful man in the kingdom — Henry VIII's right hand. In 1514 his physicians selected Hampton, which had belonged to the Knights of St John, as a suitably healthy location to escape the "sweating sickness". Here he built his country pad, where he could enjoy privacy and seclusion. However, Wolsey's wealth, ambition and self-importance went too far. By 1525 his luxurious palace had aroused the envy of the King. To preserve his position he gave Hampton Court to Henry. In the event, even this magnanimous gesture did not save his political skin; Wolsey was stripped of everything and was lucky not to die at the scaffold.

Henry adored Hampton, and it remained a royal residence for two hundred years until George III took a peculiar dislike to the place. Christopher Wren redesigned the east front of the palace for William and Mary but it remains essentially Tudor, the most magnificent example in the country. There are literally hundreds of rooms, corridors and staircases. The Great Hall with its hammerbeam roof, the Gatehouse, the kitchens, Base Court, Real Tennis Court and Tilt Yard, still with one watchtower standing, epitomize the loves of Henry VIII for eating, drinking, dancing and games-playing. 700,000 people visit the palace each year (it is on the whistle-stop tour of England), but few have time to see more than a glimpse of its treasures and intrigues. In the tortuous recesses lurk the ghosts of the victims of Henry's cruelty and fickleness. The screams of Catherine Howard as she was dragged struggling from Hampton to the Tower still echo down the gloomy passageway outside the chapel where Henry refused to hear her cries.

The grounds of Hampton Court, opened to the public in Victorian times, are less spooky, and far more influenced by the late seventeenth century. In Henry's day the estate consisted of a series of tightly knit orchards, herb, privy and knot gardens close to the palace, and beyond, naturally wooded parkland for hunting, fenced and policed but uncultivated. Charles II and William III changed all that. André Mollet, disciple of Le Nôtre, was employed to impose order and geometry to the whole 2,000 acres of the park. Here was a chance to outdo the splendour of Fontainbleau and Versailles, which Charles had admired in exile, and which St James's and Greenwich were too small to emulate. What resulted represents the grandest landscape in London. Perhaps not as clever as Chiswick or as luscious as Kew, but on a scale which is almost too big for the human eye to appreciate. Moreover, the overall concept of straight vistas and rigorous symmetry survives intact, unsoftened by eighteenth- or nineteenth-century romanticism. Hampton remains England's outstanding example of seventeenth-century design.

East of the palace Mollet created a *"patte d'oie"* (meaning goose foot) — three colossal avenues flanked by lines of lime trees radiating from a semi-circular lake pivoted on the great fountain. The central arm, running east, was constructed as a canal, the Long Water, dead straight and almost a mile long. Beside Wren's classical east front with its twenty-three bays, the Broad Walk extends for half a mile — the longest herbaceous border in the country, lined with majestic yew obelisks, each lovingly clipped and sculpted.

To the south, Henry's Privy Garden was replanted with

Opposite:
Regent's Park; the lake and Nash terraces through cherry blossom.

Facing page 65:
Epping Forest.

64

exotic evergreens and wych-elm, and terminated at the riverside by the Tijou screens. These exquisitely crafted panelled railings are a masterpiece of French artistry, each a rich composition of delicate flowers, birds and beasts miraculously fashioned out of wrought iron. It required a skill which one imagines no longer exists, like the gold-leaf treasures of Macedonia.

North of the palace William and Mary's gardener, Henry Wise, laid out the Wilderness, an extremely complicated pattern of box hedges, shrubs and parterres. Like Mollet's goose foot, it really needs to be seen from the air. That, of course, would be cheating when it comes to the Maze, Hampton's best known feature. The ravages of rampaging schoolchildren have left the hornbeam and privet hedges rather tatty and worn. Nor is the puzzle excessively contrived, being only one-third of an acre and with only five alternative routes. Yet ever since our great-great-grandfathers it has starred as the biggest crowd-puller. Beyond the Lion Gate, also by Tijou, the White Lion pub is ideally placed for couriers and teachers to leave their charges unravelling the maze while they have a quick pint.

The Tudor Gardens south of the palace were reformed in the 1920s by Ernest Law, aiming to copy as closely as possible the intricate layout of an Elizabethan knot garden. Traditional herbs and strong-smelling blooms recreate the intimate patterns and scents with which Wolsey and Henry would have been familiar. The Sunken and Pond gardens, almost bristling with squat box heges, provide a feast of disciplined geometry beside the cool elegance of the orangery. Nearby, the Hampton Court vine is another marvel, said to have been planted in 1768. Its roots stretch far beneath the foundations of the palace and garden walls, probably even below the Thames. A special greenhouse has been built to shelter the 120 feet of its longest branch. Its maintenance, and the picking and selling of 700 bunches of sweet black grapes each year, is a full-time job, but one only of the 109 staff who look after the gardens. Only Kew receives such intensive horticultural care.

The thousand acres of Hampton Court Home Park were divided inexorably by Wolsey and the old Kingston to Hampton road from the thousand acres of **Bushy Park**. This was incorporated into the plans of William and Mary, implemented by Wren, and is dominated by the imposing Chestnut Avenue. This runs virtually due north from the Lion Gate in front of the palace to Teddington Gate over a mile away. The superb phalanx of limes and chestnuts, whose flowering candles are the glory of May, is broken only by the circular basin and round pond. In the middle, fifty yards from the water's edge, the huge fountain surmounted by Diana surveys the traffic as it rumbles down the avenue. The statue was designed by Fanelli but put on its pedestal by Wren.

Both Bushy and Home Parks, stock deer, not as many as Richmond, but similarly kept for economic reasons rather than mere adornment. They even stayed during the war when the park became an American garrison. Either side of the Chestnut Avenue, Bushy Park exhibits a contented mixture of pasture, paddocks and plantations. Heron Pond and Leg of Mutton Pond to the east and the Longford River to the west, twisting through the glades of Willow Plantation and Waterhouse Woodland Garden, keep the meadows dewy lush and the mighty deciduous trees leafy green until the last throes of summer.

The passing years effect little change on the royal parks. Standards are maintained with a care and pride which are all too easily ignored. For the public they act as sacred sentinels against the passage of time. Other parts of London might change; surely never the royal parks. But who are we to know? The grounds of **Buckingham Palace**, official London residence of the monarch, remain private, accessible only by invitation to the privileged few, the honoured and the fêted. Some day, possibly, these beautiful gardens may be opened to the general public. Perhaps a future monarch will tire of the size and expense of Buck House. It happened to St James's, Kensington and Hampton Court.

Page 65:
Hampton Court,
the east front.

CHAPTER 4: Municipal Parks

Compared with the commons and heaths or the royal parks and churchyards, London's municipal parks are a recent phenomenon, a product of the last one hundred and fifty years. Commons and royal parks are ancient open spaces which at some stage have fallen into public use and survived as such. Municipal parks have been created with the specific aim of providing recreational space for the masses, using public money to do so. They are purpose-built, deemed to be a necessary part of urban life, like sewers, cemeteries, swimming-baths and libraries, controlled by committees and bureaucrats on behalf of the ratepayer.

The creation of municipal parks is still going on. In the tightly packed inner-city areas such as Hackney, Tower Hamlets and Southwark, new parks are being planned, large and small, to provide much-needed breathing spaces in districts which have been chronically deprived of open space ever since the old farmland was smothered with Victorian slums.

Between 1830 and 1880 London's population rose from one and a half million to five million. During this railway age London snowballed and the outward march of bricks and mortar threatened to engulf all. Occasionally a patch of medieval common, a small village green or the garden of an Elizabethan manor might escape the builder's spade, but the ordinary fields and meadows where Londoners used to walk and picnic, and the woods and copses where village children played were swallowed up. Cheap rail fares encouraged new dormitory towns to blossom around railway stations. Previously remote country hamlets became suburbs which rapidly merged to form a continuous sprawl of development.

The wealthier parts of north and west London were well provided with their own private gardens and squares, and were handily placed for the fashionable royal parks such as Kensington Gardens or Regent's Park. In east and south London meanly built terraces of artisans's cottages were packed together with negligible thought for public amenity. Whereas the speculative developer in Ladbroke Grove or Belgravia was only too anxious to include lavishly landscaped garden squares to attract affluent purchasers, the cheap jerry-builder in Walworth or Stepney had no such incentive.

The disgraceful conditions in London's East End and the genuine fear among well-to-do citizens that outbreaks of pestilence might spread to their own well-swept doorsteps motivated public pressure for a new park in the East End. Lack of fresh air, rather than contaminated drinking water, was believed to be the source of "miasma" which was widely held to carry disease. In 1839 a newly appointed registrar of births, marriages and deaths, concerned about devastating epidemics of cholera and typhoid, collaborated with local MPs George Young and Joseph Hume to present a petition of 30,000 signatures to the Queen. In 1841 the government agreed to proceed. **Victoria Park** was to be the first occasion where a large unprofitable amenity was provided at state expense for free use by the lowest classes.

217 acres of run-down market gardens and despoiled gravel pits were acquired east of Bethnal Green, and James Pennethorne, official architect to the government, was appointed to lay out a new park. He had learnt his trade under Nash at Regent's Park and his design for Victoria Park shows several influences (he even became the adopted son of Mrs Nash). Pennethorne thought, somewhat naïvely, that his park could also be funded by building and selling salubrious houses for the professional classes next to the park. In the event, the sooty streets and crowded tenements of Mile End and Bethnal Green failed to draw the middle classes to the East End. Victoria Park fulfilled its original intention — a park for the poor and underprivileged.

Almost immediately it brightened the lives of the teeming thousands who lived nearby; even while the lake was being dug and trees planted, it started to be heavily used. In 1862 Burdett and Grove Roads were built to improve access from Limehouse and the docks, and in 1873 Queen Victoria visited the park, one of her few public outings after Albert's death. The lake became massively popular for bathing. Very few houses had baths; each morning between six and eight o'clock ten thousand people would wash in the pool, which had to be increased in size to 650 feet by 130 feet. Huge pipes supplied 30,000 gallons of clean water each day. In summer heatwaves, up to 25,000 people squeezed in to cool down. It was replaced in 1936 by a modern lido, a quarter of the size.

Big crowds assembled on Sundays for religious and political rallies. Bonner's Fields, on which part of the park was built, had previously been used by Chartists and

Page 67:
Brockwell Park,
Herne Hill

Opposite:
Embankment
Gardens

Page 70:
King Edward VII
Memorial Park,
Shadwell; the spire
of St. George-in-
the-East behind.

Page 71:
Park Keeper's
Cottage, Brockwell
Park.

IS LIFE A BOON?
IF SO, IT MVST BEFAL
THAT DEATH, WHENE'ER HE CALL
MVST CALL. TOO SOON.
W.S. GILBERT.

evangelists. Victoria Park became the East End equivalent of Speaker's Corner. William Morris and Bernard Shaw addressed meetings, and Oswald Moseley drummed up support in the 1930s. Such forums are now a thing of the past.

Several of Pennethorne's original monuments and decorations have also disappeared. Victoria Park took a dreadful hammering in the war. Not only was it the site of anti-aircraft batteries but its sheer size attracted hundreds of stray bombs and incendiaries. The Tudor-style superintendent's lodge, splendidly ornate and rustic, and the oriental pagoda on the lake were destroyed and not rebuilt — hardly a priority in a devastated post-war East End. Fortunately the Victoria Drinking Fountain survives, a gothic octagon, fifty-seven feet high, made of granite and marble, and provided by the same philanthropic combination as the Columbia Market — Baroness Burdett-Coutts's money and H.A. Darbyshire's design. In the south-east corner of the park are two stone alcoves from the old London Bridge, demolished in 1832 (another stands in a courtyard of Guy's Hospital, rather nearer home).

Victoria Park remains the finest in east London, one and a quarter miles long by half a mile wide, bordered in the south and west by the Regent's and Hertford Union canals. Inside the sturdy railings it continues to offer great variety — swimming, paddling, tennis, gymnastics, football and cricket, and even a small aviary with pheasants and guinea fowl. Cockneys with a strong back-yard tradition have always loved their park. Surplus plants from flower beds are still given free to enthusiastic horticulturalists to cheer window boxes and balconies.

Meath Gardens is not quite an extension of Victoria Park, but very close on the other side of the canal. It was laid out in 1893 from the dilapidated Globe Town burial ground, and today has resumed a neglected feel. Smart Street, off Roman Road, is a propitious but inappropriate name for the entrance. Bleached tarmac paths, bulging and cracked with tree roots, glinting with slivers of broken glass, wind beneath elderly poplars and planes — a chilling place when the sun goes down.

The pioneer spirit of Victoria Park was soon matched by **Battersea Park**, south of the river. Battersea Fields was common land held by the manor, mainly rough pasture liable to flooding. From here Colonel Blood had tried to

assassinate Charles II as he swam from the Chelsea bank and in 1829 the Duke of Wellington and the Marquis of Winchelsea fought a ludicrous duel when both missed with their pistols. More importantly Battersea Fields played host to a notorious weekly fair, centred on the rowdy Red House Tavern, where gambling, boxing, cock-fighting and debauchery were rife. Some 40,000 people flocked there each weekend, irritating the clergy to distraction. "Surely if there was a place that surpassed Sodom and Gomorrah this was it," preached one reformer. The local vicar, Rev. Eden, together with the builder Thomas Cubitt, pressed for government action, and in 1846 £200,000 of Crown money was made available to buy 320 acres. 198 acres were set aside for a new park, the rest for mansion blocks, Cubitt's reward.

Costs soared. The whole site had to be raised above flood level, using earth excavated from the Victoria Docks at Canning Town. Prince Albert had wanted the 1851 Great Exhibition to be held at Battersea rather than Hyde Park but it was not ready in time. James Pennethorne was again put in charge of design and at Battersea he created an even more elaborate layout — avenues of elms, chestnuts and limes, a sub-tropical plantation and a lovely curving lake cleverly sheltered from the wind by mounded banks decorated with steep alpine and rock gardens.

The closure of the old fair pleased the local vestry, who were keen to promote the moral welfare of their parishioners, but the new park also spared the riverside from the third-rate dwellings which had mushroomed beside the railway and on the slopes up to Clapham. A pleasant outlook was thus ensured for the aristocratic residents of Cheyne Walk in Chelsea.

The park opened in 1858 and was an instant success, drawing people from north and south of the river. Chelsea Bridge was finished in 1850, followed by the experimental Albert Bridge in 1873. Old Battersea Bridge whose timber spans had been painted by Turner was replaced in iron and stone in 1890. The picturesque lake was popular for boating and the peripheral drive circling the park became a fashionble nursery for the novel pastime of bicycling. High society congregated at Battersea for their Sunday morning ride — "a veritable oasis in one of the dreariest and darkest spots of transpontine London" (Sexby).

Battersea, like Victoria Park, was transferred from

Crown ownership to the Metropolitan Board of Works and thereafter to the London County Council, now the Greater London Council. Today a large proportion of the park remains dedicated to active sport, including a brand-new all-weather running-track, but such is Battersea's spaciousness and variety that nothing dominates to excess. For children a miniature zoo complements the open-air deer enclosure. There are ducks and geese to feed on the lake, ponies and horses to ride, as well as the challenging playground.

The north side of the park with its leafy esplanade along the river is the quietest part. Battersea Fun-fair, so alive and noisy in the 1950s, closed after the disastrous accident on the roller-coaster and was subsequently removed. The traditional Easter Parade continues to attract big crowds, not quite as riotous or drunken as the old fair, and now very much with the blessing of any clergy who happen to be around. The new Peace Pagoda is the latest attraction, built by Buddhist monks.

Before Battersea had been finished the Crown embarked on a third park for the working classes. Until 1852 **Kennington Park** had been common land, part of Kennington manor and property of the Duchy of Cornwall, Prince of Wales. During the 1745 Jacobite rebellion it had belonged to the Duke of Cumberland, who was brother of George II. The unrelenting "butcher of Culloden" insisted that Kennington Common be used instead of Tyburn gallows to hang and disembowel the chieftain Donald Macdonald as well as dozens of other captured Scottish clansmen.

In 1818 a church was built on the site of the gibbet and the common reverted to a quiet existence of cattle grazing, disturbed only by the fiasco of the 1848 Chartist rally. Four years later, thirty-seven acres of the Common were converted into a park, the rest was built over. Compared to Battersea or Victoria parks, Kennington is small and simple, a plain area of grass enclosed by railings and dotted with fine mature trees. The best corner is the flower garden with its secluded sun-traps, and warm crazy-paving, well loved by lazy cats who prowl and bask and purr there.

In 1856 responsibility for public parks in London was delegated from governmental level to the Metropolitan Board of Works. This organization had originally been set up to carry out road schemes. The Improvement Act of 1856 empowered the Board to tackle any work for public benefit, including the provision of parks and pleasure grounds in new residential districts.

The old borough of Finsbury, south of the Angel, Islington, had become desperately overcrowded by 1850. The eighteenth-century beer- and tea-gardens of Spa Fields, Sadler's Wells and Shepherdess Walk had disappeared beneath a maze of mean streets and houses. The Finsbury Park Act 1857 proposed a new 115-acre park for Finsbury, but sited three miles north-east on what had previously been part of Hornsey Wood, owned by the Bishop of London. **Finsbury Park** gave its name to the residential neighbourhood which grew around the park. Today nobody thinks of the connection with old Finsbury borough, any more than the residents of Richmond-upon-Thames remember their Yorkshire ancestry.

The park was tightly constrained by the Great Northern Railway on the west, running in a huge cutting, and the Seven Sisters Road on the south-east. This turnpike was opened in 1830 to improve links with Tottenham and the West End, and named after a pub where seven elms had been planted by seven sisters — a romantic story for what has become a most unromantic highway. Finsbury Park is disappointingly bleak for its size, particularly the windswept football pitches, sloping down to the road, where the occasional fun-fair is held. The lake is small and often seems muddy even for the ducks, but the American gardens are nurtured to put on a good show (why American, when rhododendrons are Himalayan?). The middle of the park is high and the well-used athletics track looks out towards Wood Green and Crouch End. In the north corner the grass descends to the New River which meanders past the cricket ground and practice nets, and rows of poplars beside Green Lanes. Such verdant names flatter to deceive.

While Finsbury Park was being completed, work began on another. **Southwark Park**, laid out in 1864 at Rotherhithe, is similarly some way from Southwark though less geographically confusing, as it lies within the modern London Borough of Southwark. Sixty-three acres of market gardens behind St Olave's Hospital were commandeered for the park. Some ratepayers protested at the extravagance: surely the market gardens, which had even boasted vineyards in the eighteenth century, were good enough as open space. But there was no guarantee they would survive. The famous gardens of the Jamaica Tavern and the Cherry Garden had gone for building. Pepys had been a frequent visitor; "over the water to Jamaica House where the girls did run for wagers over the bowling green, and there with much pleasure spent little and so home".

Southwark Park today remains much as the Metropolitan Board of Works intended — an ornamental lake stocked with fish and ducks, an open-air swimming-pool (no longer with an important hygienic role), a pompous bandstand, drinking-fountain and ornate cast-iron gas lamps. The two mounds beside Jamaica Road are heaps of earth excavated from Rotherhithe Tunnel. In the last century Rotherhithe and Surrey Docks were a forest of masts and funnels. What a change now — an empty landscape of deserted wharves and lonely tenement blocks, and the racing rush-hour traffic of Jamaica Road. Southwark Park's trees, flowers and lawns are a welcome respite.

The aftermath of the Great Exhibition fortuitously provided south London with another valuable open space. Such was the sensational success of Paxton's **Crystal Palace** that the giant iron and glass pavilion was meticulously dismantled in Hyde Park in 1852 and re-erected on a carefully selected elevated site at Penge Place Sydenham Hill. For two years 6,500 workmen toiled to lay out a new one-hundred-acre park and to reconstruct the Palace — 900,000 square feet of glass, weighing 400 tons, and 4,000 tons of iron. New transepts and arching were added to the 2,000-feet-long nave which alone covered nineteen acres. Tall water towers were built at each end to feed monumental fountains. In keeping with the pedagogic spirit of the Great Exhibition, the park was designed to be scientifically instructive. Four islands in the artificial lake represented different strata of the earth's crust and were strategically adorned with life-size models of prehistoric animals. To celebrate their completion in 1854, Professor Richard Owen, who coined the word dinosaur, sat down to dinner with nineteen friends inside one of his beasts.

Londoners flooded to Sydenham as they had to Hyde Park — over one million in 1854. For eighty years the Crystal Palace was a regular resort and tourist attraction for the solid middle and working classes. It possessed a concert hall, theatre, menagerie, exhibition room and restaurant, where Messrs Schweppe secured the refreshment contract. On 1 December 1936 the palace was destroyed in a spectacular conflagration. Only the end towers were left, which acted as useful markers for German bombers until they too were demolished in 1941. All that remains now are some of the terracing and foundations. The solidified lumps of molten glass have long since been snaffled as souvenirs.

The LCC took over the park, neglected after the war, in 1952. On the southern side the National Recreation Centre with its superb athletics arena, swimming-pools and ski slope were planned and built in the 1960s. The original rock and water gardens have been beautifully restored and the fantastic Victorian monsters have recently had a fresh coat of paint. Boating and fishing in the lake and the charming children's zoo continue to make Crystal Palace popular. Towering above everything the massive television transmitter mast, like a spindly Eiffel Tower, is the modern landmark, visible on the crest of the ridge from all over London.

Below the wooded slopes of Sydenham Hill **Dulwich Park** had been part of the manor acquired in 1606 by Edward Alleyn, the famous Shakespearian actor and impresario. Here he founded Dulwich College as a hospice for the poor and a school for children. Dulwich Common vanished under new buildings and playing-fields when the school was reconstituted and redesigned by Charles Barry in 1857, and in 1885 the governors decided to give seventy-two acres of parkland to the public. Lord Rosebery gratefully accepted on behalf of the Metropolitan Board of Works.

Dulwich Park is flat, mainly grassy meadows encircled by a carriageway and giant oaks, well looked after, respectable and comfortable. The most interesting area is around the central lake which is teeming with birdlife, and pedalo boats in summer. The aviary is delightful, perhaps the best in London, full of exotically coloured birds — pekin robins, paradise whydahs, golden pheasants — all in excellent health and spirit. Neat paths confined by hoop-topped railings entwine the lake and wind through alpine and rock gardens, banks of azaleas and rhododendrons. Funny little wooden shelters appear designed to accommodate the

Opposite:
The Lost World,
Crystal Palace.

76

maximum number of people without them having to talk to each other. They might feel more at home on the prom at Worthing. Barbara Hepworth's *Two Forms (Divided Circle)* is the contribution of contemporary art to the gentility of the park. Trees and bushes often provide a better context for modern sculpture, especially Henry Moore, than stark exhibition halls. The Dulwich Picture Gallery, near the main park gates, should not be missed, however.

Brockwell Park, nearby at Herne Hill, was secured for public use at about the same time. South Brixton was developing as a fashionable middle-class suburb. In 1892 Brockwell Park came up for sale and was opened on Whit Monday, an event marred only by the sudden death at the ceremony of the local MP Thomas Bristowe from a fit.

Brockwell has magnificent contours, wide sloping expanses of grass which sweep up to the mansion on the summit rivalled by the spreading crowns of superb mature forest trees. The culverted River Effra, which rises in Norwood and joins the Thames at Vauxhall, flows through the park, feeding the lido and pond. The late-Georgian mansion is plain and solid, now used as a residence for park keepers. What a place to live, with those south-facing balconies! From the ornate clock tower there are fine views of Westminster, and to the south a good indication of how hilly south London is. What lovely countryside it must have been before all those houses were built, when badgers really did live at Brockwell.

The success of Crystal Place at Sydenham prompted a rival venture in north London at Muswell Hill. The similarities between **Alexandra Palace** and Crystal Palace are almost uncanny, and equally ill-fated. Tottenham Wood Farm had been owned by Cecil Rhodes's family, and the dream for establishing a mecca for intellectual improvement and physical recreation began to take shape in 1858. The farm was divided, 190 acres for a park, the rest for respectable housing, and in 1863 the park was opened, named after Princess Alexandra of Denmark, wife of Edward, Prince of Wales. The monumental palace which was planned to dominate the park seemed doomed from the outset. Excessive extravagance and eclecticism induced financial headaches and delay. At last on 24 May 1873 the leviathan was opened; sixteen days later it was dramatically and disastrously swept by fire. Incredibly, money was found for resurrection, but investors never recouped their

shares.

The great hall was used for exhibitions and concerts but the acoustics, even for the splendid Willis organ, were too reverberant. In 1936 the BBC occupied one wing as London's first television centre; later the Hornsey School of Art moved in too, but slowly this vast white elephant grew shabbier and sadder. In bad winters snow drifted into the organ pipes; law students sitting exams endured raindrops and pigeon droppings. The Great British Beer Festival was the best use of the cavernous space. In 1980, during an evening spectacle watched by thousands of flabbergasted north Londoners, Alexandra Palace, like Crystal Palace, was destroyed by fire, once again caused by careless workmen. Repair was estimated at £60 million; insurance raised £18 million; feasibility studies continue! Meanwhile the burnt-out hulk fills the skyline, below which the unimpeded turf of the park rolls down towards the Kings Cross railway line.

In Victorian times balloon ascents, fireworks and tightrope displays by Jean Blondin were big draws. So was horse-racing on the shortest and tightest course in the country, only five furlongs. The Alexandra Plate was run from 1868 until the course closed in 1970. In the First World War the park became an internment camp for aliens and prisoners of war. Today the activities are more mundane and parochial — cricket, tennis, pitch and putt, and artificial skiing. The air is clear and the views uplifting. Terry Farrell's temporary pavilion, a giant tent of translucent PVC fabric, now houses the beer festivals and antiques fairs. One day perhaps the Palm Court, Great Hall and Italian Gardens will breathe life again.

The Metropolitan Board of Works were keen to grasp opportunities for further open space in north London. When a large private estate was advertised for sale as building land in Stoke Newington in 1884 it was promptly acquired out of public funds. Maybe it was closer to Finsbury Park than the Board would have preferred, but there was little choice. **Clissold Park** was opened in 1889 and named after the local curate who had lived in the manor. The grounds were already full of fine parkland trees — cedars, chestnuts and copper beech — and required minimal adaptation, though a lake was dug.

Clissold and Finsbury parks both adjoin Green Lanes and help to give some credibility to this rural backwater of the

79

pre-railway age. The twists and turns of Stoke Newington Church Street and the old parish church beside the park recall the pretty medieval village of Stoke Newington. The grand spire of the Victorian church and the fairyland towers and ramparts of the waterworks to the north were new symbols to overlook the park. The pale brick mansion with its classical-columned portico, used for council offices, adds dignity to the park. The little zoo, with its fenced paddocks for deer, goats and fat rabbits which willingly eat from the hand, is a delight for children, despite problems of vandalism. The rest is quietly unassuming, statuesque trees and fields of grass.

Fortunately, with public funds being limited and mostly committed to preserving common land from development, the Metropolitan Board of Works were not the sole provider of public open space. In the second half of the nineteenth century the Corporation of London, whose coffers were flush from the profits of imperial trade and finance, assumed a highly philanthropic role. Between 1854 and 1878 the Corporation laboured hard to save and then acquire Epping Forest (see page 22). It also bought Highgate and Queen's Woods, Burnham Beeches in Buckinghamshire and Coulsdon Common in Surrey, all for the recreational benefit of the London public.

Within London the Corporation laid out two new municipal parks. The first was **West Ham Park** in 1874, partly occupying the old grounds of Upton House, since demolished, and the remainder covering run-down market gardens. Joseph Lister, instigator of antiseptic surgery, was born in the manor house, and there had been royal kennels nearby. Ye Olde Spotted Dog in Upton Lane is the only example in the area of rustic Essex ship-lap weather boarding. The park is immaculately tended and well stocked with evergreens and heathers for winter colour. Over the last century trees have been planted to commemorate successive chairmen of Common Council committees, recorded for posterity — or at least until the tree dies. The recreation ground next to Whalebone Lane unusually contains a scented garden for the blind. The rest is more predictably devoted to playgrounds, swings and tennis courts.

Queens Park, between Kensal Green and Kilburn, was purchased in 1887, a mere thirty acres but a vital oasis in an endless sea of residential streets. For several years the

football pitch was home for Queen's Park Rangers in their amateur days. When they began to attract crowds they moved to a larger ground at Shepherd's Bush. The park is pleasantly unpretentious, simply arranged in two circles to provide children's playground, miniature golf and room for locals to inhale a little air. The City Corporation still pays for the upkeep.

In 1888 the Local Government Act established the London County Council, combining parts of Kent, Surrey, Essex and Middlesex to form a new administrative unit, democratically accountable to the electorate. All the functions of the Metropolitan Board of Works were incorporated. In 1892 the LCC set up its own Parks Department, of which Lieutenant Colonel J.J. Sexby was the first superintendent (hence his magnum opus surveying London's municipal open spaces). The LCC inherited the maintenance of the large municipal parks recently created and dozens of smaller spaces which had been acquired by or given to local vestries. They also created new parks. By 1965 when the LCC became the GLC London had an unrivalled system of municipal open spaces, catering for an extraordinary range of activities. Since then responsibility for smaller parks has been devolved to local borough councils who perhaps can sense local needs more acutely, while the GLC has hung on to those of metropolitan importance.

When the Metropolitan Board of Works was scrapped, Punch's epitaph read "It drained London and gave an embankment to the Thames." The gigantic engineering feat which built the Victoria, Chelsea and Albert Embankments produced several small gardens as an off-shoot. Wren had dreamt of a riverside promenade for London, but nothing was done until the sewage crisis was tackled by the Victorians. Reluctance to tamper with the Strand led to new embankments being built on each side, almost halving the width of the Thames, to conceal colossal sewers which ran west to east and collected all London's effluent. On the north bank the cut and cover tunnel of the Circle Line was incorporated. Construction took six years, providing at ground level a broad road to carry traffic from Westminster to the City and the long and narrow **Embankment Gardens**. This thin strip of flower beds and lawns is dotted with famous statues, including ones of Robert Burns and John Stuart Mill, and fancy lamp-posts,

Opposite:
Holland Park at Easter.

Facing Page 81:
The grounds of Syon House.

sheltering under the high façades of the Savoy, Somerset House and the Adelphi. On reflection, one regrets that the Victorians lacked the foresight to put the road underground as well, as the Parisians have now done, leaving the entire surface as park. Cleopatra's Needle and the riverside would be far more appreciated.

At Westminster the Houses of Parliament were rebuilt by Barry and Pugin on the water's edge. Immediately south, **Victoria Tower Gardens** provides, where the Embankment fails, a riverside garden. It is no more than a rectangle of grass, flanked by plane trees, but the raised benches afford a splendid view of the Thames, sufficiently buffered from cars and buses. The luridly gothic drinking-fountain, erected to honour the emancipation of slaves, is a poor and diminutive companion for the massively ordered detail of the Victoria Tower; far better is Rodin's *Burghers of Calais*, vivid and emotional.

The Chelsea Embankment reverts to traffic domination, lorry fumes spiralling up into the tolerant planes. The beleaguered ornamental gardens contain a statue of Thomas Carlyle and a fountain celebrating Rossetti, who both lived in Cheyne Walk in quieter days. More tempting are the grounds of the **Royal Hospital Chelsea** whose eastern section is open to the public. This is the site of Ranelagh Gardens, closed in 1803 but annexed and re-landscaped by the hospital. The Chelsea Flower Show is held every May in enormous marquees between the hospital buildings and the Embankment, the climax of the English horticultural year.

Downstream of the city, and far removed in social status, **Wapping Recreation Ground** was laid out in 1875 by clearing slum cottages in one of London's most depressed quarters. When the Shadwell Fish Market closed in 1909, unable to compete with Billingsgate, the eight-acre Thameside site was purchased for £140,000 to provide a larger garden, **King Edward Memorial Park**. The City Corporation and the LCC shared the bill. It continues to be a pleasant refuge in a harsh enviroment. The bowling-green, paddling-pool and tennis courts entertain the active, and a plaque on the river wall marks the spot where Willoughby and Frobisher separately sailed in 1553 and 1576 to seek the North-East and North-West Passages.

South of the river, the Albert Embankment offers little except a pedestrian promenade between St Thomas Hospital and the river. Beyond Lambeth Palace Road **Archbishop Park** was originally the grounds to the palace but has been partitioned off to form a leafy public retreat. Behind the high brick walls the Archbishop of Canterbury still enjoys an enviably substantial garden. At lunchtime, fitness fanatics from County Hall and South Bank offices pack the tennis courts and football pitches or jog round the paths. At weekends the pigeons and sparrows have the place to themselves, but miss the sandwich crumbs.

Geraldine Harmsworth Park, a few hundred yards away along Lambeth Road, is less peaceful in all ways. The grass and trees surround the pompous façades of the Imperial War Museum, which is guarded by menacing fifteen-inch naval guns. These buildings were previously the notorious Bedlam lunatic asylum. Outside, hordes of shrill school-children scream and scramble, either mad with excitement or crazed with boredom, and traffic hurtles past on the criss-cross of main roads. An adventure playground completes this haven for the deaf; Archbishop Park could be a million miles away. **Vauxhall Park**, also near the river, is quieter and more geared to old folk. The newly planned rose garden and the curious little model houses and rockery show a heartening pride and enthusiasm.

South London is scattered with dozens of uneventful but irreplaceable small gardens and parks which fulfil vital local community needs. Few people other than immediate residents of Camberwell will know **Myatt's Fields**, tucked away off Knatchbull Road. A strawberry-grower called Myatt farmed a market garden here until the area became doomed to development. A local do-gooder, William Minet, put up enough cash to keep the builders at bay and paid for the artistic wrought-iron gates.

Ruskin Park on the slopes of Denmark Hill behind King's College Hospital is another example. During the day, addicted athletes and alert alsatian dogs take their exercise. Squirrels hop around the bandstand and bowling-green — perhaps a trifle mundane for high-minded Ruskin, chief priest of Victorian artistic and architectural appreciation. **Horniman Gardens**, near Dulwich Park, would be a better memorial for purely aesthetic reasons (who was Horniman anyway?). The pretty park is an adjunct to the art nouveau museum, displaying natural history and ethnography exhibits, and is spectacularly situated with an excellent view of St Paul's from the top. Its layout is cleverly varied.

Page 81:
Memorial to the greatest achievement of Victorian engineering in London.

Opposite:
The bandstand, Ruskin Park, next to King's College Hospital.

Page 84:
Burgess Park, still unfinished but taking shape. The lake opened in 1982.

Page 85:
The Grand Union Canal, Kensal Green.

The intricate water gardens flourish all year; the small menagerie, with an odd mixture of farmyard hens, crested cranes and wallabies, amuses children; and on the west side a disused railway track forms a brambly nature trail.

Mayow Park is as ordinary as the colourless suburbs of Lower Sydenham, but liked for its tennis and bowling-greens by those who shirk the climb up to Crystal Palace. **Norwood Park** straddles the high ridge and enjoys a panorama. Beyond the oaks of **Biggin Wood** the terrain falls away down to the River Graveney, which wriggles through the flat meadows of **Norbury Park.**

These open spaces give fleeting glimpses of the landscape as it once was, the natural lie of the land, views unimpeded by semi-detached houses and telegraph poles, streams and brooks which briefly burst free from their Tartarean culverts. Further west the River Wandle burbles across **Morden Hall Park.** The Edwardian suburb of Merton Park was laid out by John Innes who bought the local manor with the fortune made from his garden compost business. **John Innes Park** and **Mostyn Gardens** were his own design, small but impeccably planned and cosily suburban. Beyond the grassy expanse of **Morden Park** the dull straight road to Epsom is flanked by neo-Tudor Noddy-land, mindlessly mimicking the lost extravagance of Nonsuch.

Wimbledon Park provides a convenient buffer between the affluent mansions bordering Wimbledon Common and the cheaper gridiron streets of Southfields. It functions mainly as an up-market recreation ground, reverently in the shadow of the All England Lawn Tennis and Croquet Club. Set more solidly in the heart of Southfields between Merton Road and Garratt Lane, the ornamental trees of **King George's Park** briefly enhance the winding course of the River Wandle before its unimpressive entrance into the muddy Thames between the gasworks and **Wandsworth Park.** Directly opposite on the north bank, **Hurlingham Park** is determinedly exclusive, only partly open to the public, the rest being the private grounds of the Hurlingham Club. **South Park** close by is refreshingly commonplace with no frills or pretensions.

Further upstream **Bishop's Park** is the most attractive municipal park in this neighbourhood. Just as Lambeth Palace is the archbishop's home so Fulham Palace is the traditional residence of the Bishop of London — Fulham manor has belonged to the see since 631 A.D. The park stretches from the fifteenth-century tower of Fulham church by Putney Bridge to the twentieth-century floodlights of Craven Cottage, half a mile away. The old moat has been drained to form a lovely sunken garden but the chief delight is to watch the shifting kaleidoscope of the drifting river.

South-east London has a patchy distribution of open space. Apart from Southwark Park at Rotherhithe the inner districts north of Peckham and New Cross are badly off for parks. The thin playground of **Tabard Gardens,** surrounded by grim inter-war flats, and the tiny **Newington Recreation Ground** behind Elephant and Castle are invaluable but hardly sufficient. The seventeen-acre **Deptford Park** beside Evelyn Road is far from being a grand park but is heavily used. Celery, onions and asparagus once grew here on eighteenth-century small-holdings, part of the Deptford manor where John Evelyn lived after marrying the heiress to the estate. The fine trees, cinder running-track and paddling-pool help to soften the bleakness of present day Deptford life.

South of New Cross and Peckham the Victorians took care to provide their posher railway suburbs with a more generous smattering of public parks. **Telegraph Hill,** off Drakefell Road, was bought from the Haberdashers' Company who in 1875 had founded the Haberdasher Aske's School in Jerningham Road (since moved to Hertfordshire). The summit stands 160 feet above sea level, one of the chain of beacon and semaphore stations built in 1795 to link London with Dover for news of Napoleon's threatened invasion. It is a tiny park, but extremely steep with tiers of flower beds and terraces.

Beyond Brockley Road **Hillyfields** is a more spacious version, not quite so precipitous or pretty but appropriately named. To the north Deptford Common was devoured by the railways and brick fields of Loampit Hill. Hillyfields was purchased and landscaped as meagre compensation, too late to save the slums of Deptford but ensuring some respectability for Brockley. **Ladywell Recreation Ground** was preserved at the same time, forty-six acres of pasture beside the River Ravensbourne and railway from Catford Bridge to Ladywell station. These meadows were regularly flooded until levees and weirs were constructed. Rustic footbridges attempt to salvage the rural charm ruined by the railway embankments.

Opposite:
The Brent
Reservoir, or Welsh
Harp, looking west
to Harrow.

Flat parks, unable to rely on the natural good-looks of hilly terrain, need cunning design to disguise their simplicity. The **Forster Memorial Park** at Bellingham is a typical square suburban park, relieved only by a maze of paths and local dogs. **Sutcliffe Park** with its football posts and running-track is unrepentantly utilitarian, unhesitatingly dull unless you are intent on scoring goals or notching up a four-minute mile.

Avery Hill is perhaps best known for its teacher-training college but the adjacent GLC park is one of south London's finest. A fine open parkland of grand trees and undulating lawns is distinguished by the domed winter gardens, not quite on the scale of Kew, but containing a superb selection of tropical plants from Asia, Africa and South America. **Maryon Park** and **Maryon Wilson Park** in Charlton are blessed with hills and rills which instil a feeling of enclosure and variety and feature in the film *Blow Up*. From Little Heath Hill the park follows a coomb, broken by the irregularities of old chalk pits. Large oaks and willows flourish beside the stream. The hummock of Cox's Mound was another in the system of Napoleonic signalling posts, now cropped by deer and Jacobs sheep. It is ironic that Thomas Maryon Wilson who owned Charlton Manor should have a park named after him, having spent most of his life trying to obliterate Hampstead Heath. The villain of the north was clearly virtuous enough at home.

North Londoners rely heavily on the vast tracts of Hampstead Heath and Regent's Park for their open space. Many of the other parks seem paltry by comparison. **Highbury Fields**, where refugees camped after the Great Fire, escaped development because of the shallow railway tunnel from Drayton Park to Moorgate. Until purchased by Islington vestry in 1885, it was grazing land. Macaulay described Islington as "a solitude where poets loved to contrast its silence and repose with the din and turmoil of monster London". Today Highbury Corner and Holloway Road is an artery of that monster, and Highbury Fields, just a stone's throw from the juggernauts, is Islington's largest open space. In winter it can seem bleak, except on Guy Fawkes night when the leaping orange flames reflect in the elegant Georgian windows of Highbury Place. In summer it is green and leafy, though the much-loved open-air pool has been replaced by new indoor baths. The Victorian church at the top end, beyond the tennis and football

pitches, was righteously erected on the site of old Highbury Barn, whose raunchy tavern and bordello had become too riotous for the opulent residents of Highbury Terrace.

Further north in Haringey, the mature black poplars pre-date the founding of **Downshill Park.** Beneath the spreading trees well-tended flowerbeds give a splash of colour from spring to autumn. **Lordship Recreation Ground** is next door to Downshill, a wide expanse of grass overlooked by the awful concrete flats of the Broadwater Farm Estate. Only the remnants of an ancient hawthorn hedge and a small pond break the monotony of football pitches.

Sometimes smaller spaces have more seclusion, such as the little ten-acre garden of **Avenue House** in Finchley. Perhaps Housman knew the delights of **Cherry Tree Wood** close to Highgate:

"Loveliest of trees, the cherry now
Is hung with bloom along the bough. . . ."

Golders Hill Park is one of the prettiest of north London's parks, intimate and cultivated compared with the wildness of Hampstead Heath. Like many of the GLC parks it boasts a mini-zoo. **Hendon Park** and **Sunny Hill Park** are less ambitious, and more firmly set in solid suburbia, north of the North Circular.

Neasden, Wembley and Harrow contain all the ingredients of London's true metro-land — the Bakerloo and Metropolitan lines, arterial roads, streamlined factories, tedious hinterlands of uninspired houses, and among these, municipal parks. Somehow the tale of three highwaymen called Ned, Hal and Will who had their "dens" in these parts seems just too fanciful.

Fortunately there are hills. **Gladstone Park** enjoys an elevated position, a chance to climb above the roof tops of Dollis Hill and gulp the fresh winds from the west. A railway cuts off the southern playing-fields but to the north the parkland rises steadily up to old Dollis House. The outside, and probably the inside too, has been insensitively knocked about since the 1880s when Lord Aberdeen lived there and frequently entertained William Gladstone. The elderly prime minister might be flattered to have the grounds named after him, but he would be less gladdened by the sea of houses which replaces the view of open country. The formal garden in front of the house

Opposite:
Gladstone Park, Dollis Hill, lines of planes and playing fields.

includes a semi-circular duck pond. To one side the rich red bricks of the walled kitchen garden have been allowed to bow and crumble; how sad to see shoddy two-dimensional bodging of a carefully conceived three-dimensional design.

Roundwood Park in Willesden is also on a hill, but is smaller and has no mansion. Twisting paths snake through rockeries and spring bulbs. Wind-borne fruits and autumn leaves are blown out of the park into Willesden Cemetery next door.

Neasden Recreation Ground, Woodfield Park and the Brent Reservoir are the official names for the most famous open space in the area, otherwise known as the **Welsh Harp**. The 350-acre lake is a landmark for travellers on the North Circular, and one of the largest facilities in London for non-tidal water sport. The reservoir is fed by the dreary polluted River Brent, originally dammed as a feeder for the Regent's Canal. I prefer to think that the name derives from its shape rather than from some local hostelry. In the nineteenth century the uncluttered grassy banks were popular for pigeon-shooting and horse-racing. Today the water is the draw — wind surfing, sailing, line fishing, model boats and rowing. After a good force-seven south-westerly there are choppy waves at the eastern end, not exactly Bondi Beach but enough to swamp a canoe. Herons, swans and grebe nest here, having learnt to tolerate the constant rumble of traffic.

In Wembley both **Barham Park** and **Barn Hill Park** were once the grounds of fine mansions that have been demolished. Barham, beside the Sudbury roundabout, is modest and compact; Barn Hill spreads either side of Fryent Way, almost ten times as big but disappointingly uninteresting. With 250 acres to play with, Brent Council have the chance to make Barn Hill one of North London's best parks. Landscapes take a long time to mature. **Northwick Park** at Harrow appears drab beside the lush meadows and majestic trees of Harrow School Playing Fields, which slope up to the spires and chimneys of Harrow-on-the-Hill. Ancient hedges and pastures provide a comforting buffer of countryside between the old village and the rude glass and concrete of Northwick Park Hospital.

Beyond Harrow, the beckoning finger of the underground (by now over-ground) carries metro-land far into the Hertfordshire and Buckinghamshire countryside,

on to Watford, Rickmansworth and Chorleywood. **Pinner Park** is all that is left of the farmland dismembered by George V Avenue and the 1920s' property developers. Under feudal law Pinner Park Farm would have paid its tithes to **Headstone Manor**. The magnificent tithe barn and moated manor house survive in a peaceful park, convenient for workers in the huge Kodak factory at Wealdstone. **Bentley Priory** has strong associations with the Royal Air Force from Battle of Britain days, but its wooded grounds link Stanmore and Harrow Weald Commons and form a green wedge keeping Stanmore apart from Bushey. Real country, however, is much further off, over the hills and far away.

West London is so well endowed with large royal parks, commons and stately homes that some of the smaller municipal parks are more deserted than they deserve. In a less fortunate part of town the five-acre garden of the **Natural History Museum** at Kensington, with its extraordinary fossilized tree stumps, might not be such a Cinderella. One of the best used parks is **Paddington Recreation Ground**, set among the imposing redbrick Edwardian apartments and mansion blocks of Maida Vale. The cycling and athletics track attract the lithe and muscular, earnest boxers punishing their bodies by running in black plastic suits, sprinters tautening and limbering their hamstrings and tendons. Even the cricketers and dogs seem to play harder and faster.

At Hammersmith **Ravenscourt Park** exudes a less sweaty and energetic atmosphere. The playground at the northern end is lively enough, with the model Spanish galleon providing a limitless source of fun. The rest is a pretty and unruffled landscape of beautiful trees, smooth lawns and flowerbeds and a little lake with well contented ducks. Nothing has changed much since the Metropolitan Board of Works bought the grounds and the large French-style house in 1887. The District and Piccadilly lines were built on a low viaduct skirting the southern boundary of the park. Millions of passengers have looked enviously down at the lucky ones enjoying themselves as they trundle on to Acton Town or Hammersmith.

Walpole Park, virtually an extension of Lammas Park in Ealing, is unglamorous but pleasantly civic. Every mayor of Ealing has planted a tree in the main avenue. Pitshanger Manor in the north-east corner is now a public library but

displays a grand façade refashioned by Sir John Soane and a south wing by George Dance. The Ealing Studios where the Ealing Comedies were made also overlooks the park. Now the BBC churn out their daily diet of high- and low-brow nourishment for the intoxicated masses.

The low-lying land beside the River Brent puts an abrupt stop to the neat streets and villas of Ealing and Hanwell. Amid a succession of playing-fields, sewage farms and golf courses **Elthorne Park** and **Brent Lodge Park** both back down to the sluggish river and murky canal, unimpressive places which have lost any rural charm. Elthorne Park contains the so-called Hanwell Stone, probably the most over-rated natural phenomenon in London. This glacial boulder, dumped by the retreating ice, is moronically set in concrete, and protected by railings; the jumbos droning into Heathrow are far more fascinating.

With planes taking off and landing at one a minute every day of the year, this is not a peaceful segment of London. **Cranford Park** also has to contend with the M4 traffic noises. This little fragment of old Middlesex is desperately hemmed in by machines of the 1980s. The village church and the stables of demolished Cranford House seem desolate and forsaken. It is hard to believe that the roots of the old trees burrow deep in to a rich soil which once supported prosperous farms and market gardens. South of Heathrow, **Hanworth Park** was the aerodrome where the Graf Zeppelin landed and it has since been converted into a sports ground and lido, not exactly Nature getting its revenge.

East London relies more heavily on its municipal parks. Apart from Epping and Hainault Forests there was little common land to protect and few aristocratic estates to requisition for public gardens. **Valentines Park** at Gants Hill, just off the infamous Eastern Avenue, was a rare exception, a house and parkland grabbed by Ilford Council in 1898 to provide a municipal recreation ground with a predictable range of facilities — cricket, tennis, bowling, and open-air baths. Sadly, the great vine, said to have been 200 feet long and to have produced the cutting for the Hampton Court vine, had died in 1875. With that asset gone, not many tourists venture to Valentines, nice though it is.

Springfield Park occupies a fine steep hillside on the edge of Stamford Hill, with views out over Walthamstow

Marshes from the pond at the top. The River Lea glides past the bottom, always busy with boats from the Springfield marina, flowing temptingly on to the Anchor and Hope downstream along the towpath.

The boroughs of Redbridge, Barking and Havering have all created municipal open spaces for their ratepayers. **Bedfords, Dagham, Parsloes, Central** and **Mayersbrook** parks offer the room which any proud suburban dweller will tell you "makes the rest so worthwhile". **Havering Country Park,** run by the GLC, is more ambitious, in functional terms if not beauty. Time alone will help such places. East London is not blessed with the hills and heaths of north and south London, and its parks will never be able to match their variety and wildness. No matter.

In the nineteenth and first half of the twentieth centuries, virtually all municipal parks were fashioned out of market gardens, farmland or private estates. The Artisans and Labourers Dwellings Improvement Act of 1875 was scarcely called upon for creating recreation grounds — Wapping was a rare example. Since the Second World War, fired by the new ethos of social planning, slum clearance and the formation of public open spaces have gone hand in hand, one often opportunistically justifying the other. In the once overcrowded tenements of central London the ratio of people to open space has been improved both by reducing the numbers of inhabitants and by building new parks.

Easily the biggest and most exciting scheme is **Burgess Park** in the heart of Walworth, where for forty years the GLC have laboured to plan and build a new park, which when finished in 1995 will extend for 135 acres. It is an unprecedented project and has already involved the demolition of hundreds of houses and factories, the extinguishing of dozens of streets and alleys. Plans go back to 1945 and the blueprint for reconstructing bomb-scarred London. Work began in 1950 on the North Camberwell Open Space, as it was then known, but compulsory purchase and relocation of industries was slow and expensive. In 1965 only fifteen acres were finished, by then called St George's Park. Since then, progress has accelerated and Burgess Park (renamed after a local councillor) now boasts ninety acres, with the football and cricket sections completed in September 1985.

Stretching from Camberwell Road to Old Kent Road, the

Opposite:
New River Walk,
Islington, near
Willowbridge Road;
a lovely backcloth
for the Marquess
Estate.

length of Albany Road, there is still a lot to do. Isolated pubs, back-yard businesses and fractured roads which end in corrugated iron are distracting eyesores. Much, however, is taking shape — formal gardens on the west side, linking with Addington Square where huge flocks of starlings roost in the trees; a black and yellow concert bowl and the quaint lime kiln, uncovered and preserved. Next to the ruined St George's church, the underpass beneath Wells Way marks the line of the old Surrey canal, and the mosaic of the Camberwell Beauty glitters on the flank wall of the public wash-houses, now the Lynn Athletic and Boxing Club. Pride of place belongs to the lake, opened in May 1982, the largest post-war lake in London (though the Barbican lake was finished sooner). Already there are resident swans and seagulls, and an avant-garde fountain illuminated at night. On the quayside a plaque commemorates three of the park's landscape architects and surveyors who were killed in an air crash in 1979. How they would love to see the swallows skimming above the water on a still summer evening.

Mile End Park in Tower Hamlets is a similar venture, fifty acres at present, with forty more planned which will link Victoria Park with King George's Fields. Once again, hundreds of houses have been cleared beside the canal to make way for grass and trees. Such undertakings require immense vision, commitment and endurance. Smaller open spaces are easier and quicker to achieve. Islington, once desperately short of open space, embarked on a systematic programme in the 1970s to provide seven moderately sized parks, evenly spread throughout the borough. Caledonian Park, on the site of the old Caledonian Cattle Market, and Rosemary Gardens near the canal were duly completed but several others such as Wray Crescent in Holloway or Barnard Park in Barnsbury remain unfinished. Good housing is too valuable to be demolished for grass. Instead the council have jumped at opportunities like Northampton Buildings in Clerkenwell to provide parks on cleared sites.

Not surprisingly, many new parks seem spartan and soulless. Shoreditch Park in Hoxton, Pedler's Park in Lambeth and Weavers' Fields off Valance Road, Whitechapel, are regrettably bleak expanses of turf, exposing tatty skylines of ugly tower blocks, scrap yards and railway arches. Without mature trees or shrubs these bland stretches of grass hardly improve the dismal landscape. At Stepney Green the neglected churchyard of St Dunstan, with its broken tombs and rotting shelters, appears more attractive than the wide flat extension, devoid of folly or feature, which the bureaucrats have produced. Where are our modern Capability Browns? Just a few fast-growing silver birches work wonders, as those at the GLC's Haggerston Park in Queensbridge Road so ably demonstrate.

Until Nature softens the hard edges, tremendous effort has to be made. At Jubilee Gardens between County Hall and the Festival Hall on the South Bank the GLC have succeeded in contriving a stimulating pedestrian environment, not so much by the fey quotations set into the paving slabs but by the sculptures and planting. The Festival of Britain flagpole, the strange Oracle, the Peace statue, the concrete relief maps and the splendid ornate lamp standards all lend interest and fascination. The lawns are often festooned with marquees, trains rumble over Hungerford Bridge, skateboarders swoop and swirl beneath the shuttered concrete ramps, audiences swarm along the leafy promenade.

Adventure playgrounds and community gardens frequently occupy small temporary sites, earmarked for buildings, where local residents are encouraged by enlightened councils to do their own thing before the

Opposite:
The disused railway line from Finsbury Park to Highgate.

95

bulldozers move in. The Japanese gardens at Covent Garden, now lost for ever beneath the Odhams site, showed for an all too brief a time what volunteer labour could achieve on a shoestring budget. The little garden in Hoxton Street, Hackney, has so captured local support that the land will probably never be developed. The same goes for the **William Curtis** ecology park in the shadow of the southern ramparts of Tower Bridge, Southwark, opened in 1977 on the site of a defunct lorry-park and now established as an important scientific and educational resource.

Another recent idea in recreational planning is the country or regional park. The concept is on a metropolitan scale, to bring together existing outdoor facilities to form a structurally linked park several miles long, providing a full gamut of recreational opportunities. The **Lea Valley Regional Park** is the London prototype, projected on a vast scale to extend from Ware in Hertfordshire to the Thames. Existing playing-fields such as Hackney and Walthamstow Marshes, the Pickett's Lock Sports Centre, reservoirs, the river and canal will eventually coalesce by reclaiming derelict land to produce a linear park offering a huge range of aquatic, amphibious and terrestrial sport, from canoeing to cricket, paddling to pony trekking, sailing to soccer. On the borders of Hillingdon and Buckinghamshire, the **Colne Valley Park** is based on the same idea but enjoys more rural raw material than the Lea valley.

None of the man-made municipal parks can match the natural beauty of the heaths, commons and woods. Likewise, the **Regent's Canal**, built in 1820, is barely comparable with the majestic Thames. Nevertheless the towpath provides a remarkable walk through London, continually surprising in its orientation and detail. The central section from Regent's Park to the Islington tunnel is the most popular, past the Zoo, trendy Camden Lock and the King's Cross gas holders. But try the eastern end, from the hanging gardens of Noel Road and the Narrow Boat past Victoria and Mile End parks to the Thames at Limehouse; or venture west from Little Venice past Kensal Green cemetery to the Grand Union and the rest of England. All along the way, attempts are being made to exploit the tremendous potential for leisure, such as the canalside gardens at Stonebridge Wharf, Salmon Lane, or Thornhill Bridge Wharf, Caledonian Road. Now that the

electric cable laying is complete, the towpath is good for the attentive bicyclist, or you can take a barge trip instead. The Duke of Bridgewater would be amazed!

Even more surprising is the charming **New River Walk** in Islington, a mile-long fragment of the old aqueduct built to carry water from Hertfordshire to London in 1613 by Sir Hugh Myddelton. A series of serpentine ponds overhung by willows, ash and planes produce a lovely garden walkway from St Paul's Road to Essex Road. The rest of the course from New River Head at Rosebery Avenue is still traceable along Colebrooke Row and Duncan Terrace and along Petherton Road to the modern reservoirs off Green Lanes. North of here the New River continues to fulfil its original function, meandering through London's suburbs to distant springs.

Equally unusual is the two-mile long path which follows the disused course of the old **Finsbury Park Railway Line** to Highgate. Alternating from lofty embankment views across erratic back gardens to secretive cuttings festooned with blackberry, Old Man's Beard and elderberry, this is a delightfully overgrown track, full of town weeds and country flowers. It is hard to imagine sturdy engines puffing their way along the line, but that was long before Beeching and Serpell were names we knew. No doubt their successors will leave London with its walkways and ghost trains.

CHAPTER 5: Stately Houses

The classic image of the stately homes of England ("those comfortably padded lunatic asylums", as Virginia Woolf called them) is associated with the genial rural shires — long avenues of trees leading to distant views of hills, cattle munching contentedly beneath solitary spreading oaks; beyond the isolated mansion a wide horizon of farm and woodland. Somehow the prospect of great parkland estates hemmed in among monotonous expanses of semi-detached housing and busy roads is rather less appealing. Yet within the Greater London area there is a higher concentration of stately houses than anywhere else in the country.

Perhaps this is not so surprising given London's history. As national seat of government since William the Conqueror, and for centuries the chief port, industrial centre and generator of wealth in Britain, London has always been an irresistible magnet for the nobility and gentry. Moreover, London's competitive and extravagant society demanded that they lived in stylish residences, in the grandest manner.

In medieval times some of the richest and most powerful élite built large houses or "inns" outside the city walls, such as the Bishop of Ely's Inn at Holborn or John of Gaunt's Savoy Palace in the Strand. The Tudor monarchs retreated to their sumptuous palaces at Richmond, Greenwich, Kew and Hampton Court, enjoying the pleasures of open countryside and sport in the royal hunting forests. Easy communication by river favoured Thameside locations, so that our kings and queens could virtually commute by barge between Westminster and their favourite resort. In Stuart times, as London expanded rapidly and became an increasingly crowded and unhygienic place to inhabit, the wealthy merchant joined the aristocracy in seeking the fresher air of the high ground north and south of the city. Hampstead, Blackheath, Clapham and Islington became fashionable surburban retreats, where the horrendous outbreaks of plague could perhaps be avoided. The unprecedented affluence of Georgian London saw an even greater proliferation of country houses around the outskirts, in Middlesex, Surrey, Kent and Essex. This was the heyday of the stately mansion, and those at Osterley, Syon, Chiswick and Kenwood are the finest of their period in England.

What is remarkable is that in spite of the inexorable growth of plebeian London in the nineteenth and twentieth centuries so many grand houses have survived, and their grounds and gardens too. Dozens of surburban parks originated as the private country estates of noblemen and wealthy commoners. Most have now been taken over by the State in one form or another, some by the National Trust. Only a very few are still lived in as private mansions. Noel Coward's verse — "The Stately Homes of England, how beautiful they stand, To prove the upper classes have still the upper hand" — is hardly true for London.

Most of London's royal palaces are now set within the royal parks, covered in Chapter 3. Greatest of all is **Hampton Court Palace**, one of the finest monuments in Europe, surrounded by the magnificent 2,100 acres of Hampton Court Park and Bushy Park. **Bushy House** on the north side of Bushy Park was formerly a lavish lodge for the park ranger and is now occupied by the National Physical Laboratory with its own grounds separated off from the main park.

At Greenwich the **Queen's House**, built by Inigo Jones in 1617 for Anne of Denmark, and the first example of the Palladian style in England, is now part of the National Maritime Museum. The house used to span the road but this was moved further north by Christopher Wren when he built the Naval College, leaving the Queen's House standing proud and gleaming white on the green carpet of Greenwich Park. At the elevated south-west corner of the park near the broad expanse of Blackheath is Greenwich's **Ranger's House**, begun in 1688 but given two bowed wings in 1749. Since 1900 it has been owned by the Greater London Council, housing paintings and musical events. The open land in front, next to Shooter's Hill, is called Montague Corner. Somewhere beneath this spur lie the mysterious Point Hill caverns, obscurely carved out of the chalk bedrock by neolithic ancestors, but not accessible to the public.

At the south-east corner of Hyde Park, cut off by the tearing traffic of Hyde Park Corner, stands **Aspley House**, built in 1771 by Robert Adam but better known as the residence of the Duke of Wellington from 1805 till his death in 1852, with that memorable address, Number One London. Acquired by the nation in 1947, the grounds were incorporated into Hyde Park Corner, while the beautiful interior houses the Wellington Museum, with paintings by Turner, Bruegel and Velázquez in the Waterloo Gallery.

Page 97:
Chiswick House,
classical statues and
magnificent trees.

Opposite:
Chiswick House,
Burlington's
"Temple of Arts".

Kensington Gardens were originally the private grounds of **Kensington Palace**, bought by William III from the Earl of Nottingham and revamped by Wren and Kent. Queen Victoria was born here and lived here until she moved to Buckingham Palace in 1837. The palace remains a royal residence for various members of the royal family, and also accommodated part of the Museum of London before it was transferred to the Barbican.

The majestic palace of Richmond beside the river has long disappeared, except for a few minor outbuildings, and Richmond Park contains no major house. The grounds of Kew Palace are better known today as Kew Botanical Gardens and merit their own chapter (see page 140). The next tier below the top echelon of royal palaces and parks includes a wide range of stately mansions and their grounds which contribute enormously to London's supply of open space.

Conceivably, the prevailing westerly winds which blow London's smuts and smogs eastwards to the sea favoured settlement on the windward side of town. Whatever the reason, there is no disputing the fact that west and south-west London contain the best and most numerous examples of great houses and parkland. Among these, perhaps the most perfect in conception and construction is **Chiswick House**, unquestionably one of the sublime treasures of the metropolis, a "must" for anyone unfortunate enough never to have been there. The house itself is an extraordinary creation, "too little to live in and too big to hang on a watch chain", as Horace Walpole described it — to our eyes a landmark in architecture and a brilliant monument to eighteenth-century elegance and style.

Old Chiswick House, a nondescript Jacobean jumble, had been bought by the first Earl of Burlington. The third Earl, returning from his Grand Tour of Italy and inspired by Palladio's Villa Capra at Vincenza, built his own Renaissance "Temple of Arts". Burlington himself drew the plans and hired William Kent to design the sumptuous interior. No expense was spared in producing a magnificent collection of public rooms, octagonal, circular, rectangular and domed, all on the first floor in the true *piano nobile* manner. Completed in 1729 it was a sensation among intellectual and artistic society. Subsequently the Jacobean house was demolished and side wings added in 1788, but

these too have now been removed and Burlington's masterpiece returned to its original glory.

The gardens, covering sixty-seven acres, took William Kent twenty years to lay out and were equally futuristic for England, borrowing liberally from new Continental ideas. The park is a fantastic combination of innovative natural landscape and traditional intricate formality. Within a small area Kent contrived to accommodate an incredible variety of features and vistas. At the back of the house an amphitheatre of classical statues culminates in an apse of clipped yew niches, forming the pivot from which a series of delightful avenues and narrow walks radiate. Each vista is terminated by a temple, obelisk, folly or grotto, and lined with thick hedges of box and myrtle. Kent apparently had little hesitation in taking (some might say stealing) antique Roman sculptures from Emperor Hadrian's villa at Tivoli.

The result is a garden of endless fascination and surprise, ingeniously encompassed within mature native woodland which contrasts with the statuesque cedars of Lebanon beside the house. The intimate disciplined garden in front of the camellia house, or the sunken temple and circular lake, complete with obelisk and baby trees set in white barrels, are almost surreal. The lake, with its ludicrously ornamental bridge built by Wyatt in 1788, used to end in a cascade operated by a hydraulic archimedes screw — all part of the fantasy. No wonder these dells and glades attracted so many. Walter Scott described the gardens in 1828 as resembling a picture by Watteau. Joseph Paxton worked in the grounds as a boy apprentice. Edward VII fell in love with the place and as Prince of Wales spent much time there as guest of the Duke of Devonshire.

From 1892 to 1928 the house was occupied as a lunatic asylum until the local council stepped in to spoil Virginia Woolf's generalization. Today Chiswick is very much a public park, full of duffel-coated families, demure Dalmatians and exuberant children. When these are out of sight it is easy for the fertile mind to glimpse a ghost from the glittering past.

In the shadow of Chiswick and much worse affected by modern times is **Hogarth House**. It is an indictment of our age that Hogarth is most widely known as the name of the roundabout and flyover where the roads from the M3 and M4 converge on London. Given our predilection for road-widening it is remarkable that the Great West Road has

Opposite:
Gunnersbury Park, dilapidated follies in the grounds.

101

spared the house at all. A tiny fragment of its garden survives, including the ageless mulberry tree under which Hogarth liked to sit when this was his rural retreat from 1749 to 1764, and which had been struck by lightning even in his day.

For those speeding along the M4 who miss Hogarth House in the fury of lane-swapping, the beginning of the Chiswick flyover strides past the southern edge of **Gunnersbury Park**, offering a tantalizing vision through winter trees of the white walls of Gunnersbury House. This is one of west London's largest parks, spacious, well maintained but never too crowded. The first house, built for the daughter of George II, was demolished in 1801 and replaced by two mansions for the Rothschilds, one for themselves and one for their guests. Nathan Rothschild founded the London branch of the family bank in 1805; Gunnersbury was one of the fruits of its success, where life was lived on the grandest scale. John Claudius Loudon was employed to adorn the grounds with exotic groves, gothic follies, water gardens, rockeries and the Potomac pond.

Today the vast and pretentious house, flanked by florid conservatories, is a local museum, crammed with Rothschild memorabilia. The grounds have been municipalized with cafeteria, pitch and putt, boating ponds and a riding school full of Thelwell ponies. The old orangery is sadly derelict, every pane smashed by vandals, the "Tudor cloisters" silently smothered with ivy. Among these grandiloquent relics or kicking through the autumn leaves of sweet chestnut and copper beech one can forget the unceasing North Circular traffic beyond the eastern boundary wall.

Further west the elevated M4 offers a birdseye view of the majestic spreading cedars and mellow dark-red brick gables of **Boston Manor**. This is a gorgeous Jacobean house, compactly built in 1623, presently divided into nineteen flats. The grounds were made public in 1924 but now the motorway cuts across the middle, generating a constant swish of traffic. Underneath the concrete stilts an eerie rumble haunts the fossilized tracks of old construction vehicles. The little lake is a splendid place for young children to feed the ducks; the smooth lawns give dogs the chance to romp and chase; but for the artistic eye Boston Manor is a vivid juxtaposition of graceful civility and the new brutalism.

Opposite:
Underneath the
M4, Boston Manor.

Boston Manor's loss was **Osterley Park's** gain. Even mindless Department of Transport road planners could not impose a motorway within eyeshot of Osterley House, so the M4 had to take a northerly curve. Boston Manor suffered so that Osterley House could survive. What awful choices we give ourselves! The approach to Osterley is inauspicious. The Great West Road is the quintessential 1930s arterial dual carriageway, lined with a ribbon of self-important factories (though, alas, no longer the Firestone factory) and, beyond the service roads, serried ranks of tawdry semi-detached suburbia. Hiding behind its high walls Osterley Park is a chunk of ancient Middlesex, a rich farmland of flat fertile meadows and fine trees. The long chestnut drive from Thornbury Road to Osterley House passes through classic parkland where herds of cattle ruminate and thoroughbred horses graze, sheltering under the horizontal canopy of individually fenced oaks. Here it feels like the edge of London — a marvellous sense of open country and unrestricted horizons.

The view of the house when it appears across the upper lake is one of the most satisfying sights in England. The scale of the house and grounds is vast, perhaps not quite that of Hampton Court but incredible considering that it was established and maintained by commoners, not by royalty or aristocracy. Osterley Manor began originally in 1577 as the country retreat for Sir Thomas Gresham, immensely wealthy from his exploits in the City where he founded the Royal Exchange. Here he built an enormous Tudor mansion, posh enough to put up Queen Bess for a few nights. He even got his bricklayers to fling up a new wall overnight across the courtyard to satisfy a curious whim of his illustrious guest. The great Elizabethan stables survive from Gresham's day, a superb range of buildings around a lovely forecourt of cobbles, too substantial to be dismissed as outhouses.

The main house, however, was altered by the Childs, a prodigiously successful family of City bankers, who bought Osterley in 1711. Between 1756 and 1786 the Tudor mansion was completely remodelled, initially by William Chambers but from 1762 by Robert Adam. Only the four corner towers of the original house were kept, the rest was entirely rebuilt, including a new portico on the north-east side, a magnificent flight of steps surmounted by columns leading into the elevated central courtyard. Inside, Adam

attended to every detail, from carpet to keyhole — he even designed the furniture. Whereas most stately homes are full of paraphernalia from different periods, Osterley's unity is unrivalled. The whole estate was given to the National Trust in 1923, but the house is looked after by the Victoria and Albert Museum, almost as a memorial to Adam.

The spaciousness of the grounds befits the house. Three long lakes, all on different levels, attract wildfowl from far and wide. The exotic trees planted 200 years ago are now in full maturity. At the rear of the house a curving stone staircase sweeps down to a broad stretch of lawn, flanked by fine trees which hide the soberly classical Temple of Pan and Adam's ostentatious semi-circular orangery decorated in Wedgwood pastels. The lemon and orange bushes are plastic; somehow the fake adds to this stage set, an ornate façade with a plain brick back. The M4 cuts across the north part of the estate, thankfully not elevated, but the peace of old Middlesex is shattered more audibly by the jumbos and tristars climbing off Heathrow's runways just two miles west.

Horace Walpole on his first visit to refashioned Osterley in 1773 was much impressed — "All the Percys of Syon must die of envy", he wrote. The Childs were no doubt only too aware of their near neighbour, the Duke of Northumberland, who, barely one mile away beside the river, had employed Robert Adam to revamp his ancestral home of southern England, **Syon House**. As at Osterley this had been an Elizabethan mansion built on land given to the Percy family. By 1760 the educated Hugh Percy, well travelled and immensely rich, was tired of draughty Tudor timber and brick, and desired modern convenience and design for his home. Adam warmed to his task: "The idea was to me a favourite one, the subject great and the expense unlimited." Within an unexciting square plan Adam created a lavish interior of exceptionally ornate state rooms, perhaps his finest work. From outside the house remains deceptively dull, Victorianized with grey stone facing and battlements, enlivened only by the giant Percy lion striding across the west front, rescued from old Northumberland House near Trafalgar Square in 1874.

Syon House is the last great stately home in London, apart from the royal palaces, to be occupied by the aristocracy. It remains the private residence of the Duke of

Northumberland, perhaps explaining the slightly "Woburn Abbey" flavour, for although access to the house is limited the grounds are commercially exploited. In 1965 considerable criticism accompanied the conversion of fifty-five acres into a garden centre and modern banqueting suite, together with massive car-parks. The new butterfly safari — "the biggest of its kind in Europe" — is a further attempt to attract people who wouldn't come otherwise — a huge greenhouse where exotic butterflies and moths flutter freely in humid heat and giant spiders and ants crawl warily in glass cages.

The Tudor gardens, planted with mulberry trees, herbs and rose trellises, were remodelled by Capability Brown at the same time as Adam transformed the house, and were replaced with sweeping lawns, informal spinneys, shrubberies and two lakes. The GLC maintain these ravishing gardens which almost rival Kew across the river. Even Kew's hothouses are matched by Charles Fowler's beautiful conservatory at Syon, a lovely dome of glass and iron built in 1827, which now contains a charming little menagerie with humming birds, aquarium and reptile house. Syon thrives on its reputation as a place for all the family, and certainly pulls the crowds. At least the garish parts are grouped together; the wanderer can escape the hordes among the sylvan glades or beside the tidal Thames.

Upstream from Syon the river is lined by a string of opulent mansions and their grounds, all located for their easy water-transport to London as well as the setting. Sites had to be chosen carefully to minimize the risk of flooding. Beyond Richmond Bridge where the taverns tumble down to the water's edge the river banks spread wider and flatter at Petersham Meadows. Between old Richmond and Twickenham villages on the Middlesex side lie three stately houses subtly placed above the spring tide surges.

Marble Hill is the finest, built in 1723 in the new English Palladian style for Henrietta Howard, Countess of Suffolk and mistress of George II. The house was her country summer lodge, not particularly grand except for the double-height Great Room on the first floor, modelled on Inigo Jones's famous Cube Room at Wilton, but big enough to get away from court life and to entertain her favourite London friends in a decent manner. Two of her best friends, Horace Walpole and Alexander Pope, who happened to live nearby, helped design the gardens, which

Opposite:
Osterley House, one of the finest sights in England.

were laid out by Charles Bridgeman. Some of the original formality has been lost but they remain a delight, providing a green backcloth for the white stuccoed house and a splendid view over the river. Earlier this century Thomas Cunard, the shipping magnate, proposed covering the park, owned by him at the time, with houses. Fortunately all is now in the guardianship of the GLC.

The Cunards almost got their way next door at **Orleans House**. This is a mere shadow of the great mansion built in 1710 for the retirement of William III's minister for Scotland, and later the home for the exiled Louis Philippe of France from 1800 to 1814 and of Don Carlos of Spain. William Cunard demolished the main house in 1926, leaving only the octagonal baroque folly designed by James Gibbs in 1720. Today this is a small art gallery, set among quiet wooded gardens where the sprawling suburbs of Twickenham seem far removed.

Looking onto the houseboats and willows of Eel Pie Island, **York House** is the third mansion, enclosed by exquisite public gardens. The house, heavily restored William and Mary, is used as council offices but the grounds behind their high walls still betray the scent of less bureaucratic days. A hump-backed footbridge connects the water gardens and the river terrace. Beyond the evergreen avenue unashamed statues erected by Sir Ratan Tata, last private owner of York House, stand boldly above the fountain — seven naked nymphs and a scantily-clad Venus. This was a ready-made set for the film of Tom Jones, which was shot in the house and grounds.

The riverside path from York House to Marble Hill and the patio of the White Swan Inn afford a magnificent prospect across the Thames to **Ham House** on the Surrey Bank. At last here is a Jacobean house built in 1610 which was not tampered with by Adam, Kent, Chambers or any of their eighteenth-century fellows. Inside, a superb collection of Stuart furniture, Flemish tapestries and Italian textiles were accumulated mainly by the Duke of Lauderdale. He may have been an unpleasant politician and scheming adviser to Charles II but you can't argue with his domestic taste.

The house and gardens were given to the National Trust by Sir Lionel Tollemache in 1948, since when the grounds have been snatched back from the clutches of Nature and restored to authentic Jacobean neatness and formality.

Tragically the mighty elms had to be felled, leaving a somewhat bleak landscape. Nevertheless it is probably reminiscent of how the gardens first appeared — mathematically constructed brick paths, symmetrical flowerbeds and etched lawns, flanked with precise rows of flimsy saplings — so austere compared with the decadence of York House across the river.

Such is the wealth of parks and gardens in south-west London that it scarcely matters that **Petersham House** is not open to the public. This admirable late seventeenth-century house would be a jewel in drabber parts, yet in Richmond there is almost a surfeit of riches, and too many rival attractions.

Were it not for the ill-directed incendiary bombs of September 1940 **Holland Park**, like Ham House, might today be one of London's great stately homes. Following the disastrous fire, only the east wing and orangery survive from the Jacobean mansion begun in 1607. Nevertheless the fifty-five acres of grounds form one of London's loveliest parks, with an unexpected juxtaposition of wildness and order. The northern half of the park comprises beautiful woodland, full of birds and animals. Gravel paths meander through a sylvan idyll where tame squirrels and rabbits amble, peacocks and cockerels strut, and exotic ducks mingle with the ubiquitous pigeons and sparrows. At the junction of three paths is a seated statue of Lord Holland, who made Holland House a favourite resort for wags and wits in early Victorian society.

Immediately beside the orangery which now accommodates the Belvedere restaurant and café, the Dutch gardens are respectfully formal, a hint of the splendid floral terraces which encircled the magnificent Holland House. To the south, from the open-air theatre to the Commonwealth Institute with its parade of flags on Kensington High Street, the park is more municipal, catering for kids and active games. For its size, Holland Park is as charming and varied as any in London, much overlooked by those who go habitually to Kensington Gardens.

In north London **Kenwood House** has no peer. Superficially it is similar to Gunnersbury, but inside it equals the splendour of Osterley and Syon. Although it is separately fenced and gated, most people regard Kenwood as part of Hampstead Heath; yet for 150 years it was a private house with 200 acres of closely guarded grounds,

Opposite:
The Cedar of Lebanon, Boston Manor, planted 250 years ago.

shut off from the wild expanses of heath and common. Lord Mansfield, Chief Justice to George III, bought the estate in 1754, for its fresh air and panorama. From 1767 Robert Adam was engaged to rebuild the house. Flush with his triumph at Syon and Osterley, Adam obliged with an imposing exterior and a sumptuous interior. In 1925 Kenwood was acquired by Lord Iveagh, who two years later gave the whole estate, his collection of paintings and a lump sum endowment to the public. Iveagh's bequest was an act of supreme generosity and magnanimity. With its fabulous library and great masters — Reynolds, Rembrandt, Vermeer, Gainsborough and Stubbs — Kenwood is one of the nation's most select art galleries, and a lovely venue for Sunday evening concerts. In front of the house the promenade terrace overlooks lawns which sweep down to the lake, where in one corner Humphrey Repton's sham Chinese bridge completes this perfect landscape. On balmy summer Saturday evenings the woods behind echo to the *1812 Overture* and the *New World Symphony*, those perennial potboilers of Kenwood lakeside concerts.

Alongside the house the ivy tunnel excites every child while the magnolias, azaleas and rhododendrons in May and June are a riot of colour. Hidden and almost unnoticed, Dr Johnson's summer house was moved here from Streatham in 1968, rethatched after arsonists did their worst. The eminent doctor had never had much to do with Kenwood until then. Beyond the trickling rill which runs red with iron among the thin copse of silver birch and the monolithic Henry Moore, the long hay fields of Kenwood climb up to merge with the wild grass and scrub of the heath through the metal fence.

Compared with Kenwood, **Fenton House** is tiny and hemmed in by the higgledy-piggledy lanes and alleys of Hampstead village. This National Trust property, dating from 1693, is best known for its assortment of early keyboard instruments — harpsichords, clavichords, spinnets and virginals — and Constable's painting of Hampstead Heath, but outside is a beautiful walled garden, sheltered and ordered.

Highgate is Hampstead's salubrious twin, on the east side of the heath. Here, near the top of Highgate Hill, stands Lauderdale House and its grounds, better known as **Waterlow Park**. The house is not grand compared with the Duke of Lauderdale's other London home at Ham. Pepys

when he visited in 1666 "went to Lord Lauderdale's house and find him and his lady and some Scotch people at supper; pretty odd company". Lauderdale in fact spent most of his time away persecuting Scottish protestants, and Charles II reputedly boarded Nell Gwynne here in his absence.

In 1871 Lauderdale House was nearly pulled down, as the adjacent cottage of Andrew Marvell, the poet, had been twenty-two years earlier. Its future was assured by Sydney Waterlow, an apprentice engineer and self-made man who worked his way to wealth and presented the estate to the public in 1891 as "a garden for the gardenless". His statue proudly presides over his park and gazes further to the great wen where he was once Lord Mayor. Perhaps these shades of Dick Whittington attracted him to Highgate. Camden Council does its best to fulfil his wishes, providing tennis courts, bandstand, an aviary with mina birds and a well-stocked lake. The hilly and varied terrain make Waterlow one of London's jolliest parks, and seemingly far larger than its twenty-seven acres. What a contrast this is to the rampant jungle and spooky tombs of Highgate Cemetery next door, guarded by its sinister railings.

Tottenham is not noted for its stately homes, or anything much except football. **Bruce Castle**, within sight and sound of Spurs' stadium, is a surprise. Robert Bruce was once Lord of Tottenham Manor, and inside the house the local history museum contains the old Tottenham Rolls going back to 1318. This is one of a strange medley of exhibits, including trophies of the Middlesex Regiment (the Diehards), and philately, honouring Rowland Hill, who lived here. The castle is disappointingly unpugilistic. Perhaps the detached round red-brick tower is part of the original fortification; the main building is a rag-bag of styles and materials, patchily restored. At the back the bold coat of arms looks on to the pleasant if unspectacular park with wide spreading oak trees and prolific spring bulbs.

A little way north, just off Fore Street, **Pymmes Park** was a splendid Elizabethan mansion, totally destroyed in 1940. Only the mellow garden walls remain, enclosing well-manured rose beds and evergreen shrubs. An ornamental lake and bandstand complete this municipal scene, a welcome haven from monotonous Edmonton streets and grinding traffic on the North Circular Road. A mile west, **Broomfield House** and **Park** is girdled by the respectable suburbs of Palmers Green and Southgate. The

Opposite:
Kenwood House, beautiful in any season.

Page 110:
Tea-rooms and cafeteria, Kenwood.

Page 111:
Waterlow Park, "a garden for the gardenless".

THE OPEN SPACES OF LONDON

seventeenth-century house, now a local art gallery, has been bashed about and patched up, certainly not a masterpiece, although a fine timber staircase painted by Thornhill survives. The park boasts mature forest trees and broad acres of grass, popular with local dog-owners and joggers.

Forty Hall at Forty Hill Enfield deserves to be better known, for this is an architectural gem, nestling in a beautiful park. Forty Hall and **Whitewebbs Park**, which is contiguous, were both once part of Enfield Chase, a vast stretch of natural forest and hunting ground for Plantagenet and Tudor kings. Potter's Bar was one of the entrances into this royal domain. Forty Hall was built in 1629 on the site of an Elizabethan lodge, and refaced with russet William and Mary bricks capped with lofty chimneys. The seventeenth-century panelling and plaster inside is intact, well restored in 1962. The classical façades, complemented by pretty outbuildings and stables, are the focus for long avenues of limes and superb lakeside views framed by cedars of Lebanon.

Whitewebbs Park was also partitioned out of Enfield Chase as a 230-acre private estate of natural parkland whose massive oaks are direct descendants of the native forest. The large white house in the middle was built in 1791 in a French colonial style, rather less impressive than Forty Hall. The new M25 now separates Whitewebbs from **Theobald's Park**, flanked by Hugh Myddelton's New River and notable for containing the old Temple Bar. This was removed from Fleet Street to ease traffic congestion and re-erected a dozen miles north, sadly neglected and allowed to crumble. Now there is a plan to re-erect Wren's grand gateway next to St Paul's in the heart of the City.

The humble suburbia of Walthamstow is an unpromising area for grand houses, yet Water House in Forest Road and **Lloyd Park** behind it are well worth the tedious journey from central London, a must for pre-Raphaelite students and north-east Londoners. This bay-windowed Georgian house was the home of William Morris, who was born in Walthamstow in 1834 and became an ardent campaigner in the battle to save Epping Forest. Morris deplored the erosion of the forest which he loved "yard by yard from Wanstead to the Theydons and from Hale End to the Fairlop Oak". It is hard to imagine that the gardens at the side and back of Water House, now a delightful urban park,

Opposite:
Charlton House;
the pavilion next to
the mulberry tree.
112

were in Morris's day a clearing on the edge of the forest. Morris left Walthamstow in 1871 and retired to Kelmscott in Oxfordshire. How he rejoiced in the 1878 Epping Forest Act, but how appalled he would have been to see the authoritarian architecture of Walthamstow Town Hall near his old home.

Further east on the outer fringes of London, **Rainham Hall** is a superb early Georgian house, modest in size and exquisitely finished, but though owned by the National Trust it is not normally open to the public. **Langtons**, nearby in Hornchurch, is a slightly later house, set among elegant lawns, geometric flowerbeds and an ornamental lake, maintained by the local council.

East London was not a popular residence for the nobility, either north or south of the river. Those who did look east mostly ventured deeper into the fertile countryside of Kent or Essex, away from the damp mists and odours of the Thames estuary. The exceptions repay the search, even such small treasures as **Manor House Gardens** in Lee. This stylish brick house, now a local library, presides over an endearing park with smooth lawns sloping down to a little lake where ducks and geese strut and squabble. What a splendid rural retreat this must once have been.

Two miles east, along Eltham Road, the medieval remains of **Eltham Palace** lie inconspicuously off Court Road. The Army Education Corps occupy the buildings, but on Thursdays and Sundays the public are allowed in to admire the venerable sixteenth-century hall with its breathtaking hammerbeam roof. The gardens were laid out by Sir Stephen Courtauld in 1930 and contain fragments of old palace walls and red-brick ramparts, combined delightfully with trees, flowers and lawns. The whole complex is protected by the encircling moat, complete with deep murky water and patrolled by black swans. Left of the main gate a narrow drive leads to the Royal Parks Training Centre, private but worth a peek if you're nosy. As expected each tree is meticulously labelled, lawns are manicured and hedges clipped to perfection, not a weed in sight. East of Court Road Eltham Lodge, dating from 1663, is now part of Blackheath Golf Club, a suitable age for this ancient institution, though it moved here only in 1923.

North of Shooters Hill and the Old Dover Road, **Charlton House** occupied an elevated position which commanded fine views westwards to London before being

blotted out by modern flats and houses, masking the natural lie of the land. This must have seemed a magnificent house when finished in 1607, with its tall chimneys, proud turrets and mullioned windows. James I was so impressed that he ordered a new mulberry tree to be planted near the house, claiming to be the oldest in England. Sadly, not much of the interior, now used as a library and community centre, is worth inspecting. In front of the house a lonely stone archway stands on the close-cropped grass among vivid flowerbeds. At the rear the terrace is popular with kids practising wheelies on their chopper bikes. The sheltered walled garden south of the main house next to the dutch-gabled outbuildings is a refuge for rose bushes, four cherry trees and a circular pond. The rest of the forty-acre park is flat and rather dull, mainly football pitches. Even the old ha-ha has been spoilt by a fence, no doubt erected by a safety-conscious park-keeper.

Danson Park, almost engulfed by the dreary avenues and crescents of Welling, was also once a grand estate. The mansion was built in 1760 for Sir John Boyd and surrounded by infant cedar saplings which have grown into giant sentries. Today the white stucco is smothered in scaffolding, and the old stables have been left to rot. If only the Council had renovated them instead of building nasty new sheds for their mowing machines. The grounds are big, over 185 acres. The traditional English rose garden near the mansion and the rock garden are palpably the attendant's pride and joy; the rest is mainly taken up by a huge expanse of windswept grass between the house and the lake, punctuated by a solitary oak. Beyond the lakeside poplars traffic thunders along the A2 to Dover.

After just a mile and a half these same vehicles roar past the grounds of **Hall Place**, on the very edge of Bexley. It is almost 450 years since the first wing of the house was built on the site of a mill, reusing ragstone from "dissolved" Kentish monasteries mixed with chequer-board patterns of knapped flint. The southern half of the house was added between 1649 and 1666, using fashionable red brick and roof tiles. Inside, the timbered Tudor hall and gallery were decorated with elaborately moulded plaster. This strangely beautiful house is encompassed by equally lovely gardens, superbly maintained by Bexley Council and worthy winner of the Landscape Heritage Award in 1975. The warm brick

paths and immaculate lawns are the stage for a remarkable tableau of topiary. Perhaps it is a little hard to differentiate between the lions, unicorns and other heraldic beasts — some indeed could well be Yogi Bear or Brer Rabbit — but the abstract cubist sculptures are magical.

If it were not for the incessant noise of traffic this would be an idyllic place, the formal gardens divided from rural pasture by the meandering stream. Instead the road builders, as at Boston Manor and Hogarth House, have done their damnedest. How tranquil might these water meadows be if all the cars would go away, and let the River Cray flow peaceably to the Darenth and the sea.

Once these stately homes were set in country parks, half a day from town by cart, where gentle twilight and hoary dew were set to music by a thousand birds. Alas, no longer; our noisome weapons do their worst.

"Yet nature lives even here, and will not part
From her best home, the lowly-loving heart."
(Coleridge)

CHAPTER 6: London Squares

Page 115:
St. James's Square,
and the statue of
William III.

Opposite:
Covent Garden,
Punch-and-Judy or
hide-and-seek?

Squares are by no means a uniquely London feature. Every great city has its grand civic spaces, like La Place de la Concorde in Paris or New York's Times Square, but no other city has used the square quite so exhaustively as a design for development in both residential and commercial areas. Nor was the idea of the square — a rectangular open space surrounded and overlooked by terraces of buildings with gaps for side roads — a British invention, whatever some might have you believe. But it was a concept so readily adopted and liked by Londoners that they now regard it as traditional and naturally English. London still abounds with architects and planners keen to have a hand in forming the newest London square. As an address the suffix "square" has assumed unrivalled prestige, and as a result it is a much abused name. Hence it is virtually impossible to say how many squares London has; a simple scan of the A-Z leads to many disappointing culs-de-sac.

London squares have no guiding uniformity in size, shape or function. Some are large leafy places available for public recreation, some are open only to keyholders from private estates, some are little more than traffic islands, so polluted with noise, lead and carbon dioxide that only pigeons and drunkards stay there for long. They do, however, contribute enormously to London's character and variety of open space.

Historically London's first square was the forum built by the Romans in the centre of their Londinium. This was an open paved market-place, some 200 yards across, surrounded by the main public buildings, notably the basilica, located due north of London Bridge roughly in the area of the present Leadenhall market. It did not, of course, survive. Saxon and medieval London which grew up on top of the ruins of the abandoned and plundered Londinium did not attempt to recreate the Roman layout and experienced no overall planning. Instead houses, churches, workshops, taverns and markets crowded together in a disorganized labyrinth of narrow streets and alleys. This was a dark age when the classical ideals of urban space and structure were lost beneath the primitive and hectic instincts of survival. Within the patched-up city walls impoverished tenements huddled together in a chaotic jumble. Space, when it was needed for fairs, sport, pageants or cattle markets, was found on open unprotected land outside the city, at Smithfield, Moorfields or at Southwark. The nearest thing

to a square within the city was the ecclesiastical cloister of Greyfriars or **Amen Court**, or perhaps the cobbled courtyard in front of the **Guildhall**. Only when London burst free of the restraining strait-jacket of the city walls was it possible to contemplate more spacious and elegant forms of development.

Until the dissolution of the monasteries most of the countryside around London had been owned or occupied by the church. Henry VIII confiscated the lot, without mercy, and what he didn't keep for his own royal hunting parks he handed out in large chunks as rewards to helpful noblemen and lackeys. The successors of these complicitous courtiers and cronies dictated the growth of Stuart and Georgian London and established the London square.

The land north of the Strand which ran beside the river from Temple Bar to the separate palace of Westminster had been a convent garden supplying Westminster Abbey. In 1550 it fell into the possession of John Russell, first Earl of Bedford, and it was the fourth duke, Francis Russell, who eighty years later realized its potential for building. Inigo Jones, Surveyor of the King's Works and the most revered architect of the time, was appointed and with the consent of his employer produced drawings for **Covent Garden Piazza** in 1630.

Jones was only nine years younger than William Shakespeare and similarly a genius far in advance of his time. Much influenced by visits to Italy in his formative years, he had introduced the Renaissance style of the Italian Palladio to England. His Queen's House at Greenwich and Banqueting House in Whitehall were a revelation, breaking uncompromisingly with Tudor and Jacobean tradition. On his travels Inigo Jones had admired the classical church square at Livorno with its colonnaded façades. He was possibly also influenced by the Place des Vosges in Paris, built for the French court in 1610, a large, perfectly square courtyard surrounded by uniform tall, narrow houses with arcaded pavements. The enlightened Francis Russell probably had this in mind when he vetted the scheme and agreed to Jones's insistence on the Italian rather than Gothic style.

Covent Garden Piazza today gives little idea of what it originally looked like, 350 years ago. Although the general outline survives, only a rebuilt facsimile of the north-west section remains of the arcaded houses which lined the

north, south and east sides of the great square. The fifth Duke of Bedford, when neither his father nor Inigo Jones were alive to protest, instigated the most radical change when in 1670 he obtained a charter from Charles II to hold a market in the middle of the Piazza for the sale of horticultural produce. During the next century, much to the irritation of local residents, the market expanded rapidly and permanent wooden huts appeared for storing and selling fruit and vegetables. By 1800 there were 15,000 acres of market gardens within ten miles of Covent Garden and each night hundreds of farmers loaded their carts for the market. The shouts of buyers and sellers, the rumble of barrows and the smell of cabbages and apples overwhelmed the smart domesticity of the Piazza and drove away the respectable resident. Jones's colonnaded houses around the Piazza were gradually replaced by more commercial properties, and in 1830 Charles Fowler erected new market buildings, much added-to in this century.

The market was one of London's great institutions, crowded with besmocked countrymen, aproned costers and greengrocers with their carts and barrows, porters struggling under the weight of piles of baskets balanced on their heads, Irish apple-sellers, flower girls, pea-shellers and urchins. So it remained until November 1974, when the market moved to a purpose-built complex at Vauxhall. Suddenly in the heart of London, where previously there had been chronic traffic congestion, overcrowded warehouses and pubs packed with market folk there was an emptiness, a vacuum into which developers, planners, politicians and community leaders plunged in a headlong battle over the future of the area. After two uncertain years the conservationists won and the Piazza was saved, together with Fowler's elegant market halls.

Ten years on, Inigo Jones's Piazza is once again the place to go, London's most popular haunt. Everything has been meticulously renovated, neat and graceful. Gone are the uncouth oaths of the porters and that unique mix of bananas and ballerinas. Even the buskers and jugglers are auditioned before they can perform on their allocated patch of smooth clean cobbles. Only the Jubilee Market offers a reminder of the earthiness of former days, a hint of tattiness among self-conscious boutiques, restaurants and dance workshops.

One important element of Jones's initial plan does

Opposite:
Street theatre in front of St. Paul's, Covent Garden.

survive as the focal point of Covent Garden Piazza — the great portico of St Paul's church on the west side. The Duke of Bedford required a church for the new residents but something simple to minimize costs — "I would have it not much better than a barn." Inigo Jones came up with "the handsomest barn in England". In front of these mighty columns where Eliza Doolittle was found, the Punch-and-Judy shows and the acrobats keep hundreds of onlookers amused. The Piazza has come full circle, reclaiming its original role as a place where the beau monde while away their evenings and weekends.

The success of Inigo Jones's design and the Duke of Bedford's profits were such that other landowners quickly jumped on the bandwagon. The Piazza was the prototype for dozens of new London squares to be built over the next two centuries. Having finished his own mansion near St James's Palace in 1632, the Earl of Leicester decided to preserve a rectangle of open land before selling off the remaining parts of Leicester Fields for development in 1635. Although Leicester House was demolished in 1790 **Leicester Square** endured, enclosed by railing since 1690. William Hogarth and Joshua Reynolds both lived and died in houses overlooking the square, but by the 1850s the properties had become shabby and the gardens neglected. The Metropolitan Board of Works rescued the square from the clutches of property developers in 1863 and reopened the gardens in 1874. Today Leicester Square epitomizes West End theatre-land — flashing lights, neon pizza parlours, the whirr of taxis. It's much better for being closed to through traffic, and has recently become a popular afternoon hang-out for punks, themselves a considerable tourist attraction. Perhaps they also attract the huge flocks of starlings which roost in the trees. The statue of Shakespeare in the centre looks on benignly.

In 1638 the meadows between Covent Garden and the disreputable suburb of Holborn, known as **Lincoln's Inn Fields**, came under threat. For centuries these had been an undisputed recreation ground for law students resident at the Inns of Court clustered just outside the old city wall. Inigo Jones had even supervised the planting of trees in 1618. The fields and the Inns of Court were owned by the Crown, having previously been monastic institutions suppressed by Henry VIII. Charles I, constantly short of funds, unhesitatingly sold a licence for building, incurring the fierce wrath of the Society of Lincoln's Inn, who succeeded in securing the preservation of seven acres, soon surrounded by houses. Thus London's third, and largest, square was formed, more by luck than judgement. By 1641 the south and west sides were built of which nos. 59-60 are survivors, reputedly by Inigo Jones, though now disguised under stucco. The north side was constructed later, including Sir John Soane's house at nos. 12-14, now a museum of his accumulated art treasures and Egyptian relics. It is even said that the Fields are the same size as the base of the Great Pyramid in Egypt. I haven't bothered to check, and I'm sure its truth or otherwise matters little to those who enjoy its facilities — least of all to Lord William Russell, who was executed in the middle of the Fields in 1683 after his abortive assassination attempt on Charles II.

After the Napoleonic wars the Fields became infested with cripples who intimidated passers-by with their crutches, and beggars who imitated the maimed to solicit charity. In this murky Dickensian context (the Old Curiosity Shop is nearby in Portsmouth Street) Charles Barry proposed rebuilding the Law Courts over the Fields. His immodest plans were rejected and instead the gardens were taken over by London County Council in 1894. Lincoln's Inn Fields are much loved for the huge plane trees and grassy shade, the outdoor café and lunchtime netball — stirring stuff for lunching lawyers. The maples in Canada Walk commemorate the Canadian wartime centre of operations, and comfort any homesick North American in the fall. Within Lincoln's Inn itself **New and Old Square** offer a tantalizing glimpse of pre-war Oxbridge, where the quads ring with the confident step of black leather shoes and the plummy cheer of barristerial baritone voices.

Gray's Inn Fields survived in similar fashion to Lincoln's Inn Fields, originally pasture land used for archery and other outdoor sports (as the alley Jockey's Fields suggests) and subsequently protected vehemently by conservative lawyers. The gardens were laid out by Francis Bacon when he was treasurer of the Inn in about 1600, but became enclosed by buildings later that century. They remain more private than Lincoln's Inn Fields, open to the public only during the working day. Through the iron railings in Theobald's Road sloping terraces of velvet lawn, ancient catalpas supported on props and slatted wooden benches cast a spell on any prepared to stop and look, as wisps of gardener's bonfire smoke drift through soft afternoon sunshine. Nearby in High Holborn **Staple Inn** was also once a Chancery Inn until 1884, and behind the rickety Tudor façade a tiny garden square lives on.

The yards and courts of the **Temple** are more akin to the squares inside Lincoln's Inn, set among delightful old buildings with quaint titles such as Crown Office Row and Paper Buildings. All is private, within the City of London yet beyond its jurisdiction; access for the general public is carefully controlled, restricted to certain courts and certain times. In these sequestered gardens Shakespeare made the rival Houses of York and Lancaster pluck their emblems of the white and red roses, and Boswell wrote his glowing words: "A most agreeable place. You quit all the hurry and bustle of the City in Fleet Street and the Strand, and all at once find yourself in a pleasant academical retreat of handsome walks; you view the silver Thames, you are shaded by venerable trees and crows are cawing above your head." Little has changed in this bastion of the Establishment, though the roses are not for the picking.

After the Civil War and Cromwell's regime had temporarily halted new buildings the Restoration brought back not only the monarchy but also confidence for development. North-west of Lincoln's Inn, the Earl of Southampton laid out **Bloomsbury Square** early in 1665 before fleeing from the growing scourge of plague, and when he died two years later his estate was inherited by the Duke of Bedford, who completed the square. By then, however, London had suffered its greatest calamity, the Great Fire of 1666. Four-fifths of the half-timbered medieval city was destroyed, including 88 churches and 13,000 houses. With most of London's despondent population camping out in makeshift tents, here was the chance to replan London.

Christopher Wren's ideas for rebuilding the city with triumphant boulevards and majestic squares fell foul of petty squabbles over land ownership. Instead the devastated city was reconstructed on virtually the same old undisciplined street lines, except that brick and stone replaced timber and plaster. Wren had to content himself with adorning the city with 51 new churches and St Paul's Cathedral. Meanwhile in the meadows and woods of Soho, Mayfair, Marylebone and St James's the landowners grabbed the opportunity to provide a more elegant and

Opposite:
Charles Chaplin,
Leicester Square.

spacious way of life for the monied merchants and gentry who did not relish returning to the cramped and cluttered City.

Each landholder meticulously planned his estate as a complete entity, adopting the Covent Garden blueprint, with a combination of handsome mansions, more modest houses in secondary streets, plentiful mews for servants and ostlers, a church, market-place and burial ground. The focus was the square, on to which all the finest houses faced, the consummation of opulent living. As each new estate competed with the last in attracting the élite and genteel, so the squares became ever grander and more lavishly landscaped.

Development was speculative but cleverly arranged so that the landowner retained the real estate or freehold and raised cash for building by selling long leases. Subsequently the freeholder collected low ground rents until the lease expired, when more profitable terms could be dictated. London's squares today are a remarkable legacy of this speculative building boom, all painstakingly designed as cohesive units, yet all formed in a time when there was no overall town planning, no green-belt policy, and precious few building regulations. London squares became the envy of the world.

Soho Square, today rather tatty and seedy, was highly fashionable for several years after it was built in 1681, "having very good buildings on all sides which are inhabited by nobility and gentry". Few of the old houses are left now, but the trees in the square have grown to cast pleasant shade. The landowner Richard Frith, Earl of Macclesfield, and builder Thomas Neale were aided and abetted by the ambitious Nicholas Barbon, son of "Praise the Lord" Barbon, whose talents lay in the more profane and earthy skills of property speculation. In 1684 Barbon proceeded to develop land he had bought near Gray's Inn, much to the annoyance of the lawyers, and laid out **Red Lion Square**. Legend has it that Oliver Cromwell's body lies somewhere under the square, having been dug up from Westminster Abbey in 1661 on the Restoration, taken to Tyburn for ceremonial mincing and then ignominiously buried in unconsecrated ground. No stone or obelisk stands to add precision to this yarn, but no matter. The square today has a curious charm of its own and a long thin garden full of pigeons and sparrows. The western end is ruined by

thundering traffic but the east is quiet and secluded. In one corner is the South Place Ethical Society and the Conway Hall, host for those delightful Sunday evening concerts. For three years Gabriel Rossetti, William Morris and Edward Burne-Jones shared a house and avant-garde pre-Raphaelite thoughts at no. 17, overlooking the gardens.

Two other squares were also laid out in 1684, but in very different styles. **Golden Square**, south of Beak Street, is one of central London's smallest and least known squares, hidden almost apologetically in the maze of narrow Soho streets. Dickens described it in *Nicholas Nickleby* as "not exactly in anybody's way to or from anywhere. It is a great resort of foreigners. The dark-complexioned men who wear large rings and heavy watch-guards and bushy whiskers, and who congregate under the Opera Colonnade, all live in Golden Square. Two or three violins and a wind instrument from the Opera band reside within its precincts. The notes of pianos and harps float in the evening time round the head of the mournful statue, the guardian genius of a little wilderness of shrubs, in the centre of the square. On a summer's night windows are thrown open and sounds of gruff voices practising vocal music invade the evening's silence, and the fumes of choice tobacco scent the air."

St James's Square, south of Piccadilly, remains one of London's finest, perfectly symmetrical and surrounded by magnificent houses. Its dignity and location, near to St James's Palace and Westminster, attracted the leading aristocrats and politicians from the 1680s to the late nineteenth century. Three prime ministers, Pitt, Derby and Gladstone, lived in Chatham House, no. 10 St James's Square. The centre of the square was originally embellished with a circular pond and an elegant fountain. Later this was replaced by a statue of William III and a garden planted with trees and enclosed with ornate railings. The refined quality of the square survives intact, including most of the original houses, now occupied mainly by learned institutions such as the London Library. The Libyans have proved a regrettable excepton.

The end of the Duke of Marlborough's successful campaign against the French in 1712 sparked off a further building boom north and south of the Oxford Road (today's Oxford Street). First to act was the Earl of Scarborough, who promptly asked the new King George I (Elector of

Opposite:
Lincoln's Inn Fields, London's largest square and lawyers' playground.

Hanover) for the privilege and prestige of using the royal name. **Hanover Square** was begun in 1717 to a spacious and formal design which pleased the German-speaking court. From the square, the statue of William Pitt enjoys a magnificent view down the wide vista of George Street to the projecting portico of St George's church. Hanover Square was immediately the height of fashion, and today you can still feel a stolid Germanic calm in the square.

Westwards, as far as the royal Hyde Park, the land was owned by Lord Grosvenor who had successfully suppressed the ancient May Fair in 1708. The debauchery and drunkenness of this licentious carnival were superseded by the propriety of the Grosvenor Estate. Central to the entire development was **Grosvenor Square**, six acres of trees, lawns and flower gardens, second in size only to Lincoln's Inn Fields. The site, known as Oliver's Mount, was levelled and drained, having been disturbed by earthworks hastily thrown up to defend London from Charles I in 1643. The gardens are as immaculate now as when opened in 1725, but the buildings around have changed. During the last war this was London's "little America". The terrace on the north side of the square was General Eisenhower's headquarters from 1942-4, remembered by the memorial to Franklin Roosevelt in the gardens. The west side is dominated by the strident United States Embassy, designed by Eero Saarinen in 1955 — hence the hordes of American students milling around the square or lolling on the grass, waiting for visas and permits.

The buildings around Grosvenor Square took twenty-five years to complete, by which time **Berkeley Square**, a little south and east, had been built, more of an oblong than a square. Tales of nightingales have made this one of London's most famous squares, certainly with no ornithological justification. The huge gnarled trunks of the massive plane trees, planted in 1780, are its best feature, thriving on London's grime, while the constant roar of vehicles round the square would drown the massed braying of a dozen donkeys, let alone the song of a solitary nightingale.

Simultaneously with Grosvenor Square Robert Harley, Earl of Oxford, embarked on **Cavendish Square** north of Oxford Street, the cornerstone for the Harley Estate. Sadly, the central circular garden is now a beleaguered island in a sea of traffic, and undermined by an underground car-

park. A few of the fabulously opulent Georgian houses remain on the north side, where portrait-painter George Romney lived in luxury. But, alas, the square is not the peaceful refuge for Oxford Street shoppers that it might be. Nevertheless Cavendish Square established Marylebone as a fashionable part of town. Completion of the New Road (Marylebone Road) in 1756 and the end of the Seven Years War with France paved the way for the building of **Portman Square** in 1764 and **Manchester Square** two years later. In Manchester Square the superb proportions of the houses and elegant central gardens indicate the powerful influence of John Wood, who had perfected the art in Queen's Square and the Circus at Bath. If Bath stone had been available in London they would have used it here to produce the exquisite decoration which brick cannot match. Portman Square was slower to be finished, and less uniform, though Robert Adam designed some of the houses. The garden is large and well maintained, but being sandwiched between the traffic maelstroms of Baker Street and Gloucester Place it is not a spot to linger long, even if you have a key to get in.

North of Marylebone Road the Portman Estate added **Dorset Square** and leased the oval open space to Thomas Lord in 1767 who had previously run a cricket club at White Conduit Fields in Islington. At Dorset Square Lord founded the Marylebone Cricket Club, where no doubt lots of windows were smashed until a larger site further north in St John's Wood was bought in 1814. Turf from Dorset Square was dug up and relaid at Lord's.

Henry Portman's Dorset residence at Bryanston gave the name for one of the last two Marylebone squares. **Bryanston Square** and its twin **Montagu Square** virtually completed the grid-iron of streets between Oxford Street and Marylebone Road. Formed and protected by Act of Parliament in 1813, both are unusually long and thin, very far from square, the gardens almost acting like a generous central reservation on a dual carriageway. None the less they provide leaves and colour for those lucky enough to live there and somewhere to sit and stroll for those residents with keys.

The Georgian predilection for squares spread to all quarters. When the rough marsh of Moorfields was finally drained, George Dance constructed **Finsbury Square** in 1777. The plan survives but none of the old houses. Instead

this rather bleak space, accommodating a bowling green, café and underground car-park, is now faced by sombre Portland stone office blocks built in the 1930s and '50s. Trees are noticeably stunted, presumably prohibited by the car-park. Georgian terraces surrounding the old plague pits at Smithfield enclosed **Charterhouse Square**, which became a "neat and comely" address. Diagonal rows of planes were planted across this oddly pentagonal space, some of which have grown into mighty giants, flourishing on the bones and humus beneath.

Just north of Fleet Street, tiny **Gough Square** was lined with Georgian houses, one of which was rented by Dr Johnson. Similarly, in Clerkenwell the ancient courtyard of St John's Priory was renamed **St John's Square** and faced with elegant houses, but keeping the medieval gate on the south side. Today both are overrun by cars, motorbikes and parking-meters, with no room for a blade of grass or a single flower.

The greatest opportunity, however, was the green fields of the Duke of Bedford's estate from which blossomed Bloomsbury and Fitzrovia. 112 acres were developed, of which twenty were parcelled off as public gardens, all in the form of squares adorned with trees and grass. **Bedford Square**, dating from 1776, was the first and perhaps the finest of its period. The duke and his designer Thomas Leverton ensured vigilantly that all the houses looked the same from outside, though individual whims could be satisfied inside. Miraculously the square survives intact, and the circular garden has now been augmented by additional paving to restrict traffic. Until 1893 the squares of Bloomsbury were protected by gates, keeping out all who had no business there, maintaining peace and quiet. After those intellectual Edwardian salad days of Virginia Woolf and the "Bloomsbury set", many of the original houses disappeared beneath utilitarian university blocks and modern hotels. Bloomsbury was well and truly raped in the 1930s; only the leafy garden squares, oblong and circular, live on.

Russell Square is the largest Bloomsbury garden, big enough to offer genuine sanctuary from the traffic behind its curvy-topped railings and hedges. Being so close to the British Museum and University it is a popular summer retreat for tourists and students to sprawl on the grass or imbibe at the cafeteria beside the fountain. Humphrey

Repton's design included the absurdly pretentious statue of Francis Russell, Duke of Bedford, wreathed and toga-clad like a Roman emperor. He stares straight down Bloomsbury Way into the Whiggish eyes of Charles James Fox who sits smugly on the north side of Bloomsbury Square, which of course had already existed for 136 years. Behind the towering Imperial Hotel on the east side of Russell Square you will find **Queen Square**, near the hospitals and examination halls of Great Ormond Street. This slender garden is a favourite last resort for revision crammers, a place to fret away anxious minutes.

James Burton, who was to collaborate with Nash (and father Decimus) at Regent's Park, was employed by Russell to extend his estate. **Tavistock Square** lies just north of Russell Square, a slightly sunken garden now with a statue of Mahatma Gandhi in familiar pose. Charles Dickens lived in this square when writing *Bleak House* and *Little Dorrit*, just one of so many Dickens abodes that one wonders whether he had shares in blue plaques! Either side of Thomas Coram's Foundling Hospital Burton laid out **Brunswick** and **Mecklenburgh Squares**, both named after Hanoverian principalities. Today they are very different, Mecklenburgh Square having retained most of its fine terraced houses and the residential privacy of its garden, while Brunswick Square is more public and surrounded by modern buildings, notably the controversial Bloomsbury Centre. Between the two is **Coram's Fields**, not exactly a square but nevertheless one of Bloomsbury's most valued open spaces and still run by the Thomas Coram Foundation for Children, begun in 1739. Behind the Georgian colonnades in Guildford Street a splendid playground entertains young children, and excludes unaccompanied adults.

Further north still, **Argyle Square** extended the estate up to the doorstep of Kings Cross, an area now sadly down at heel. The square is pleasantly if functionally organized for games, at its worst frequented by intoxicated Scotsmen, shifty kerb-crawlers and plain-clothed police — not inviting at night. **Euston Square** in 1828 and **Gordon Square** in 1850 completed the development of Bloomsbury. The oblong garden at Gordon Square remains largely unaltered, open only to keyholders and surrounded by a mishmash of old houses and new university buildings. Euston Square has changed beyond recognition, with the

Opposite:
Russell Square in autumn.

127

tragic demolition of the Euston Arch in 1960 and the massive modern redevelopment of the station and forecourt in glass, steel and concrete — hardly the most restful place in London.

Fortunately, the perfect restorative for the conservationist is not far away. **Fitzroy Square**, south-west of the nightmarish Tottenham Court Road underpass, is one of London's better-preserved nooks, sensibly closed to traffic and sensitively paved and planted. The gleaming stucco of the grand terraces, built by Henry Fitzroy in 1792, illuminate the whole square with a joyous light, but don't raise your eyes too high if you want to avoid the Euston and Post Office towers which soar above the mansard roofs.

At the end of the Georgian period the formal terrace began to be replaced by more varied house designs. Detached and semi-detached villas became fashionable in Regency suburbs such as St John's Wood, but always the square retained its position as the most tried and tested form of development. While London's inner suburbs differ greatly in character and building design the communal garden square is omnipresent, churned out repeatedly by speculative builders as a sure way to success and profit.

The leading developer of the Regency and early Victorian era was Thomas Cubitt, master builder and father of the modern construction industry. In 1820 work started on a highly ambitious project to develop the remainder of the Duke of Grosvenor's estate, the hitherto marshy waste of Belgravia and Pimlico. Surplus spoil from excavations at St Katharine's Dock was used, as at Battersea Park, to raise land levels; George Basevi drew up the designs, and Cubitt provided the bricks and mortar and hired the muscle. Such was the scale of building that it was nicknamed "Cubittopolis".

Magnificent squares were crucial to the scheme, most of which survive as they were intended, luxurious and exclusive. **Belgrave Square** is the finest, with a beautiful sunken garden shaded by mature trees. Alas, for the general public it is purely an amenity to be viewed from the road. Admittance is restricted to those with keys who live or work in the prestigious stuccoed embassies and penthouses; even then, a curt notice forbids fireworks, ball games, flower-picking and a dozen other possible sources of nuisance or pleasure. Nothing is allowed that could remotely offend anyone. **Chester Square**, **Eaton Square**

and **Cadogan Square** and **Gardens** are the same, for the private use of lessees and tenants of the Grosvenor Estate; all very right and proper, but no comfort for the stranger. At **Lowndes Square** the Sun Life Assurance Society are the turnkeys, offering no apparent special favours for policy-holders. The drunks and undesirables whom they fear must stagger into Hyde Park or down to dusty **Sloane Square**, which is little better than a traffic roundabout.

Things are slightly rosier for the visitor in Pimlico. **Warwick Square** and **Eccleston Square**, with their pompous porticoes and elaborate balconies, possess private gardens hidden behind thick hedges, but **St George's Square** is open to the public. So too is petite **Ebury Square**, discreet and sheltered near Victoria Coach Station, as nice a place to sit in the sun as you will find without a lengthy walk. Even less frequented is **Pimlico Gardens**, isolated between the embankment race track and the river. It offers nothing to startle the botanist but there's a good view of Battersea, the smell of Thames mud, and a curious statue of the statesman William Huskisson, born in the same year as Beethoven but distinguished in death by being the first person to be killed by a railway train, idiotically run over at the official opening of the Manchester — Liverpool line.

Across Vauxhall Bridge Road **Vincent Square** is occupied by the private playing-fields of Westminster School, visually refreshing and wonderfully convenient for the school. This district is poorly-off for public open space. **Millbank Gardens** behind the Tate Gallery and **Westminster Hospital Gardens** in Horseferry Road are worth the search, garden squares in nature if not in name. Do not be misled by **Smith Square** and **Dolphin Square** which offer only indoor entertainment and virtually no outdoor space.

The squares of the Hyde Park Estate in Bayswater, built in 1836, continue in similar vein to Belgravia, but a little less grand. The best preserved is **Connaught Square**, surrounded by superb terraces with thirteen lofty plane trees filling the central space and a winter-flowering cherry to provide an unexpected splash of blossom. What a place to live — a stone's throw from Hyde Park and Marble Arch with the bonus luxury of a garden square. **Oxford Square**, **Norfolk Crescent** and **Cambridge Square** are less impressive, having been totally rebuilt since the war and rather minimally landscaped. More money has been spent on floodlighting the trees at night than on imaginative

Opposite:
Lonsdale Square, Islington; pretty gardens surrounded by grey gothic houses.

gardening. **Sussex Square**, where Winston Churchill lived for three years, and **Hyde Park Square** are susceptible to traffic noise; one gets the impression that these green pockets are more for looking on to than for sitting in. North of Bishop Bridge Road, more distant from the wide expanses of Hyde Park, **Porchester Square** is a welcome exception to the typical west London square, being open to the public, courtesy of Westminster Council. This strip of open space, lined with limes and planes, boasts an excellent children's playground, brightly painted swings, slides and climbing-frames.

Further west, towards Queensway and beyond, the squares take on a monumental quality of mid-Victorian grandeur; ostentatious terraces rise to six storeys, caked with icing-sugar decoration, the pavements are wide, the roads heavily cambered. **Cleveland**, **Leinster** and **Princes Squares** are magnificent and unspoilt examples, all built in the 1850s. An innovative layout provided rear access for the houses, so that their fronts open straight on to the communal gardens without having to cross a road. These are preciously guarded enclaves, scrupulously locked to keep out tramps, dossers and burglars. Ornamental shrubs and weeping ashes break the monotony of umpteen plane trees.

In North Kensington the imperial splendour has faded. These monster mansions with their tripartite round-headed windows are divided into flats and bedsits, a jaded picture of cracked and peeling stucco and collapsing porticoes. Both **Powis Square** and **Colville Square** are open to the public, but like the houses, would benefit from renovation.

Notting Hill has recovered its smartness, if it ever lost it. **Campden Hill Square**, rising steeply from Holland Park Avenue, is a delightfully leafy arbour, pre-dating the development of the rest of the area. From this superior position Turner painted the sunset sinking over Shepherd's Bush, long before **Norland Square** was laid out further down the hill. **Pembridge Square** is rather severe, with heavy detached villas facing a plain garden enclosed by hedges and railings. It is spartan compared to the glories of **Ladbroke Square** gardens, one of the loveliest private open spaces in London. Dense tall privet hedges conceal an exquisite landscape of lawns, shrubberies, copses of exotic trees, herbaceous borders and tennis courts, linked together by gently tempting gravel paths. On the north side the sumptuous houses of Kensington Park Gardens, flaunting their precocious conservatories, have the greenest southerly aspect in London. The dawn chorus is loud and long. Here and in the wooded dells of Lansdowne Road and Elgin Crescent you see the ultimate rhapsodic amalgamation of town and country after which the affluent Englishman has long hankered. Perhaps one day the "subscribers only" signs will come down, but it is a distant and revolutionary dream.

Kensington and Chelsea too have their sprinkling of choice squares. At Knightsbridge **Montpelier Square**, **Trevor Square** and **Brompton Square** were built in the 1820s, with opulent houses and leafy spinneys, much enjoyed by the poet Mallarmé when he lived there. **Kensington Square**, a quiet backwater behind Barker's department store in Kensington High Street, is lovely too, with a funny mock-Grecian summer-house, but regrettably private. The same goes for select **Edwardes Square**; lucky that Holland Park is so close for the lesser fry! The crunchy gravels and dripping limes of **Royal Avenue** off the King's Road, Chelsea, are open for all to wander and admire; not so the leafy seclusion of **Paultons Square**, **Carlyle Square** or **The Boltons**.

Chelsea Physic Garden, though not exactly a square, is the most unusual open space in the area, privately owned but open to the public. This is the oldest surviving herb garden in London, laid out by the Apothecaries on land leased by Sir Hans Soane. Until Kew Gardens usurped its position it was the receiving ground for newly discovered plants like cotton and tea, brought home by explorers, and a nursery to propogate saplings and seedlings for export to new colonies. Today the collection of traditional and exotic herbs and plants is almost like a miniature Kew, and exquisitely tended.

In north London a more socialistic attitude ensures that nearly all the communal garden squares of Islington and Camden are open to the general public. Usually this is because the original estate has become fragmented and sold off, often with large chunks to the local council. In west London most of the old freehold estates survive, unflinchingly and unassailably in private hands. Nevertheless Islington's remarkable collection of squares, varied and idiosyncratic, were an important factor in its refound

Page 130:
Ladbroke Grove, the luxuriant gardens behind Elgin Cresent.

Page 131:
Lansdowne Road Gardens.

Opposite:
Chelsea Physic Garden, immaculately maintained.

popularity in the 1960s and '70s. The strange mixture of new owner-occupiers and council renovation saved these decaying Victorian terraces from total demise and slum clearance. Property prices spiralled as nowhere else.

Canonbury Square was the earliest, designed in 1800 by Leroux to lie either side of the New North Road, which then was an innocent if sometimes muddy rural track. Today the gardens are superbly tended, a constantly changing display of vivid blooms, but alas, that little farm road now groans under the weight of juggernaut lorries disgorging from Channel ports, ruining the lives of all who live along their path. **Northampton Square** which followed two years later is visually spoilt by modern City University buildings, if not by traffic.

South of Pentonville Road, five squares were built in the 1820s: **Lloyd Square**, still in the ownership of the Lloyd Baker Estate, **Wilmington Square** with its municipal benches and flowerbeds, **Myddelton Square**, handy for Sadler's Wells, **Claremont Square**, dominated by its water reservoir, and **Granville Square** sitting unconcerned on top of the Metropolitan railway. Islington's finest and quirkiest squares are in Barnsbury, north of Pentonville Road. The central space of **Cloudesley Square** was quickly filled with Barry's Holy Trinity church, but all the others retain public gardens. In **Gibson Square**, elegant and narrow, a curious brick folly disguises an air-vent shaft for London Transport's Victoria line, which passes directly beneath the gardens, too deep to hear or feel. North out of Gibson Square is the extraordinary **Milner Square**, designed in 1841 by Roumieu and Gough. Their eccentric hard-edged neo-classical style, almost oppressively vertical, smacks more of Glasgow than London. The central garden, a logical component in the plan, had deteriorated into a cabbage patch fifty years ago but was restored together with the houses by Islington Council in 1978 as a busy little playground.

Across Liverpool Road **Lonsdale Square** could scarcely be more different; dignified grey-brick houses display an unusual blend of collegiate Tudor and railway gothic, and overlook a spacious and serene garden. **Barnsbury Square** is less formal, a verdant enclave surrounded haphazardly by dissimilar villas. Largest of the Islington squares is **Thornhill Square** with its elliptical crescent, a splendid space for children to run and play, and big enough to make

the encircling terraces seem quite small. **Arundel Square** beside the North London railway dates from about 1850, with shades of Bayswater grandeur, but the adventure playground and hard-worn grass are more typically Islington.

In Camden Town **Camden Square** is pleasant and grassy, shaded by chestnuts and limes, but the miniscule gardens of **Harrington Square** and irregular **Oakley Square** are disappointingly exposed to traffic. **Chalcot Square** at Primrose Hill has lovely trees, pretty railings, new swings and no through traffic — and house prices to match.

To the prejudiced north or west Londoner who has never been tempted to explore the unknown territory of the East End or south of the river, it may come as a surprise to learn that these "arid wastes" contain a host of delightful oases. Though few in number, the squares of Kennington and Borough are gems. **Cleaver Square**, sandwiched between the hustling arteries of Kennington Road and Kennington Park Road, is an unexpectedly quiet space, simple and uncluttered. **Courtenay Square** is even more secluded, with petite cottages exquisitely restored, facing on to double rows of pollarded limes. Both are unfenced and surfaced in gravel, ready made for French boules. **Albert Square** in Stockwell is as fine as any in Kensington, while nearer the Elephant and Castle **West Square** is a tiny but bowery retreat for basking in lunchtime sunshine. **Nelson Square**, off Blackfriars Road, was probably its equal until wartime bombing destroyed all the old houses bar one small fragment. Today it is a dismal space, gigantic plane trees rising unnaturally out of barren tarmac, overshadowed by faceless post-war blocks of flats. Inigo Jones, where were you? Perhaps **Trinity Church Square** near Borough High Street would restore his faith, especially the mellow stone church restored as Henry Wood Hall, or the branching boughs of **Merrick Square** next door.

So to the east, where a dozen Victorian garden squares provide some relief among a dislocated landscape of high-rise flats and misguided post-war planning. In **Beaumont Square** and **Trafalgar Gardens** utilitarian council blocks have replaced the old houses, leaving only the central gardens, but in **Tredegar Square** there is a glimpse of how some Islington squares must have looked in the 1950s, shabby but intact terraces and a neglected garden with rusting play equipment. What potential there is here for

Opposite:
Courtenay Square, Kennington.

Page 136:
West Square.

Page 137:
The National Gallery, Trafalgar Square.

restoration, and also at **Sidney Square** with its planes, weeping ash and solitary holly tree. Forlorn **Ford Square** is battered almost beyond redemption but **Albert Square** with its coy Edwardian statue fronting Commercial Road is much smarter. Across the road **Arbour Square** almost lives up to its name, presided over by the blue-coated boy and girl on the façade of the Raines Foundation School. A former Stepney Borough gardener clearly had a penchant for holly trees; every square has one.

York Square, Limehouse, shows what can be done. The council have scrubbed the yellow-brick houses, relaid the turf and painted the garden railings, while Young's Brewery have spruced up the Queen's Head, well worth a visit. No doubt in twenty year's time the other East End squares will be as spick and span.

The convenience of working in the City has already earmarked **Albion Square** and **De Beauvoir Square** in Hackney as "desirable residences" for professional types. The perfect circle of solid Victorian railings which enclose mature lime trees, gentle lawns and a toddlers' playground, and the ornate villas sporting gothic gables and honeycombed lattice windows, make De Beauvoir a most attractive open space by any standard.

Discerning readers will have noticed that all the squares mentioned so far were built as part of residential development. It has omitted the likes of **Finsbury Circus** in the City, a neat oval garden complete with bowling green and surrounded by Edwin Lutyens's imperial commercial buildings, packed with office workers in weekday lunchtimes, deserted at weekends. Several of London's most famous squares were deliberately planned as grand civic spaces. **Trafalgar Square** was conceived by Nash as an extension to Pall Mall and The Mall, sweeping away the ancient royal stables of Whitehall and the churchyard of St Martin's-in-the-Fields. Although not particularly green, it is one of London's celebrated sites, and the foreground for many show-piece buildings, a traditional gathering ground for demonstrators, Scottish football supporters, Hogmanay revellers, camera-clicking tourists and over-fed pigeons. 185 feet above it all stands Nelson, 17 feet tall, immune to all except the higher flying pigeons. Ever since the dinner party was held on the column's top platform to mark the statue's completion in 1843 their lofty perch has been unchallenged. Down at ground level the mounted statue of Charles I, cast in 1633 and cunningly concealed from puritan iconoclasts, stares sadly towards Whitehall where he met his end. Present mortals clamber over the recumbent lions or drench themselves in water pools and fountains — one of London's more sophisticated adventure playgrounds. **Piccadilly Circus** is a much smaller but equally famous focal point, frequented by the footloose and vagrant.

Parliament Square also sees its full share of rallies and protestors, but is rather too dominated by the nearby landmarks to be much appreciated in its own right, and too ensnared in traffic to be much of a refuge. Statues are the least complaining users of this space. A defiant Winston Churchill is the latest addition to this hall of fame which includes Palmerston, Peel, Lincoln and Cromwell. Disraeli's feet are decked with primroses each year on the anniversary of his death. The ancient sequestered cloisters of **Westminster Abbey Gardens**, where monks once grew their herbs, offer reverent silence, and a blissful sanctuary from the din and the politicians.

Further down Victoria Street, massive redevelopment of the street frontage has opened up a magnificent prospect of the west front of Westminster Cathedral by forming a new piazza. Pedestrian precincts have been a popular ingredient in the post-war redevelopment recipe. **Paternoster Square**, north of St Paul's Cathedral, which before the war was a warren of narrow streets, is as good example as any of the planners' dream. The art of creating squares is not dead; the concept smoulders in the heart of every well-educated architect. Westminster Cathedral piazza will surely not be the last addition to London's squares.

CHAPTER 7: Kew Gardens and The Zoo

No book about outdoor London should miss the chance to eulogize on the wonders of Kew Gardens and the Zoological Gardens. Among all of London's open spaces they are the most extraordinary, the most visited and the most widely loved. Without doubt they demand the special attention of a chapter on their own, and although so different in size, location and atmosphere they form a natural pairing. Both have long and fascinating histories and both have strong academic and scholastic foundations and intentions.

The Zoo is one of London's great attractions, for tourists and Londoners, most of whom have at some stage in their life (usually childhood) had a day at the Zoo. Few conscientious parents can escape the trip. Most tourists who stay in London for more than just a day or two will visit the Zoo. Like the Tower, Buckingham Palace and Trafalgar Square, it is a national institution, world-famous. Kew is more for the connoisseur, one of Britain's loveliest gardens with a unique collection of plants and exotic buildings. Even on the wettest, drabbest winter's day it is never dull; in spring and early summer when the sun shines, it is the most glorious place to be in all London.

Kew Gardens

For the dedicated horticulturalist and botanist, Kew is a place of pilgrimage, their Mecca; for the ignorant, both old and young, it is a place of unending fascination, a bewildering complex of plants, landscapes and buildings.

From outside there is little hint of the treasures within. If you approach from the quaint and rustic railway station, walking past comfortable well-kept Edwardian homes, only the loftiest trees and the top of the strange pagoda peep above the high brick boundary walls of Kew into the suburban side streets. The route to the main entrance crosses Kew Green on the south side of Kew Bridge. Despite the traffic and aircraft, the familiar cricket pitch, the affable old pubs and the uncomplicated landscape of grass and perimeter trees produce the tranquillity of an English village green, giving no clue to the exotica beyond.

At the fine heavy wrought-iron gates transistor radios, musical instruments, dogs and footballs are politely turned away, ensuring peace and cleanliness within. The neat clattering turnstiles and the nominal entrance fee deters

the vagrant and troublesome, and contributes towards the wages of the gatemen. On decimalization it was one of the few things that actually went down in price, from 3d. to 1p. Now it's gone up to 10p. — in for a florin. Once inside, you enter a different world, a seat of study and learning as well as a panorama of visual delight. Walk on the velvet grass by all means, but don't pick the wild flowers, " which are as much a source of enjoyment to the visitor as are the cultivated plants".

Kew's supremacy over all other botanic gardens is partly due to its age. For over 200 years plants have been propagated, nurtured and tended; we are now lucky enough to see the maturity of earlier labours. In the early eighteenth century the whole south bank of the Thames from Richmond to Kew was owned by the Crown. For the king and the nobility seeking the sweeter air of the country, the ease of transport to Westminster and Whitehall palaces by river as opposed to road greatly favoured residences beside the Thames. From Lambeth Palace to Hampton Court the riverside was dotted with grand houses and mansions.

At Kew in the 1730s there were two estates, Richmond Lodge and Kew Palace. The former was used as a rural retreat by George II and his wife Queen Caroline, who employed her favourite architect, William Kent, to landscape the grounds. Kew Palace next door was occupied by George's eldest son, Frederick Prince of Wales (never to be king), and his strong-minded wife Princess Augusta. Frederick's tutor, the Earl of Bute, encouraged his pupil's mild interest in botany but it was Princess Augusta who proved the more enthusiastic, developing a passion for foreign and exotic plants. On her husband's premature death she formally established a botanical garden in 1759, with Bute as its director. William Chambers, romantic, ingenious and fanciful, was instructed to adorn the grounds with buildings illustrating architecture of the world, and he obliged with classical temples and ruins, a Turkish mosque, a Moorish Alhambra and a Chinese pagoda.

Meanwhile Augusta's son had become King George III and taken over Richmond Lodge. Not to be outdone by his mama, he employed Capability Brown to remodel Kent's layout in a more naturalistic style with a long irregular lake, dells and plantations of trees. After his mother's death

Opposite:
Kew in winter.

140

George merged both estates and appointed Sir Joseph Banks to succeed Bute as director of the enlarged Kew Gardens. Richmond Lodge was pulled down and George moved with Queen Charlotte into Kew Palace, where the poor man withdrew from public life as insanity and senility encroached.

The gardens were in good hands. Banks had accompanied Captain Cook on several voyages and under his dedicated guidance Kew expanded its worldwide collection of plants. In 1841 Queen Victoria sensibly bequeathed Kew to the nation. Now accessible to the public and under the inspired directorship of Sir William Hooker and his son Joseph, Kew developed into the finest garden of its type in the world. As Britain explored and conquered the world, accumulating a far-flung empire, so the Hookers collected and catalogued a vast number of new species of plants, brought home by the likes of Charles Darwin. Kew must have been an exciting place to be then as weird and wonderful unknown specimens arrived, like samples of rock from Mars today. Rubber-plant saplings were smuggled to Kew from Brazil to be propagated and shipped out to Malaya to break the Portuguese domination of rubber production.

Today Kew Gardens is astonishing in its variety, not just for the plants but also for the buildings and monuments which have survived. Near the main entrance beside the river stands Kew Palace, unlived in since 1818. Dating from 1631 this homely Dutch red-brick house is the oldest building at Kew, and now full of eighteenth-century furniture and Hanoverian paraphernalia. Behind the house is the Queen's Garden, a delightful seventeenth-century knot garden of immaculately clipped box hedges and borders of heavily scented herbs, recently redesigned for the disabled and neatly labelled with amusing medieval herbal remedies for peculiar ailments.

Several of William Chamber's fanciful follies survive, none more famous than the Pagoda, for many the emblem of Kew. Ten storeys and 160 feet high, it was constructed to provide Princess Augusta with lofty views over her beloved gardens. The balconies were originally decorated by Chippendale with eighty wooden dragons but these have disappeared. The whole structure is now too fragile and rickety for public access, but remains nevertheless one of London's most extraordinary buildings. The Orangery, also dating from 1761, is altogether sturdier and has been

splendidly restored with its ornamental stucco as an exhibition centre.

Least accessible, in the south-west corner of Kew, hidden away in deliberately untamed natural woodland, lies Queen Charlotte's cottage, her secret summer refuge to escape the madness of her husband's dotage. Timbered and thatched, it snugly matches Keats' autumnal ode — "the vines that round the thatch-eves run; to bend with apples the moss'd cottage-trees..." — for on the little garden lawn stands a costard tree, the native apple from which our hybrids came and whence old costermongers took their name.

Exotic plants flourish in exotic climes. Joseph Banks recognized the necessity of reproducing different conditions at Kew, but the Aroid House, near the main gate, was one of the first attempts. Designed by Nash for Buckingham Palace, it was moved in 1836 to Kew, where it fulfils the hothouse needs of tropical plants like ginger and yam which love heat and humidity. However it was nowhere near large enough for the huge trees of the equatorial rain forests. Decimus Burton, who had assisted Nash at Regent's Park and who had designed the main entrance gates, was appointed to erect a new gigantic greenhouse, or "stove", as it was called at the time. His Palm House, built in 1844-8, is a remarkable bulbous creation of glass and iron, a small and voluptuous Crystal Palace. Inside, it is filled with a steamy jungle of luxuriant foliage — banana, cocoa, coconut and bamboo trees — and a few lucky birds. Burton also added the Temperate House in 1860 in a less curvaceous but supremely elegant style, now exquisitely renovated. Here the sub-tropical flowers and fruits of Australia, South Africa and America can be viewed from the heady heights of the gallery. Now the Palm House too is being restored, temporarily emptied of plants and its iron carcase exposed for surgery.

Nearby is Nesfield's Kew Lodge, an innovatory precursor of Norman Shaw's "William and Mary" style built in 1866, and the Marianne North Gallery, crammed with her meticulous paintings of rare plants. Beyond the herbaceous, aquatic and alpine gardens, nestling beside the eastern boundary wall is Cambridge Cottage, housing a museum of timber and wood with some incredible exhibits. One of the more recent and odd additions to Kew is the Japanese Gate of the Imperial Messenger, a scaled-down

Opposite:
Inside Decimus Burton's Palm House.

model of the real thing, presented by the Japanese government and located near the Pagoda, presumably as a friendly gesture of Oriental solidarity.

A guide or résumé of the trees, shrubs and flowers must depend very largely on the season, but some sights should not be missed. In early spring, harebells and bluebells carpet the floor of the Queen's Plantation with a shimmering haze of pale azure. The magnolias and cherries foam with pink and white blossom in April. The rhododendron dell, excavated by Capability Brown but stocked by Joseph Hooker with hundreds of exotic species from the Himalayas, is a gluttonous riot of scent and colour in May. In high summer the rose terraces beside the Palm House and the herbaceous borders blaze with reds and yellows. In autumn the maples turn to fiery browns while cheerful heathers smother the rock gardens. And when the deciduous trees are bare the sombre cedars and redwoods line the great avenue to the Pagoda like mighty sentinels. Midweek in winter the gardens are quiet and deserted. Canada geese strut pompously across the lawns and pheasants venture nervously from under bushes. From the lakeside, softened with golden weeping willows and delicate maidenhair trees, winter exposes the marvellous view west to the façade of Syon House, capped with its resplendent lion. The dividing Thames acts as a giant ha-ha, tricking the eye into seeing Syon as part of Kew.

Always, when the heavens open or when an icy February wind numbs the feet and hands beyond endurance, there are the hothouse oases. Never on a visit to Kew have I failed to be drawn by the magnet of the great Palm House, reliving those disjointed childhood memories, to stand in the stifling heat among vast dripping and perspiring leaves, the mazy network of hot pipes, the filigree tracery of the spiral stairs and balcony, and that distinctive noise of shoes walking over grating. Suddenly one is a small child again, in a dream world, seeing it for the first time. . . .

Surely no one could ever tire of Kew, not even the party of school children screeching like parrots in the cactus house or the earnest art student sketching in pencil. The donkey-jacketed gardeners who dig and weed there every day take years before they know all the sequestered treasures hidden among its 280 acres. The weather and the seasons guarantee that no two visits are the same. Time alone demands the constant forming and fading of flowers, fruit and foliage. People may come and people may go, but Kew goes on for ever.

The Zoo

The Zoo was 150 years old in 1978, and owes its foundation not to royalty as at Kew but to the early nineteenth-century respectability of scientific endeavour and the growing desire among the middle classes to see and understand natural phenomena. Learned societies were set up, and one such was the Zoological Society of London, founded in 1824 by the explorer Sir Stamford Raffles. Premises for a museum and library were acquired in Bruton Street but the Society's ambition was to establish an open-air menagerie where animals could be studied and exhibited. Many of the original members of the Society were influential people, several conveniently being Regent's Park residents. In 1826 a formal request was made to the Crown Estate for twenty acres of Regent's Park.

There was haggling over the location. Raffles wanted the Inner Circle (now Queen Mary's Gardens), but there were objections. Eventually a triangular site in the north-east corner was chosen, at the foot of Primrose Hill, well removed from Nash's grand terraces and villas. "We do not know how the inhabitants will like the lions, leopards and lynxes so near the neighbourhood," speculated the *Literary Gazette*. The young Decimus Burton, Nash's protégé, was appointed architect and set about designing a garden where animals and birds could be kept safely and attractively. Within a remarkably short space of time the ambitious plans of 1824 were realized; the Zoological Gardens of London were opened on 27 April 1828.

In itself there was nothing new about keeping and exhibiting exotic animals. Bears, monkeys, lions and tigers had long been popular curiosities at travelling fairs and circuses. Since the fourteenth century the monarchy had kept a Royal Menagerie in the Lion Tower at the Tower of London — largely a prestigious public relations exercise to impress visiting ambassadors. This was closed in 1831 and moved to the new Zoo.

Initially the grounds were open only to Fellows of the Society and their guests. Membership was two guineas per annum (a lot then, though it had risen to only three guineas

Opposite:
Queen Charlotte's Cottage at bluebell time.

Facing Page 145:
Kew Gardens.

Top left:
Decimus Burton's Temperate House.

Top right:
One of William Chamber's follies.

Bottom left:
Tropical jungle.

Bottom right:
Water lilies.

by the early 1960s). Guests paid one shilling. Income was increased by opening to the public in 1847 and the Zoo quickly became one of London's most popular outings. Fellows retained exclusive use on Sundays.

At first all the animals were gifts, often as gestures of goodwill by foreign emissaries, but as funds grew new acquisitions were made. In 1836 giraffes were transported from Africa and huge crowds escorted them as they walked from the docks through the streets of East London to the Zoo. Chimpanzees aroused similar excitement when they arrived in 1837. Decimus Burton added new buildings as necessary, including a special house for the giraffes and camels, and dug a tunnel under the outer circle road which bisects the site. The gardens were extended in the 1840s and again in the 1860s to house new collections of Indian animals. A new elephant house was built in 1868 and new open enclosures for the big cats. 900,000 people visited in 1876; "Walking in the Zoo" was a smash hit of the day. The most famous Victorian attraction was Jumbo the elephant, whose name has become part of our language. Public outcry accompanied his sale in 1882 to a circus in North America, where sadly he was killed in a train crash in 1885. An unfortunate taxidermist had the Herculean task of stuffing poor Jumbo so that he could still be a money-spinner.

The range and variety of animals grew, with an increasing emphasis on rare and endangered species. Lubetkin's innovative penguin pool was built in 1936 and giant pandas arrived in 1938. During the war the larger animals were evacuated to Whipsnade, the aquarium was drained and all the poisonous snakes and insects destroyed for safety.

Since the war, redevelopment has been achieved in a piecemeal fashion and today the Zoo possesses a great mixture of architectural styles. Decimus Burton's original camel and giraffe houses, with clock tower, elegant round arches and pronounced eaves, have been rightly kept, as have his ravens' aviary and east tunnel, though only the ornate south portal survives. The Crown have been unwilling to lease more land to the Zoological Society, so new buildings have been squeezed alongside the old. The best of these is the Charles Clore (pure coincidence) Mammal House, a low brown-brick structure full of wallabies and weasels, leaping lemurs with long black tails

and perky marmosets snug under their ear-warmers. There is a pleasant sensation here of the animals outside with homo sapiens behind glass. Downstairs is the fascinating nocturnal world of bats, badgers, mice and foxes, synchronized to make the animals active during our daytime.

The Michael Sobell Pavilion for apes and monkeys is also good for the public. The equipment in the gorilla and orang-utan pens is similar to an adventure playground, though scarcely enough to test their arms or brains. The new lion terraces replaced the Old Lion House of 1876, keeping only the entrance inscription. Of all the animals the great cats seem the most caged, pacing to and fro or lying quietly and unruffled, sheltering from the English climate. The terrain of wet grass and dock leaves is a far cry from the savannah. Information boards extol the great power, speed and agility of these cats but there is no space here for them to demonstrate. Nearby, the wolves look distinctly sheepish in their "forest". Their sunset howls for foreign forests are one of London's more poignant sounds.

Sadly, the birds of prey cannot display their prowess and are forbidden/denied the space and freedom of Lord Snowdon's magnificent aviary. Their cages are elegant but restrictive. How wonderful it would be to see the eagles, buzzards and condors glide and wheel in the sky. Snowdon's angular geometry of steel booms, wires and netting is now a famous landmark, though it often looks sparsely inhabited, and some of the occupants are sparrows and pigeons. The braver birds and squirrels of Regent's Park do well out of the Zoo.

Least compromising architecturally is the concrete elephant and rhinoceros house, which inside has a warm rich smell of dung and hay. Accommodation is really too tight for these mighty animals, who fortunately can have a holiday at the more spacious Whipsnade Zoo, also owned by the Zoological Society. Other animals, such as the flamingos, ducks and flightless birds, have relatively much more room. The ostrich has a long back garden behind its house where it loves to peer over the fence with its enormous eyes and beak set in prejudiced defiance.

It takes a whole day to see the Zoo, maybe more if you read every caption. Don't miss the reptile house with its gigantic pythons and anacondas, monitors and iguanas, or feeding time for the sea lions and penguins. Smell the sea

Page 145:
The Michael Sobell Pavilion, London Zoo.

Opposite:
Rhinoceroses, unamused.

water in the strange world of the aquarium and see how long you can bear to stay in the parrot house, a bedlam of screeches and squawks mimicking and amplifying the squeaking door and screams of children. Today the Zoo houses about 9,000 animals, an amazing number when you stop to think just where it is, right in the heart of London. The logistics of feeding, heating and cleaning are mind-boggling, looking after inmates who are more pernickerty and discerning than in any other institution. The animals are better cared for here in terms of diet and warmth than most humans; longevity and good health are essential.

Despite Sir Hugh Casson's modernization programme of the last twenty-five years there are constant demands for new displays, better conditions for animals and lower running costs. The Zoological Society is a registered scientific charity and receives little government support. Unlike most of London's open spaces and artistic institutions the Zoo has to finance itself from the people who visit it, and it struggles to make ends meet. 1982 was a disastrous year, when higher admission charges resulted in very low attendance, only 1,026,759. The hot summer and reduced entrance fees of 1983 restored numbers to $1\frac{1}{2}$ million. The salvation has been sponsorship. The "adoption" of individual animals has been a very successful sales pitch. Neat plaques beside several cages and enclosures state who is looking after whom. It's a nice idea, and one which could help to keep entrance charges down.

Everybody has their own individual view about zoos and London Zoo in particular. Children adore it, indignant animal rights supporters dislike it, guardians of wildlife regard it as a regrettable necessity for endangered species. The media never lose an opportunity to appeal to the sentimental animal-loving side of the British public. Goldie the eagle, Chi-Chi and An-An the giant pandas and Guy the gorilla were in their day as well known as most cabinet ministers. Obviously the Zoo is an artificial place, but then, you might argue, so is a city like London. Some of the animals would clearly relish a more natural and less restricted habitat, and look bored and jaded; the same goes for many Londoners. Desmond Morris once said "the city is not a concrete jungle, it is a human zoo". If you ever tire of peering at yet another Mexican stick insect or Bolivian Lesser Spotted Frog, remember that the Zoo is an ideal place to study the habits of human beings.

CHAPTER 8: Churchyards and Cemeteries

As we city dwellers hurry through our hectic urban lives, how rarely we pause to think or plan for death. Today, to contemplate burial is unfashionable, or perhaps too frightening; yet our forefathers, weighed down by religious indoctrination or superstition, took the greatest care to ensure a peaceful resting place for themselves. Their churchyards and cemeteries are an extraordinary bequest and an enormous contribution to London's open space.

There are 300 churchyards and cemeteries in London, covering over 3,000 acres of land. To some people, including a good many clerics, they are a liability, neglected and abandoned for Nature to run riot. To others who love their sentiment, strangeness and wildness they are a precious asset for rest and play, less grand than the expansive royal parks, less formal than the genteel squares of Georgian and Victorian London and less organized than the utilitarian recreation grounds, but with a peculiar beauty of their own.

Burial has been a crucial part of the human ritual of death since long before London was established by the Romans. Inevitably, London's graveyards are an important component in its history. For centuries churchyards were the domain of the gravedigger and the dead. While distinguished parishioners might be buried within the church, the rest were found a humbler plot outside, where a lifetime's savings might pay for a headstone. Before the Great Fire of 1666 the City of London boasted 108 parish churches, each with its own graveyard. In addition, plague pits outside the city walls had been used for mass burials of the victims of the Black Death in 1348 and the Great Plague in 1665. During the Black Death the city churchyards simply could not cope with the death toll, which reached 40 per cent in congested parts of the town. Previously known as "No Man's Land", where criminals and outlaws had been interred in a small pardon grave, **Charterhouse Square** became the largest extramural plague pit, holding some 30,000 corpses. Charterhouse and **Bunhill Fields** (a corruption of Bone Hill) buried 200 bodies each day, carried out through the city gates on horse-drawn carts covered by rough black sacking, and with jangling bells broadcasting their approach.

After the Great Fire John Evelyn had advertised Wren's idea for establishing a huge necropolis outside the city,

divided into portions for each parish, and "with ample walks of trees adorned with monuments". Like many of Wren's other theories for replanning London, it fell on deaf ears.

By 1800 London's churchyards were a public scandal, chronically overcrowded and a hazard to all those unfortunate enough to live nearby. Bodies were dumped on top of existing graves and soil was imported in a feeble attempt to cover exposed corpses. In the crypts, mounds of bodies piled up into putrid heaps of rotting human compost. The pestilence and squalor was horrific. Respectable folk dreaded the legendary "miasma", believing that to breathe the polluted air invited disease and death. Medical evidence in fact suggests that certain malignant viruses were transmitted from the dead to the living. The "curse of the tomb" is not necessarily just the fantasy of the cheap horror movie.

With over 40,000 deaths per annum, London's churchyards were overflowing to bursting point, fuelled by cholera epidemics and a booming population. Dickens's description of "St Ghastly Grim" in *Sketches of Boz* and *Bleak House* sums up the reality: "Over yinder, among them pile of bones and close to that there kitchen winder, they put him very nigh the top and was obliged to stamp upon it to git it in."

Such indignity was intolerable for the middle and upper classes. In 1804 the great Parisian cemetery at Père Lachaise had been established and this provided the inspiration for London. Based entirely on private and non-ecclesiastical money, **Kensal Green Cemetery** was opened in 1832 and, though expensive (the cheapest grave was thirty shillings), it was immediately successful. Kensal Green was the first of seven private cemeteries — the magnificent seven — opened in the outskirts of London during the next eight years.

In an age of imperial pomposity and self-indulgent materialism, these cemeteries heralded a new approach to burial, extolling and glorifying death. The whole concept was different from the obnoxious graveyards of old London. Fresh air, plenty of space and natural beauty were the new ideals, championed by John Loudon, a landscape gardener from Scotland. "A general cemetery in the neighbourhood of a town, properly designed, laid out, ornamented with tombs, planted with trees, shrubs and

Page 149:
St. James's,
Piccadilly.

Opposite:
The burial ground
at The Royal
Hospital, Chelsea.

herbaceous plants all named, and the whole properly kept, might become a school of instruction in architecture, sculpture, landscape-gardening, arboriculture, botany, and in those important parts of general gardening, neatness, order and high keeping," wrote Loudon piously and persuasively in 1843.

Considerable trouble was taken to attract custom by careful landscaping, creating luxuriant gardens and arboreta. Thousands of trees were planted — oak, poplar, elm, plane, willow and yew — and elaborate formations of rock plants, waterlily ponds, artificial waterfalls and shrubberies were constructed. Among the plants, mammoth chapels and gatehouses were erected and space for everlasting memorials and monuments to the dead. These flamboyant mausoleums employed the leading architects of the day, such as Barry, Tite, Gilbert Scott and Bunning, who displayed extraordinary whims of style — Byzantine, Egyptian, Grecian, Italian, Romanesque, Gothic, Baroque, Rustic — and used the most extravagant building materials available — marble, polished granite, terracotta and Bath stone.

In 1843 plans were unveiled for a 150-acre cemetery at Primrose Hill, constructed as a pyramid on ninety-four levels, higher than the dome of St Paul's Cathedral. Fortunately the £2½ million was never found to build it. Instead the sylvan cemeteries became desirable places to take the air and to enjoy the gardens, until the owners were inundated with applications for keys for the privilege of walking in the grounds.

Edwin Chadwick's public health reforms and the Burial Act in 1851 banned further burials in London's 400 churchyards. Burial, like sewage and water supply, suddenly became a civic responsibility and dozens of municipal cemeteries were laid out in the suburbs for the thousands of dead who could not afford a private burial. They were more mundane affairs than the opulent Kensal Green or Highgate, with serried ranks of graves set among regularly mown grass, rose beds and yew trees. Hugh Mellor's splendidly comprehensive survey of London cemeteries lists one hundred within a nine-mile radius of Charing Cross, comprising an area of about four square miles. Such was the industry of death!

Meanwhile, during the thirty years after the Burial Act many of the ancient churchyards grew moss and weeds or

Opposite:
Hampstead
Cemetery.

were sold off for building land. In 1884, the Disused Burial Grounds Act stopped further incursion and the Metropolitan Public Gardens Association set about converting derelict graveyards into gardens and playgrounds. By 1912, 135 new public gardens had been created in London by this method.

Civic conversion was varied. Some managed to retain a churchyard atmosphere, nestling beside their mother church. Others changed beyond recognition, with the tombs and gravestones cleared away or the church demolished, to be boxed in by new buildings or dismembered by road widening.

In the City of London alone over seventy churchyard gardens survive. Here, among the towering financial palaces, a few square yards of lawn or flagstone paving and a solitary tree can be a more intensively used and valued refuge than a hundred acres in suburbia. These tiny oases, tucked away out of sight or hemmed in by modern buildings, provide sanctuary, solitude and refreshment for hundreds of thousands of City workers, as well as a remarkable link with medieval London.

St Paul's Churchyard beside the cathedral used to be the largest in the City, once extending south to Carter Lane and west almost to Ludgate. Sir Christopher Wren reduced its size and enclosed a smaller yard around his new cathedral with high ornate iron railings. In medieval times the churchyard was used as an extension of the long Cheapside market; stalls and barrows huddled round the cathedral and some even sheltered inside. The north side, known as Paternoster Row, became the centre of the publishing and bookselling trade. After the severe bombing in the Second World War, **Paternoster Square** was redeveloped with Holford's uncompromising office blocks, but to the south and east new gardens were laid out, opening up fabulous views of his magnum opus. Wren's railings survive, but outside them the older tower of St Augustine-by-the-Gate and the new St Paul's choir school sit happily in this enlarged space amid flowerbeds, benches and fountains.

At the other end of the City, next to an equally well-known tourist honey-pot, is **All Hallows-by-the-Tower**, with its terraced garden affording fine views of the Tower of London. Until the Reformation the church was owned by the Abbey of Barking, but then reverted to a parish

153

church. The churchyard was immediately next to the executioner's block at Tower Hill and served as a temporary burial place for many famous and unfortunate men who fell into disfavour and paid with their lives. The position of the scaffold is marked in **Trinity Square Gardens** across the road together with the names and dates of the best-known victims — Edward Earl of Warwick, Sir Thomas More, Archbishop Laud and James Duke of Monmouth. The rest is a memorial to 24,000 merchant seamen lost at sea in the last war.

Two of the largest and most unspoilt churchyards lie beside old gateways into the medieval city. **St Botolph, Bishopsgate**, named after the patron saint of travellers, has one of the loveliest gardens. The vigorous endeavours of the rector, William Rogers, transformed the churchyard in 1888 from "a dirty unwholesome receptacle for all the dead cats and dogs of the neighbourhood" into "one of the brightest spots in the City". St Botolph's Aldersgate is better known as **Postman's Park**, lying in the shadow of the headquarters of the Post Office in St Martin's-le-Grand, close to the Museum of London. This is one of my favourite places, shaded by the luxuriant foliage of giant plane trees which shield the quaint wooden bellcote of Nathaniel Wright's church. In one corner a curious veranda displays memorial plaques recording fifty tragic and heroic Victorian self-sacrifices; in another is an aggressive minotaur sculpture by Michael Ayrton. Take your fill of this heaven while you may, for if the City Corporation do as they say then the dilapidated buildings of Little Britain, where Dickens's Jaggers had his dusty chambers and where John and Charles Wesley received their evangelical conversion, will be swept away for a new road. Postman's Park would never be the same again.

A short walk up the north arm of Little Britain leads to the Tudor gateway of the churchyard of **St Bartholomew-the-Great**. The yard occupies what was once the nave of the huge priory church (as big as Rochester Cathedral), of which the chancel forms the present beautiful church. The garden, with its tilting headstones, is overlooked by rare Jacobean timber houses in Cloth Fair, built before the Great Fire.

Several other City gardens occupy space vacated by church buildings. **St Dunstan-in-the-East** is still in ruins after the blitz of 1941; only the tower with its spire supported on flying buttresses remains, while the nave has been amalgamated with the churchyard to make a beautiful garden. The fallen stones of **St Mary Aldermanbury**, near the Guildhall, were transported lock, stock and barrel in 1970 to Fulton, Missouri, USA, where they like to re-erect all things English. Among the exposed foundations, trees and shrubs now adorn a delightful spot to while away the time. In the maze of little alleys behind Carter Lane, the churchyard of **St Anne Blackfriars** continued to take burials until 1849, even though the church had not been rebuilt after the Great Fire. The entrance off Church Entry marks the division between nave and chancel which is now home for a tree of heaven. **St Alphage, London Wall** was pulled down in 1924 except for a portion of the fourteenth-century tower, but the tiny churchyard lingers on, a neat garden flanked by a section of the ancient Roman city wall and a perfect sun-trap in summer.

The smallness of most of the City churchyards is compensated by their careful landscaping and impeccable maintenance. **St Anne and St Agnes**, Gresham Street, which used to be known rather more romantically as St Anne-in-the-Willows, has vivid flowerbeds and copious seating in the colourful garden beside the rich red-brick church. Sir Thomas Gresham, founder of the Royal Exchange, is in fact buried at **St Helen Bishopsgate**, a lovely medieval building which miraculously escaped fires and bombs, where the grass and trees on the west side of the church provide softness and shade for the weary.

If you are fuming in Fenchurch Street seek out the enclosed graveyard of **St Olave, Hart Street**, off Mark Lane. The entrance is from Seething Lane where the wall is topped by forbidding iron spikes to deter plunderers. The church too is lovely, though much rebuilt after war damage, and contains the tombs of Samuel Pepys and his attractive wife who died aged twenty-nine after fifteen years of marriage. **St Bride's**, near Ludgate Circus, offers peace and solitude from the stop-press hubbub of Fleet Street, nestling beneath Wren's fantastic wedding-cake steeple, while **St Peter Cornhill** with its planes and yorkstone is equally unexpected, unseen behind Gracechurch Street and accessible only from St Peter's Alley.

Some hidden churchyards can be reached only by going through the church itself. Fifteenth-century

St Ethelburga, Bishopsgate, is the City's smallest church, ridiculously dwarfed by its neighbours, yet beyond the snug vestry lies a secret cloister garden. Similar are **St Katherine Cree**, Leadenhall Street, which nutures the City's tallest plane tree, and **St Stephen Walbrook**, tucked behind the Mansion House, where Sir John Vanbrugh, dramatist and architect of Castle Howard and Blenheim Palace, is buried.

The old churchyards of **St Mary-le-Bow** and **St Mary Abchurch** have been paved over, unfenced and incorporated into pedestrian concourses. In the Barbican a lavatorial treatment has been imposed on the surrounds of **St Giles' Cripplegate**, paved with hard glazed brick sets in which flattened tombstones lie unconvincingly. Road-widening accounted for the churchyard of St Magnus the Martyr, which existed for 650 years beside the approach to old London Bridge. More recently, the City Corporation completed an atrocious scheme at Wren's Christchurch Newgate, demolishing most of the ruined nave merely to improve one-way traffic flow around St Martin's-le-Grand. Such is progress; Postman's Park next.

The same fate almost engulfed the large yard of **St Andrew Holborn**, Wren's biggest parish church. Holborn Viaduct, built in 1863, left just a sliver of sunken garden beside the resurrection stone on the north side of the church, where candidates for the Last Judgement climb out of their coffins — or perhaps they can't sleep because of the traffic. Let's hope it doesn't disturb William Marsden, founder of the Royal Free, or Thomas Coram, famed for his Foundling Hospital at Coram Fields, who both lie here too. They deserve a better rest.

Apart from the odd square and the even odder Barbican complex, old graveyards provide all the public open space within the City. Throughout the remainder of London there are scores more churchyards, but here they compete with hundreds of larger parks, gardens, commons and woodlands, a few of which are actually owned and maintained by the City Corporation at their expense. Inevitably, visits to "suburban" churchyards tend to be undertaken somewhat more selectively.

Several larger churchyards are big enough to serve as small local parks. **St Mary Paddington**, once part of a compact village set in fields and meadows close to the sinister Tyburn gallows, still has its original churchyard although the medieval church has gone. Its replacement, built in 1791, is charming inside and out. The Great Western Railway managed to miss it, and the elevated West Way. **St Pancras** churchyard off St Pancras Road was less lucky. The church is 600 years old, though not recognizably so because of tasteless Victorian restoration, and sits on a gentle mound surrounded by a graveyard which was much enlarged in the eighteenth century. The Midland Railway tried to buy the lot for a goods depot, but when thwarted proceeded willy-nilly to construct a viaduct across the eastern half of the churchyard. Parliamentary furore over the inadequate reburial of bodies clumsily unearthed by the navvies did nothing to deter the railway company. Today it is a strange juxtaposition of viaduct arches, trees and gravestones, including those of Sir John Soane and Johann Christian Bach, J.S.'s youngest son.

St John's Wood churchyard, just across Wellington Road from Lord's Cricket Ground, began as an overflow for Paddington and Marylebone parishes. The church was added seven years later in 1814 when Park Road was built to connect with Marylebone Road. The six-acre churchyard is now divided into two, the north as a functional playground, and the south kept as it was. A thick canopy of trees shelters tidy lawns and paths which meander among laurels, japonicas and jasmine. In spring hundreds of bulbs shoot up between the weathered headstones, and cheerful blackbirds hop for cover under the bushes.

Marylebone itself filled two graveyards in the eighteenth century, both of which survive as pleasant gardens. The older is in **St Marylebone High Street**, next to the culverted Tyburn stream (hence Mary-le-bourne), where James Gibbs and George Stubbs are buried. The other is nearby down **Paddington Street** and now a friendly playground. The old church, where Byron was baptized, was rebuilt in 1817 with a grand portico facing Marylebone Road.

One of the largest, and also the last churchyard to be consecrated in London, is **Holy Trinity** Brompton, behind the famous (some think hideous) Oratory. Twenty years of well-heeled burials did not overcrowd it and a peaceful village atmosphere survives, shielded from the incessant roar of traffic on Brompton Road.

In East London, open space is a precious commodity among unrelieved swathes of houses, factories,

Opposite:
St. John's Wood churchyard.

157

warehouses and railways. Hawksmoor's two great East End churches, built to rival the zealous non-conformist tabernacles in the 1720s, both have unusually spacious churchyards. **St George-in-the-East**, between Cable Street and Ratcliff Highway, has seven acres, rescued from dereliction by the Metropolitan Public Gardens Association in 1887. They also took over the three acres at **St Anne Limehouse** which now display elegant railings to replace those ripped down for the war effort.

South of the river, Thomas Archer's **St Paul's Deptford** was another of the fifty new churches commissioned by Parliament in 1711, and its sublime round porch and spire in white stone shines like a radiant lighthouse in a sea of mediocrity. The churchyard is a fine walled arbour where flowers bloom all year round and dignified tombs, like that of musicologist Dr Charles Burney, recall remote days when Deptford was a fishing village and country retreat for those who preferred a little privacy from the pompous naval gentry at Greenwich. There, a mile away, the spire of **St Alphege** is Hawksmoor's most conventional, and vies with Archer's as a riverside landmark. Thomas Tallis was a chorister here, but was never, I suspect, allowed to kick a football around the churchyard garden behind St Alphege's Passage as they do today, irritating the park-keeper, who is proud of his spruce flowerbeds and manicured lawns.

Some of London's largest graveyards are detached from their church, or never even had one. Perhaps the finest is **Bunhill Fields**, originally a plague pit but from 1623 to 1852 the principal burial place for non-conformist believers in London. It was a suitable site, occupying marshy ground near Moorfields, just north of Artillery Fields. Here many vigorous dissenters were laid to rest — John Bunyan who collapsed and died at Smithfield in 1688 on a rare visit to London, Daniel Defoe, Susanna Wesley (mother of John and Charles), the hymn-writer Isaac Watts, and William Blake, poet, painter and rebel genius. John Milton died fifty yards away in Bunhill Row, and opposite in City Road John Wesley built his Chapel, centre of the Methodist faith. Since 1869 it has been a public garden, tended by the City Corporation. Leafy veils of plane trees dapple the gigantic slabs of stone paving with sunbeams and speckle the row upon row of headstones, their carved letters blurred with age. Such unspoilt beauty has not inspired others nearby. Behind **Wesley's Chapel** in Tabernacle Street the tiny burial ground containing Wesley's tomb has been ruined by a modern office block, the old trees and iron railings torn down for steel, glass and concrete.

In the West End either lack of space or decorum often dictated that the churchyard be sited some distance away from the church. Graveyards were smelly and unsightly places, haunted by grave-robbers and body-snatchers, best avoided. London's most fashionable place of worship in the eighteenth century for the nobility and gentry was **St George's Hanover Square**, which buried its genteel parishioners on a piece of land in South Audley Street. A small chapel was erected as part of the Grosvenor Square development in 1730. Similarly **St George's Bloomsbury**, the *à la mode* Hawksmoor church next to smart Bloomsbury Square, located its graveyard discreetly north. Today you will find it behind Kingsway Princeton College, Sidmouth Street, with its entrance from Handel Street, a peaceful haven of flowers and mature plane trees. Nearby in Gray's Inn Road, beside Marsden's first Royal Free Hospital, is the overflow graveyard of **St Andrew Holborn**, decorated with lawns and roses.

In Clerkenwell, **Spa Fields**, south of Exmouth Market, gives no clue to its varied past. In the Middle Ages it was called Ducking Pond Field but later became noted for its bowling greens, near the spa of Sadler's Wells. Gradually hemmed in by slums, it was a burial ground for eighty years until 1850, when the Middlesex Regiment took over the space for drill practice. After the Great War it was converted into a public park, recently extended on to cleared land on the far side of Rosoman Street. South of Clerkenwell Road, sandwiched between Britton Street and Turnmill Street, **Benjamin Street Gardens** once belonged to St John Clerkenwell, no longer a parish church. Now it is thickly planted with trees and shrubs, perfectly sheltered by the higgledy-piggledy backs of Britton Street and the sleek lines of York, Rosenberg and Mardall's offices.

Further west, **Whitfield Gardens** facing Tottenham Court Road is the site of the old burial ground for Whitefield's Tabernacle, founded in 1756. The Rev. Toplady, composer of the Hymn "Rock of Ages", is buried here. For centuries before that, Tottenham Court Fair and Gooseberry Fair had featured as a mecca for London's low-life. The graveyard in **Drury Lane**, once notorious for overcrowding, is now a modest playground in a drab street

158

of grimy tenement blocks. The secluded **Nelson Recreation Ground**, off Kipling Street in unpretentious Bermondsey, was originally where Guy's Hospital buried their dead.

Strangest of all the motherless churchyards is **Old Dulwich Graveyard** on the corner of Dulwich Village and Court Lane, a picturesque spot with splendid gates and sturdy tombs. Edward Alleyn, the wealthy Shakespearian theatre tycoon who owned Dulwich Manor and founded most things to do with Dulwich, gave the land in 1616 for those locals who could afford nothing better. Old Bridget, queen of the gypsies, who camped with her tribe each year on Gipsy Hill, was buried here in 1768, while the last was Betsy Goodman in 1898, daughter of the landlord of the Crown Inn.

The most conventional churchyards nestle beside their church, where the two combine and complement. In central London **St Paul's Covent Garden** takes some beating, scarcely altered since laid out in 1638. While the east portico of the church is the focal point of the Piazza, Inigo Jones deliberately hid the churchyard round the back. A wide path leads to the west door of the church, softened by trees and shrubs and flanked by ornate gas lights. Narrow alleys lead in from Henrietta and King Streets. St Paul's is famous as the actors' church, but Grinling Gibbons, Thomas Arne and Thomas Rowlandson were buried here too. For centuries it has been a beloved refuge, previously from the bustle of the vegetable market, now from the thronging herds who pack the trendy boutiques and brasseries.

South of the Strand the **Queen's Chapel of the Savoy** is a wonderfully secluded niche. Still owned by the Duchy of Lancaster, once John of Gaunt, this delightful garden, lined by tombstones, is shaded by a single fig tree. Far noisier and busier is **St James Piccadilly**. West of the church a pretty garden of remembrance commemorates the fortitude of Londoners in the blitz; the north side, fronting Piccadilly, is paved and supports a disused outdoor pulpit and a weekly bric-a-brac market — not the quietest sojourn but good for bus-spotters. Hygienic rose-beds surrounding **St Giles-in-the-Fields**, Holborn, conceal a squalid history. Originally a hospice in open fields, like St Martin's, where lepers and beggars hung out, St Giles became London's worst slum, spawning the Great Plague and the ghastly gin-drinking epidemic of the early eighteenth century. Today the occasional wino is the sole reminder of Hogarth's Gin Lane.

Idyllic country churchyards survive in the suburbs. Hogarth lies in **Chiswick Churchyard** near the river, together with Lord Burlington who built Chiswick House, William Kent who landscaped the gardens, and James Thornhill the painter. James McNeill Whistler was buried in 1903 in the adjacent cemetery. The grave of that most English of English painters, John Constable, stands in the churchyard of **St John's Hampstead**. Of all the places he lived Hampstead was his favourite, as his paintings and drawings of the village and heath suggest. "Here let me take my everlasting rest," he wrote in his diary, and why not, for this place breathes an elegiac tranquillity. In the evening the dense yews and sombre evergreens cast long shadows across the tightly packed tombs of Hampstead worthies, while the church tower catches the sinking sun.

Chelsea Old Church, Cheyne Walk, has the smallest churchyard outside the City, and one of the prettiest, just a patch of grass and three seats, but ablaze with flowers. Once, when Sir Thomas More lived nearby, there was a muddy footpath down to the river; today Cheyne Walk is shattered by traffic along the Embankment. **St Mary Abbots**, Kensington, is a welcome refuge from the High Street fumes, tucked away behind Holland Street and Church Walk. So too is the leafy garden of **St Mary Islington** off Upper Street, and its parochial sister, **St Mary Magdelene**, between Holloway Road and Liverpool Road.

Frequently, old-fashioned graveyards have been re-vamped or enlarged by local councils eager to provide parks with a wider range of facilities. **St Martin's Pratt Street** has been converted into an adventure playground, with hillocks, palisades and swinging ropes. **St James Clerkenwell** now reveals all sides of the church, once hemmed in with humble houses and tatty workshops, as well as a section of ancient nunnery wall. **St James Pentonville** possesses an imaginative new garden, but, alas, no church: abandoned, decayed, demolished. Luckily, Joe Grimaldi's gravestone was rescued from the iconoclasts. Churchyards too can lie neglected, like the derelict **St Luke's**, Old Street, or **Christchurch Spitalfields**, which may see better days. **St Anne Soho**, one of three Wren churches outside the City, stands as it did after the bombs rained down. The dilapidated yard faces Wardour Street, a suitably scruffy oasis among Soho's shabby dives.

Facing page 160:
Highgate Cemetery.

Opposite:
Autumn in
Ladywell Cemetery.

161

While the Metropolitan Public Gardens Association succeeded in the late nineteenth century in rescuing and renovating most of the abandoned churchyards, sadly the same has not happened this century with London's cemeteries. The carnage of Flanders wiped away the grandiose Victorian and Edwardian values and changed public opinion as to the glory and sentimentality of death.

The enthusiasm and money needed to maintain the elaborate gardens and ornate monuments gradually dwindled. In the municipal cemeteries, tightening civic purse-strings brought insensitive economy measures, producing uninspired landscapes lacking even the bleak austerity and numberless regularity of war graves. The private cemeteries meanwhile fell to rack and ruin, the original owners bankrupt, the obelisks and mausoleums toppled by vandals, and the chapels smothered in ivy. Belated efforts have been made in some to check the march of Nature, or at least to make the best of them as nature reserves. Today the atmosphere of neglect and decay gives these places an eerie and poignant quality, unlike any of London's other open spaces.

Kensal Green, first of the "magnificent seven", is also reckoned by many to be the finest architecturally. In its 56 acres, between Harrow Road and the Grand Union Canal, stand an unsurpassed forest of monuments and mausoleums, with an overall design reminiscent of Nash's Regent's Park, an inner circle surrounded by quadrants. In this unruffled open-air museum lie some of the greatest Victorians — William Makepeace Thackeray, Anthony Trollope and Wilkie Collins, Decimus Burton and John Loudon, Isambard Kingdom Brunel, Henry Mayhew and Emile Blondin, tightrope-walker extraordinary who crossed Niagara Falls and died unremarkably in Ealing.

Norwood Cemetery followed Kensal Green five years later, but suffered badly from misdirected Luftwaffe bombing and subsequent "modernization". Several superb monuments and sepulchres remain, worthy of Westminster Abbey, but urgent repairs are needed. Both chapels have been demolished, and now it is enjoyed mainly for its space and magnificent trees. Thomas Cubitt, Henry Doulton, Horace Jones and Henry Tate (who founded his gallery out of his sugar profits) are buried here, among thousands less eminent.

Probably for the single reason of Karl Marx's grave

Highgate East
Cemetery.

Highgate is London's most celebrated cemetery. When opened in 1839 it was also for a time the most fashionable, not only for burials but as a place for the able living to stroll. Behind its massive protective walls and gates a network of winding paths meandered through an Elysian landscape of groves and glades, an elevated paradise for viewing the abyss of London. When full, an extension was added to the east side of Swain's Lane. What a change since then! Inexorably engulfed by a jungle of moss, creeper, ivy and sycamore, the west cemetery was closed in 1975, too dangerous for public admittance. The owners were only too glad when a voluntary group sprang to its belated rescue. The west section remains closed, except for infrequent guided tours, but the Friends of Highgate Cemetery have made an impression in selected spots, clearing the ground around the graves of Michael Farraday, Gabriel Rossetti, George Eliot and the Dickens family. Once again one can admire the tamed lion on the tomb of George Wombwell, the menagerist, and read the MCC's epitaph to the cricketer Lillywhite, "bowled out". It is a continual struggle to keep the rest at bay, an impenetrable undergrowth of rampant wildness and dank putrefaction. In this terrible Valhalla weeping angels lie choked by infernal weeds, and the rusted doors of family vaults in the columbarium stand unhinged for souls to flee abroad.

The east side is open to the public, and maintained after a fashion. Here the tourists swarm round the giant bearded bust of Mr Marx, posing for photographs beside those famous words, "Workers of the World Unite". Wild flowers line the paths in spring and summer, encouraged by the Friends. Oxslips, celandine, wood anemone and wild garlic carpet the floor and, above, the pigeons murmur and sparrows twitter in the trees.

Brompton Cemetery was opened in 1840, an ambitious plan covering disused brick fields. Its harmonious circle of elaborate catacombs and its imposingly domed Bath-stone chapel attracted the most self-conscious families, exiled Russian princes and a smattering of well-known names — Richard Tauber, Emmeline Pankhurst and John Fowler, who built the Forth railway bridge. Now it's looked after by the Department of the Environment, who have at least preserved that air of pretentious dignity, so different from the razzle of Fulham Road and Stamford Bridge outside. Perhaps the quaint "in memoriam" for Isabella David —

Right:
Highgate, nature untamed.

Page 164:
Highgate West Cemetery.

Page 165:
London's most famous grave, Highgate East Cemetery.

"Have a good sleep, dear" — anticipated that she'd have trouble on Saturday afternoons!

The same cannot be said of the last three of the seven, where Nature has been left to take its course. **Abney Park**, Stoke Newington, is now owned by Hackney Council, who have restored the splendid east gates and Egyptian lodge, but not much more. Like many cemeteries it is at its most melancholic in autumn. Grassy gravel paths curve past battalions of stone angels and marble cherubs, swamped by thickets of hawthorn, blackberry and dog rose which hang limp with dewy berries, hips and haws. Lofty Lombard poplars sway in the gentlest breeze above the sheltered wisps of willow herb, where a sweet smell of fallen leaves lingers. The thrush and blackbird are king, free from the fuming noise of Stoke Newington High Street. Somewhere in this tangle-wood is William Booth, general of the Salvation Army, and unknown Mary Hillum who lived for all 105 years of her life in the same house in Church Street and never travelled more than ten miles away. A clutch of recent graves in a tiny clearing sport vivid plastic flowers and shiny polished granite which time will soon dull and fade.

Nunhead is sadder still, its sophisticated cairns and chapels in desperate decay. It occupies a fine hilltop site near the old Nun's Head Tavern, once a popular rural resort, but after the first fifty prosperous years it has fallen into dismal decline. Even James Bunning's entrance in Linden Grove is in a parlous state. The railings went in the war and now the cenotaph piers threaten collapse. From these noble gates a majestic avenue of limes leads up to the ruined chapel. But these planted trees are also past their prime. The whole place smells as though it's rotting. Newly tarmacked tracks are a last attempt to keep the wilderness at heel, and a touching enclave of Great War graves, trimmed by veterans. Elsewhere foxglove, teazle, cow-parsley, elder and bracken grab their chance to flourish. Over fifty species of plant have been counted at Nunhead, an unusually rich flora caused, some say, by distant relatives carrying seeds on their funeral shoes. Southwark Council bought all fifty-two acres in 1975 for £1 with long-term plans for nature trails and a new park. How Bunning would weep to see it now.

The seventh and last private cemetery at **Tower Hamlets** is equally overgrown, an incredible profusion of foliage which shelters nearly a hundred types of birds. Opened in 1841, its East End location was partly philanthropic. A fair proportion of its thirty-three acres was for paupers — victims of virulent cholera epidemics, sailors and boatmen drowned at sea and labourers killed in dockside accidents. The Greater London Council have controlled it since 1960 but abandoned their ideas for converting it into an all-purpose park after local objection. The tawny owls and nightjars appear safe.

The East End was accustomed to cemeteries long before Tower Hamlets. The Jews who crowded into ghettos in Whitechapel, Stepney and Bethnal Green could not entertain a burial in the gentiles' churchyard. The **Old Sephardi Cemetery** in Mile End Road at Stepney Green near the Charrington's brewery was their earliest. This minute cramped garden was acquired with Cromwell's blessing in 1656 by refugees from the Spanish Inquisition. Many others followed and burial grounds proliferated, usually sequestered nooks kept locked and barred. The Jewish cemetery in **Brady Street** is among the biggest, but even this is secretive, and packed with Hebraic memorials, including the grave of Nathan Meyer Rothschild, father of the London branch of the family bank. Gradually the East End Yiddish community dissipated, moving north to Stamford Hill or newer suburbs. The secluded cemetery at **Kingsbury Road**, Dalston, illustrates the shift, full of Goldsmids, Sterns and Levy's, including Joseph Levy who started the *Daily Telegraph* in 1855.

The Huguenots were another persecuted sect, fleeing Catholic oppression. A small group of these strict French protestants settled in the remote village of Wandsworth in the 1690s, and their burial ground survives near the north end of Wandsworth Common, just off **Battersea Rise**. Over the years, intermarriage and integration saw the names change from French to English.

After the old parish churchyards were closed, dozens of municipal cemeteries were established, occupying enormous expanses of land throughout the outer suburbs. The **City of London** was the quickest to act when they realized in 1849 that the eighty-eight City churchyards, totalling a mere 8½ acres, were soon to be closed by Parliament. By 1856 they had bought 176 acres of natural woodland near Wanstead Flats at the southern tip of Epping Forest and laid out a magnificent new cemetery. William Heywood, the

Opposite: Nunhead Cemetery, a clearing in the wilderness.

City Engineer who later designed Holborn Viaduct, supervised the work, even erecting his own mausoleum near the blue entrance gates in Aldersbrook Road. Half a million people have since been buried there, thousand upon thousand of City elders, livery-men and their families. Sparkling granite tombs stand proudly beside broad weedless drives, among close-mown lawns, avenues of trees and Gothic chapel spires. City funds ensure that all is well kempt; vandals find easier pickings elsewhere nearby, for example at **Manor Park**, **Woodgrange** or **West Ham** cemeteries. At **Chingford Mount**, originally an extension to Abney Park, the magnificent plane trees are the best thing left.

The other inner London boroughs followed the City's example. **St Marylebone Cemetery**, now run by Westminster Council, was founded in 1854 in East End Road, Finchley, and enclosed by great black railings. Beneath the spreading cedars lie the good burghers of Marylebone, including Leopold Stokowski (*né* Stokes), with space yet for more. In the same year the **St Pancras and Islington** opened nearby, biggest of all London's cemeteries. 182 acres of Horse Shoe Farm and Finchley Common were commandeered to produce an immense rambling necropolis. Here many old Islingtonians were reinterred when Upper Street was widened outside St Mary's in 1880. Below the trees, undergrowth has invaded large sections today, but sparing the fabulous Mond Mausoleum in the centre.

North London seems popular terrain for cemeteries. The **Great Northern** at Southgate gobbled up another sixty acres of farmland, to be planted with rhododendron drives and yews. A sobering monument remembers the hundreds of young Germans who died during internment at the Ally Pally in the First World War. At Mill Hill the **Paddington Cemetery** contains a tragic bronze memorial to 270 Dutchmen killed in the Second War, in a small well maintained garden. **Tottenham Cemetery** in Prospect Place (somewhat ironic) is a delightful retreat next to Bruce Castle gardens, in an otherwise dreary area. Manageable size clearly helps maintenance. The thirty-seven acres of **Hampstead Cemetery** off Fortune Green are immaculately tended by a dozen gardeners. Among stately cedars and homely mulberries you can find many well-known names — Dennis Brain, Joseph Lister, Gladys Cooper and Marie Lloyd.

In west London the cemeteries pale rather against the alternative delights of other open spaces. **Kensington Cemetery**, overlooked by the Chiswick Flyover at Gunnersbury Avenue, is a bleak place compared to the adjacent beauty of Gunnersbury House and Park. The black Katyn obelisk is a recent and stark memorial to 14,000 Poles who perished in 1940 in Russian camps, later unearthed in mass graves, a uniting symbol for the strong Polish community in West London. The two cemeteries at **Hanwell** either side of the Broadway are little frequented, with the lure of Osterley and Boston Manor so close. **Ealing and Old Brentford** in South Ealing Road is worth seeing for its springtime magnolias, and **St Mary's RC** cemetery, squeezed between railway and canal off Scrubs Lane, contains Sir John Barbirolli's grave, little else of note.

The cemeteries of South London are by and large uncosmopolitan and unglamorous. **Streatham Park** is the epitome, seventy ornately landscaped acres laid out in 1909, intended to cater for one-fifth of all south London burials. Once known as the Great Southern, it is full of music-hall musicians and cockney comedians who died in the 1930s and '40s — famous in their day, virtually forgotten in our television age. The dowdy suburbs of Kennington and Camberwell seemed to breed these men and women like Wales bred fly-halves. Many pre-war memories of fun and laughter are buried here among the decrepit ponds and pergolas.

Putney Vale, separated from Richmond Park by the A3 road, is dense with cypress, yew and holly, but well maintained. It is stuffed with affluent Victorians, Sir This and That, and is still a popular burial place for south Londoners. The comfortable suburb of Sydenham furnished the **Crystal Palace** cemetery with lavish rose gardens and an artificial waterfall. Sydenham was a respectable spa, hence the numerous graves of doctors, including W.G. Grace, whose last job was as coach at Crystal Palace. **Hither Green** cemetery is located promisingly in Verdant Lane, but despite its extent the verdure is disappointingly restrained, unimaginative and drab. One could hardly conceive a greater contrast than the rural charm of **Richmond** cemetery, serene and beautiful. In spring the ubiquitous yews sink into a thick pile of wild flowers. In this Eden lies Tom Richardson who "bowled his best but was himself bowled by the best on July 2nd 1912".

Opposite: Tower Hamlets Cemetery, last of the "magnificent seven".

Many of south London's cemeteries occupy hilltop sites, inspired by the example of Highgate, as well as being nearer to God. **Greenwich Cemetery** in Well Hall Road, **Plumstead Cemetery** in Wickham Lane and **Woolwich Cemetery**, once part of Plumstead Common, all offer spectacular panoramas west to the jagged City skyline and north across the river. **Camberwell New Cemetery** in Brenchley Gardens sprawls along the Brockley ridge, affording a glorious setting for Aston Webb's chapel. Nearby is the **Old Camberwell Cemetery** in Forest Hill Road, a fertile habitat for horsetail, blackberry and conker, and the voluptuous evergreens of **Ladywell** and **Brockley** cemeteries, lying quietly at the foot of Hilly Fields.

For the less predictable, seek out the tiny burial ground in **Bolingbroke Grove,** Battersea, where poplars and planes stand guard over the forlorn graves of railway workers, or the small elusive Roman Catholic cemetery at **Mortlake**, where beneath the splendour of a bizarre Arab tent lie the embalmed remains of the explorer Richard Burton, translator of *The Arabian Nights*. The faint-hearted would do well to avoid the macabre shadows of **Barnes Cemetery**, now merged with the sandy heathland of the Common, where reports of vandalism and violence mingle with tales of headless nuns and highwaymen.

Today most people are cremated, rather than buried — it's cheaper, easier and takes far less space. Never again will the business of death consume such tracts of land. Most functioning municipal cemeteries now include a crematorium, and a garden of remembrance in which to sprinkle the ashes. The best known is the **Golders Green Crematorium** in Hoop Lane, consisting of a trim garden of flowering trees, and a simple cloister lined with memorial plaques recording many of this century's famous names: Rudyard Kipling, Sigmund Freud, Neville Chamberlain, Hugh Gaitskell and Ernest Bevin, Marie Stopes, Anna Pavlova, Kathleen Ferrier and Ralph Vaughan Williams — just a few of the thousands incinerated here, reduced in seconds from flesh and bone to dry grains of carbon.

London's burial grounds are a multifarious treasure — the neat City churchyard, the spacious public cemetery, the lonely wilderness of Nunhead, the tranquillity of the crematorium garden. How curious to know that these contain the bones of nearly everyone who has ever lived in London, the rich, the poor, the famous and the anonymous.

As you wander and explore these open spaces, a faint inscription from Bunhill Fields puts us in our time and place:

Behold thyself by me,
Such one was I, as thou;
And thou in Time shall be
Even dust, as I am now.

BIBLIOGRAPHY

Blunt, W. *In for a Penny*, London, Hamish Hamilton, 1978.

Braybrooke, N. *London Green*, London, Gollancz, 1959.

Carrington, R. *Alexandra Park and Palace, a history*, London, Greater London Council, 1975.

Davies, H. *A Walk Round London's Parks*, London, Hamish Hamilton, 1983.

Dickens, C. *Nicholas Nickleby*, London, 1839.

Edlin, H.L. *The Public Park*, London, Routledge & Kegan Paul, 1971.

Evelyn, The Hon. C. *London Parks and Gardens*, London, Archibald Constable, 1907.

Forshaw A. and Bergström, T. *Smithfield, Past and Present*, London, Heinemann, 1980.

Hackman, H. *London Churchyards*, London, Collins, 1981.

Hibbert, H. *London, the Biography of a City*, London, Longmans, 1969.

Housman, A.E. *A Shropshire Lad*, New York, Holt, Rinehart and Winston, 1939.

Jenkins, S. *The Companion Guide to Outer London*, London, Collins, 1981.

Larwood, J. *The Story of the London Parks*, London, 1881.

Mellor, H. *London's Cemeteries*, London, Avebury, 1981.

Poulsen, C. *Victoria Park*, London, Journeyman Press, 1976.

Rasmussen, S.E. *London, the Unique City*, Harmondsworth, Penguin, 1960.

Saunders, A. *Regent's Park*, Newton Abbot, David and Charles, 1969.

Sexby, J.J. *Municipal Parks, Gardens and Open Spaces of London*, London, Elliot Stock, 1895.

Stevenson, B. *Middlesex*, London, Batsford, 1972.

Trevelyan, G.M. *English Social History*, London, Longmans, 1942.

White, J.T. *Country London*, Routledge and Kegan Paul, 1984.

Williams, G. *London Walks*, London, Constable, 1981.

Wittich, J. *Discovering London's Parks and Squares*, Aylesbury, Shire Publications, 1981.

Wroth, W. *The London Pleasure Gardens of the Eighteenth Century*, London, Macmillan, 1896.

GAZETTEER

THE CITY

Name & Address	Map Ref.	Public Transport	Size (acres)	Opening Hours	Remarks	Page Ref.
All Hallows By-the-Tower, Byward Street, EC3	27/Q	Tower Hill	$1/4$	Daylight		153
Amen Court, Warwick Lane, EC4	25/P	St Paul's	$1/4$	Always		116
Benjamin Street Gardens, Britton Street, EC1	25/P	Farringdon	$1/2$	Daylight		158
Bunhill Fields, City Road, EC1	26/O	Old Street	4	Daylight		150, 158
Charterhouse Square, EC1	25/P	Barbican	$1/2$	Private Keyholders		127, 150
Clerkenwell Green, EC1	25/O	Farringdon	$1/4$	Always		32
Finsbury Circus, EC2	26/P	Moorgate	1	Daylight	Bowling Green	138
Finsbury Square, EC2	26/P	Moorgate	2	Always	Open-air café	124
Gough Square, EC4	25/P	Chancery Lane	$1/4$	Always		127
Guildhall Yard, Gresham Street, EC2	26/P	St Paul's	$1/2$	Always		116
Myddelton Square, EC1	25/O	Angel	1	Daylight		135
Northampton Buildings, Skinner Street, EC1	25/O	Farringdon	2	Daylight	Newly opened	95
Northampton Square, EC1	25/O	Angel	$1/2$	Daylight		135
Paternoster Square, EC4	25/P	St Paul's	$1/2$	Always		138, 153
Postman's Park, King Edward Street, EC1	26/P	St Paul's	$1/4$	Daylight		154
St Alphage Garden, London Wall, EC2	26/P	Moorgate	$1/4$	Always		154
St Andrew's Churchyard, Holborn Circus, EC4	25/P	Farringdon	$1/4$	Always		157
St Anne and St Agnes Churchyard, Gresham Street EC2	26/P	St Paul's	$1/4$	Always		154
St Anne, Blackfriars Churchyard, Off Blackfriars Lane, EC4	25/P	Blackfriars	$1/4$	Daylight		154
St Bartholomew-the-Great Churchyard, West Smithfield, EC1	25/P	Barbican	$1/4$	Daylight		154
St Botolph Churchyard, Bishopsgate, EC2	27/P	Liverpool Street	$1/4$	Always		154
St Bride's Churchyard, Off Fleet Street, EC4	25/P	Blackfriars	$1/4$	Daylight		154
St Dunstan-in-the-East Churchyard, Great Tower Street, EC3	27/Q	Monument	$1/4$	Daylight		154
St Ethelburga Churchyard, Bishopsgate, EC2	27/P	Liverpool Street	$1/4$	Daylight	Access through church	157
St Giles' Cripplegate Churchyard, Barbican off Wood Street, EC2	26/P	Moorgate	$1/2$	Always		157
St Helen Bishopsgate Churchyard, Great St Helens, EC3	27/P	Liverpool Street	$1/4$	Always		154
St James's Clerkenwell Churchyard, Clerkenwell Close, EC1	25/O	Farringdon	1	Daylight		161
St John's Square, EC1	25/O	Farringdon	$1/2$	Always		127

Name & Address	Map Ref.	Public Transport	Size (acres)	Opening Hours	Remarks	Page Ref.
St Katherine Cree Churchyard, Leadenhall Street, EC3	27/P	⊖ Aldgate	1/4	Daylight	Access through church	157
St Luke's Churchyard, Old Street, EC1	26/O	⊖ Old Street	1/2	Daylight	Part disused	161
St Mary Abchurch Churchyard, Abchurch Lane, EC4	26/Q	⊖ Cannon Street	1/4	Always		157
St Mary Aldermanbury Churchyard, Love Lane, EC2	26/P	⊖ St Paul's	1/2	Always		154
St Mary-le-Bow Churchyard, Cheapside, EC2	26/P	⊖ Mansion House	1/4	Always		157
St Olave Churchyard, Seething Lane, EC3	27/Q	⊖ Tower Hill	1/4	Daylight		154
St Paul's Cathedral Churchyard, Paternoster Row, EC4	26/P	⊖ St Paul's	1/2	Daylight		153
St Peter Cornhill Churchyard, Cornhill, EC3	26/P	⊖ Bank	1/4	Daylight	Access through church	154
St Stephen Walbrook Churchyard, Walbrook, EC4	26/P	⊖ Bank	1/4	Daylight		157
Spa Fields, Rosoman Street, EC1	25/O	⊖ Farringdon	2	Daylight		158
The Temple, Off Fleet Street, EC4	25/Q	⊖ Temple	1	Daylight	Part private	120
Trinity Square Gardens, Tower Hill, EC3	27/Q	⊖ Tower Hill	1/2	Daylight		154
Wesley's Chapel Graveyard, Tabernacle Street, EC1	26/O	⊖ Old Street	1/4	Daylight		158

THE WEST END

Name & Address	Map Ref.	Public Transport	Size (acres)	Opening Hours	Remarks	Page Ref.
Aspley House, Hyde Park Corner, W1	22/R	⊖ Hyde Park Corner	1/2	10am-6pm	Charge for admission	98
Argyle Square, WC1	24/O	⊖ King's Cross	1	Daylight		127
Bedford Square, WC1	23/P	⊖ Goodge Street	2	Private Keyholders		127
Belgrave Square, SW1	22/R	⊖ Hyde Park Corner	3	Private keyholders		128
Berkeley Square, W1	22/Q	⊖ Green Park	2	Daylight		124
Bloomsbury Square, WC1	24/P	⊖ Holborn	1	Daylight		120
Brunwick Square, WC1	24/O	⊖ Russell Square	1	Daylight		127
Bryanston Square, W1	21/P	⊖ Marble Arch	1	Private keyholders		124
Buckingham Palace Gardens, The Mall, SW1	22/R	⊖ Green Park	40	Private. By invitation only		66
Cadogan Square and Gardens, SW1	21/R	⊖ Sloane Square	2	Private keyholders		128

Cavendish Square, W1	22/P	⊖	Oxford Circus	1	Daylight		124
Chester Square, SW1	22/R	⊖	Victoria	¹/₂	Private keyholders		128
Coram's Fields, Guildford Street, WC1	24/O	⊖	Russell Square	8	9am - dusk	Children and accompanying adults	127
Covent Garden Piazza, WC2	24/Q	⊖	Covent Garden	2	Always		116
Drury Lane Burial Ground, Drury Lane, WC2	24/P	⊖	Covent Garden	¹/₄	Daylight		158
Eaton Square, SW1	22/R	⊖	Sloane Square	1	Private keyholders		128
Ebury Square, SW1	22/S	⊖	Sloane Square	¹/₄	Always		128
Eccleston Square, SW1	22/S	⊖	Victoria	¹/₂	Private keyholders		128
Embankment Gardens, Victoria Embankment, WC2	24/Q	⊖	Embankment	2	Daylight		42,81
Fitzroy Square, W1	23/O	⊖	Warren Street	¹/₂	Private keyholders		128
Golden Square, W1	23/Q	⊖	Piccadilly Circus	¹/₂	Daylight		123
Gordon Square, WC1	23/O	⊖	Euston Square	1	Private. Often open lunchtime		127
Granville Square, WC1	24/O	⊖	King's Cross	¹/₂	Daylight		135
Gray's Inn Fields and Square, Off High Holborn, WC1	24/P	⊖	Chancery Lane	2	Private but open 8.15am - 5.00pm weekdays		120
Green Park, Piccadilly and Constitution Hill	22/R	⊖	Green Park	53	Always		48
Grosvenor Square, W1	22/Q	⊖	Bond Street	4	Daylight		124
Hanover Square, W1	22/P	⊖	Oxford Circus	¹/₂	Daylight		124
Leicester Square, WC2	23/Q	⊖	Leicester Square	1	Always		119
Lincoln's Inn Fields, WC2	24/P	⊖	Holborn	7	Always	Open-air café	119
Lloyd Square, WC1	25/O	⊖	Angel	¹/₄	Private keyholders		135
Lowndes Square, SW1	21/R	⊖	Knightsbridge	¹/₂	Private keyholders		128
Manchester Square, W1	22/P	⊖	Bond Street	¹/₂	Private keyholders		124
Mecklenburgh Square, WC1	24/O	⊖	Russell Square	1	Private keyholders		127
Millbank Gardens, John Islip Street, SW1	23/S	⊖	Pimlico	¹/₂	Daylight	Behind Tate Gallery	128
Montagu Square, W1	21/P	⊖	Marble Arch	1	Private keyholders		124
New Square, Lincoln's Inn, WC2	24/P	⊖	Chancery Lane	¹/₄	Open during working days		120
Old Square, Lincoln's Inn, WC2	24/P	⊖	Chancery Lane	¹/₄	Open during working days		120
Parliament Square, SW1	24/R	⊖	Westminster	1	Always		138
Piccadilly Circus, W1	23/Q	⊖	Piccadilly Circus	¹/₄	Always		138
Pimlico Gardens, Grosvenor Road SW1	23/T	⊖	Pimlico	¹/₂	Always		128

Place	Grid	⊖ Station	Size	Access	Notes	Page
Portman Square, W1	22/P	⊖ Marble Arch	1	Private keyholders		124
Queen Square, WC1	24/P	⊖ Russell Square	½	Daylight		127
Red Lion Square, WC1	24/P	⊖ Holborn	½	Always		123
Russell Square, WC1	24/P	⊖ Russell Square	4	Daylight	Open-air café	127
St Andrew's Graveyard, Gray's Inn Road, WC1	24/O	⊖ Russell Square	1	Daylight		158
St Anne Soho Churchyard, Wardour Street, W1	23/P	⊖ Piccadilly Circus	¼	Daylight		161
St George's Bloomsbury Gardens, Sidmouth Street, WC1	24/O	⊖ Russell Square	1	Daylight		158
St George's Hanover Square Churchyard, South Audley Street W1	22/Q	⊖ Bond Street	¼	Daylight		158
St George's Square, SW1	23/S	⊖ Pimlico	½	Daylight		128
St Giles-in-the-Fields Churchyard, St Giles High Street, WC2	23/P	⊖ Tottenham Court Road	¼	Daylight		161
St James's Churchyard, Piccadilly, SW1	23/Q	⊖ Piccadilly Circus	¼	Daylight		161
St James's Park, The Mall, Birdcage Walk, Horse Guards Parade SW1	23/R	⊖ St James's Park	93	Always		44
St James's Square, SW1	23/Q	⊖ Piccadilly Circus	1	Private keyholders (Libyans permitting)		123
St Marylebone Churchyard, Marylebone High Street, W1	22/P	⊖ Baker Street	½	Daylight		157
St Marylebone Graveyard, Paddington Street, W1	22/P	⊖ Baker Street	1	Daylight		157
St Paul's Covent Garden Churchyard, Bedford Street, WC2	24/Q	⊖ Covent Garden	½	Daylight		161
Savoy Chapel Graveyard, Off the Strand, WC2	24/Q	⊖ Aldwych	¼	Daylight		161
Sloane Square, SW1	21/S	⊖ Sloane Square	¼	Always		128
Smith Square, SW1	24/R	⊖ Westminster	¼	Always	Filled by church	128
Soho Square, W1	23/P	⊖ Tottenham Court Road	½	Daylight		123
Staple Inn Garden, Holborn WC1	25/P	⊖ Chancery Lane	¼	Daylight		120
Tavistock Square, WC1	23/O	⊖ Russell Square	1	Daylight		127
Trafalgar Square, WC2	24/Q	⊖ Charing Cross	2	Always		138
Victoria Tower Gardens, Millbank SW1	24/R	⊖ Westminster	2	Daylight		81
Vincent Square, SW1	23/S	⊖ Pimlico	6	Private School playing-fields		128
Warwick Square, SW1	23/S	⊖ Victoria	½	Private keyholders		128
Westminster Abbey Gardens, Broad Sanctuary, SW1	24/R	⊖ Westminster	½	Daylight		138
Westminster Hospital Gardens, Horseferry Road, SW1	24/S	⊖ Pimlico	½	Daylight		128
Whitfield Gardens, Tottenham Court Road, W1	23/P	⊖ Goodge Street	¼	Always		158
Wilmington Square, WC1	24/O	⊖ Angel	½	Daylight		135

NORTH LONDON

Name & Address	Map Ref.	Public Transport	Size (acres)	Opening Hours	Remarks	Page Ref.
Abney Park Cemetery, Stoke Newington High Street, N16	27/K	≷ Stoke Newington	35	Daylight		166
Alexandra Palace Park, Muswell Hill, N22	23/G	⊖ Wood Green ≷ Wood Green	190	Daylight	Palace closed for repair	79
Arundel Square, N7	25/M	⊖ Highbury and Islington	1	Daylight		135
Avenue House Park, East End Road, N3	19/G	⊖ Finchley Central	15	Daylight		89
Barnard Park, Copenhagen Street, N1	25/N	⊖ King's Cross	6	Daylight		95
Barnsbury Square, N1	25/M	⊖ Highbury and Islington	1	Daylight		135
Broomfield House and Park, Powys Lane, N13	24/E	⊖ Arnos Grove ≷ Palmers Green	54	Daylight	Free Museum	109
Bruce Castle Park, Lordship Lane, N17	27/G	≷ Bruce Grove	20	Daylight		109
Caledonian Park, Market Road, N7	24/M	⊖ Caledonian Road	20	Daylight		95
Canonbury Square, N1	25/M	⊖ Highbury and Islington	1/2	Daylight		135
Cherry Tree Wood, Great North Road, N2	21/H	⊖ East Finchley	17	Daylight		89
Claremont Square, N1	25/N	⊖ Angel	1	No access	Reservoir	135
Clissold Park, Green Lanes/Stoke Newington Church Street, N16	26/K	⊖ Finsbury Park ≷ Stoke Newington	55	Daylight	Children's Zoo	79
Cloudesley Square, N1	25/N	⊖ Angel	1/4		Church only	135
De Beauvoir Square, N1	27/M	≷ Dalston Junction	2	Daylight		138
Downshills Park, West Green Road, N17	26/H	⊖ Turnpike Lane	40	Daylight		89
Elthorne Park, Hornsey Rise, N19	23/J	⊖ Archway	6	Daylight	Newly opened	95
Finsbury Park, Seven Sisters Road/Endymion Road, N4	25/J	⊖ Finsbury Park	115	Daylight		75
Finsbury Park Railway Line, Oxford Road, N4; Crouch End Hill, N4; Northwood Road, N6; Shepherds Hill, N6	22/J-25/J	⊖ Finsbury Park ⊖ Highgate	15	Always		96
Forty Hall, Forty Hill, Enfield	27/A	≷ Turkey Street ≷ Enfield Town Bus 135, 231	262	Daylight	House Free	112
Gibson Square, N1	25/N	⊖ Angel	1	Daylight		135

Great Northern Cemetery, Brunswick Park Road, N11	22/D	⊖ Arnos Grove	60	Daylight		169
Hadley Green and Wood, Hadley Highstone, Barnet	18/A	⊖ High Barnet	33	Always		32
Highbury Fields, Highbury Place, N5	25/L	⊖ Highbury and Islington	29	Always		89
Highgate Cemetery East and West, Swains Lane, N6	22/K	⊖ Archway	42	East daylight West by appointment		163
Highgate Wood, Muswell Hill Road, N6	22/I	⊖ Highgate	70	Daylight		34
Islington Green, Upper Street, N1	25/N	⊖ Angel	1/2	Daylight		32
Kingsbury Road Cemetery, N1	27/M	⇌ Dalston Junction	1/4	Daylight		166
Lonsdale Square, N1	25/N	⊖ Highbury and Islington	1/2	Daylight		135
Lordship Recreation Ground, Lordship Lane, N17	26/G	⊖ Turnpike Lane ⇌ Bruce Grove	120	Daylight		89
Milner Square, N1	25/M	⊖ Highbury and Islington	1/4	Daylight		135
New River Walk, St Paul's Road/Canonbury Road/Essex Road, N1	26/M	⊖ Highbury and Islington ⇌ Essex Road	4	Daylight		96
Priory Park, Middle Lane, N8	23/H	⇌ Hornsey	10	Daylight		79
Pymmes Park, Silver Street/Victoria Road, N18	27/E	⇌ Silver Street	50	Daylight		109
Queen's Wood, Wood Lane, N10	22/I	⊖ Highgate	30	Always		34
Rosemary Gardens, Southgate Road, N1	26/N	⇌ Essex Road	7	Daylight		95
St James's Pentonville Churchyard, Off Pentonville, Road N1	24/N	⊖ King's Cross	1	Daylight		161
St Mary Islington Churchyard, Upper Street, N1	25/N	⊖ Highbury and Islington	1	Daylight		161
St Marylebone Cemetery, East End Road, N3	19/H	⊖ Finchley Central	40	Daylight		169
St Mary Magdelene Churchyard, Holloway Road/Liverpool Road, N7	25/M	⊖ Highbury and Islington	4	Daylight		161
St Pancras and Islington Cemetery, North Finchley High Road, N12	21/G	⊖ East Finchley Bus 104, 263	182	Daylight		169
Shoreditch Park, New North Road/Pitfield Street, N1	26/N	⊖ Old Street Bus 76, 141, 271	25	Daylight	Not fully completed	95
Stoke Newington Common, Stamford Hill, N16	27/K	⇌ Stoke Newington	5	Always		32
Theobald's Park, Off Flamstead End Relief Road, Hertfordshire	27/A	⇌ Theobalds Grove	80	Daylight		112
Thornhill Square, N1	24/M	⊖ Caledonian Road	2	Daylight		135

Name & Address	Map Ref.	Public Transport	Size (acres)	Opening Hours	Remarks	Page Ref.
Tottenham Cemetery, Church Lane, N17	27/F	⇌White Hart Lane	50	Daylight		169
Trent Park, Cockfosters/Bramley Road, Enfield	23/A	⊖Cockfosters ⊖Oakwood	410	Daylight	Horse riding	34
Waterlow Park, Highgate High Street, N6; N19	22/J	⊖Archway	27	Daylight		109
Whitewebb's Park, Whitewebb's Lane, Enfield	27/A	⇌Turkey Street Bus 135, 231	230	Daylight		112
Whittington Park, Holloway Road, N19	23/K	⊖Archway	15	Always	New	95
Wray Crescent Open Space, Tollington Park, N4	24/K	⊖Finsbury Park	5	Daylight	Uncompleted	95

NORTH WEST LONDON

Name & Address	Map Ref.	Public Transport	Size (acres)	Opening Hours	Remarks	Page Ref.
Barham Park, Harrow Road, Wembley	11/L	⊖Sudbury Town	25	Daylight		90
Barn Hill Park, Fryent Way, NW9	13/J	⊖Kingsbury	250	Daylight		90
Bentley Priory, Common Road, Stanmore	9/D	Bus 142, 258	163	Daylight		90
Big Wood, Northway, NW11	19/I	⊖Golders Green Bus 102, 244	15	Always		34
Camden Square, NW1	23/M	⊖Kentish Town ⇌Camden Road	2	Daylight		135
Chalcot Square, NW1	22/M	⊖Chalk Farm	½	Daylight		135
Dorset Square, NW1	21/O	⊖Baker Street	½	Private keyholders		124
Euston Square, NW1	23/O	⊖Euston	1	Always		127
Fenton House, Off Heath Street, NW3	20/L	⊖Hampstead	¼	Feb-Nov 11-5 Sat 2-5 Sun	Charge for house	109
Gladstone Park, Dollis Hill Lane/Kendal Road, NW2	16/L	⊖Dollis Hill	100	Always		89
Golders Green Crematorium, Hoop Lane, NW11	19/J	⊖Golders Green	12	Daylight		170
Golders Hill Park, West Heath Avenue, NW11	19/K	⊖Golders Green	38	Daylight	Children's Zoo	21,89
Hampstead Cemetery, Fortune Green Road, NW6	18/L	⊖West Hampstead	37	Daylight		169
Hampstead Churchyard, Church Row, NW3	20/L	⊖Hampstead	1	Daylight		161
Hampstead Heath, Highgate Road/East Heath Road/Hampstead Lane/West Heath Road, NW3 and NW11	21/K	⊖Hampstead ⇌Hampstead Heath	825	Always	Includes Kenwood, Parliament Hill etc.	17

Harrington Square, NW1	23/N	✆ Mornington Crescent	1/4	Daylight		135
Harrow Weald Common, Old Redding, Harrow	8/D	✆ Hatch End	50	Always		31
Headstone Manor Park, Parkside Way, Harrow	7/H	✆ Headstone Lane	60	Daylight		90
Hendon Park, Queen's Road, NW4	17/I	✆ Hendon Central	29	Daylight		89
Horsenden Hill, Horsenden Lane North, Greenford	9/M	✆ Perivale	245	Always		39
Kenwood House, Hampstead Lane, NW3	21/J	Bus 210		Daylight. Part of Hampstead Heath. House free. Lakeside concerts		21, 106
Northwick Park, Watford Road/Norval Road, Wembley	10/J	✆ South Kenton	66	Daylight		90
Oakley Square, NW1	23/N	✆ Mornington Crescent	1/2	Daylight		135
Paddington Cemetery, Willesden Lane, NW7	18/N	✆ Queen's Park	25	Daylight		169
Pinner Park, George V Avenue Pinner,	7/G	✆ Headstone Lane	250	Daylight		90
Primrose Hill, Albert Road, NW8; Primrose Hill Road, NW3	21/N	✆ Chalk Farm	70	Always		58
Queen's Park, Harvist Road, NW6	18/N	✆ Queens Park	30	Daylight		80
Regent's Park, Outer Circle, NW1	22/O	✆ Baker Street ✆ Regents Park ✆ St John's Wood	470	Daylight	Includes Zoo and Queen Mary Gardens	56
Roundwood Park, Longstone Avenue, NW10	16/M	⇌ Willesden Junction	35	Daylight		90
St John's Wood Churchyard, St John's Wood High Street, NW8	21/O	✆ St John's Wood	5	Daylight		157
St Martin Pratt Street Churchyard, Camden Street, NW1	23/N	✆ Camden Town	2	Daylight		161
St Mary's R.C. Cemetery, Scrubs Lane, NW10	15/O	⇌ Willesden Junction	30	Daylight		169
St Pancras Churchyard, Pancras Road, NW1	23/N	✆ King's Cross	6	Daylight		157
Stanmore Common, The Common, Stanmore	8/D	Bus 142, 708, 719	120	Always		31
Sunnyhill Park, Off Church End, NW4	16/G	✆ Hendon Central	54	Daylight		89
Watling Park, Abbots Road, Edgware	14/F	✆ Burnt Oak	21	Daylight		74
Welsh Harp, Cool Oak/Birchen Grove, NW9	15/J	✆ Wembley Park	390	Daylight		90
Zoological Gardens, Outer Circle, off Albert Road, NW1	22/N	✆ Camden Town	36	9am - 5.30pm summer 10am - dusk winter. Admission charge		144

WEST LONDON

Name & Address	Map Ref.	Public Transport	Size (acres)	Opening Hours	Remarks	Page Ref.
Acton Green, South Parade, W4	14/S	⊖ Chiswick Park	7	Always		31
Boston Manor Park, Boston Manor Road, Brentford	10/S	⊖ Boston Manor	35	Daylight	House private	102
Brent Lodge Park, Church Road, W7	8/Q	⇌ Hanwell	25	Daylight		93
Brook Green, W6	17/R	⊖ Hammersmith	5	Always		34
Cambridge Square, W2	21/P	⊖ Edgware Road	1/4	Private keyholders		128
Campden Hill Square, W8	18/Q	⊖ Holland Park	1	Private keyholders		133
Chiswick Churchyard, Church Street, W4	15/T	⊖ Turnham Green	1/2	Daylight		161
Chiswick Common, Chiswick Common Road, W4	14/S	⊖ Turnham Green	5	Always		31
Chiswick House, Burlington Lane, W4	14/T	⇌ Chiswick Bus 290, E3	67	Daylight	Admission charge for house	101
Cleveland Square, W2	20/P	⊖ Bayswater	1/2	Private keyholders		133
Colne Valley Regional Park, West Drayton to Rickmansworth				12 miles long		96
Colville Square, W11	18/P	⊖ Ladbroke Grove	1/4	Daylight		133
Connaught Square, W2	21/P	⊖ Marble Arch	1/2	Private keyholders		128
Cranford Park, Cranford Lane, Hayes	3/T	Bus 81, 82, 105, 111	150	Daylight		93
Duke's Meadows, Great Chertsey Road, W4	14/U	⇌ Chiswick	25	Always		42
Ealing and Old Brentford Cemetery, South Ealing Road, W5	11/S	⊖ South Ealing	18	Daylight		169
Ealing Common, Gunnersbury Avenue/Uxbridge Road, W5	12/Q	⊖ Ealing Common	50	Always		31
Edwardes Square, W8	18/R	⊖ High Street Kensington	1/2	Private keyholders		133
Elthorne Park, Boston Road, W7	9/R	⊖ Boston Manor	37	Daylight		93
Gunnersbury Park and House, Pope Lane, W3	12/S	⊖ Acton Town	190	Daylight	Free Museum	102
Hanwell Cemeteries, (Kensington and Westminster), Broadway, W7	9/Q	⇌ Hanwell	50	Daylight		169
Hanworth Park, Uxbridge Road, Feltham	5/Y	⇌ Feltham	145	Daylight		93
Hogarth House, Hogarth Lane, W4	15/T	⊖ Turnham Green Bus 290	1/4	Daylight	Admission charge for house	101
Holland House and Park, Kensington High Street/ Abbotsbury Road, W8	18/R	⊖ Holland Park	55	Daylight		106
Hounslow Heath, Staines Road/Hanworth Road, Feltham	6/W	⇌ Hounslow	200	Always		31

Hyde Park, Bayswater Road/Park Lane/Rotten Row, W2	21/Q	⊖ Marble Arch ⊖ Lancaster Gate ⊖ Hyde Park Corner	360	Always	Includes Serpentine and Speakers' Corner	48
Hyde Park Square, W2	21/Q	⊖ Lancaster Gate	½	Private keyholders		133
Kensal Green Cemetery, Harrow Road, W10	17/O	⊖ Kensal	56	Daylight		150, 162
Kensington Cemetery, Gunnersbury Lane, W4	13/S	⊖ Gunnersbury	30	Daylight		169
Kensington Gardens and Palace, Bayswater Road, W2/ Kensington Gore, W8	20/Q	⊖ Queensway ⊖ High Street Kensington	275		Admission charge for Palace	52, 101
Kensington Square, W8	19/R	⊖ High Street Kensington	½	Private keyholders		133
Ladbroke Square Gardens, Kensington Park Road, W11	18/Q	⊖ Notting Hill Gate	8	Private keyholders		133
Lammas Park, Culmington Road/Northfield Road, W13	11/R	⊖ Northfields	27		Daylight	31
Leinster Square, W2	19/P	⊖ Bayswater	½	Private keyholders		133
Norfolk Crescent, W2	21/P	⊖ Edgware Road	¼	Private keyholders		128
Norland Square, W11	18/Q	⊖ Holland Park	½	Private keyholders		133
Osterley Park and House, Thornbury Road, Isleworth	8/S	⊖ Osterley	140 plus farm	Daylight	Admission charge for house	102
Oxford Square, W2	21/P	⊖ Edgware Road	¼	Private keyholders		128
Paddington Recreation Ground, Randolph Avenue, W9	19/O	⊖ Maida Vale	27	Daylight		90
Pembridge Square, W2	19/Q	⊖ Notting Hill Gate	1	Private keyholders		133
Porchester Square, W2	19/P	⊖ Royal Oak	½	Daylight		133
Powis Square, W11	18/P	⊖ Ladbroke Grove	¼	Daylight		133
Princes Square, W2	19/Q	⊖ Bayswater	1	Private keyholders		133
Ravenscourt Park, Paddenswick Road, W6	16/R	⊖ Ravenscourt Park	35	Daylight		90
St Mary Abbots Churchyard, Kensington Church Street, W8	19/R	⊖ High Street Kensington	¼	Daylight		161
St Mary Paddington Churchyard, Paddington Green W2	20/P	⊖ Edgware Road	1	Daylight		157
Shepherd's Bush Common, Shepherd's Bush Green, W12	17/R	⊖ Shepherd's Bush	8	Always		31
Sussex Square, W2	20/Q	⊖ Lancaster Gate	¼	Private keyholders		133
Syon House and Park, Park Road/London Road, Brentford	11/U	⇌ Syon Lane	200	Daylight	Garden Centre Admision charge for house	105
Turnham Green, Chiswick High Road, W4	14/S	⊖ Chiswick Park	4	Always		32

Name & Address	Map Ref.	Public Transport	Size (acres)	Opening Hours	Remarks	Page Ref.
Walpole Park, Mattock Lane, W5	11/Q	Ealing Broadway	30	Daylight		90
Wormwood Scrubs, Scrubs Lane/Du Cane Road W12	16/P	East Acton	200	Always	Includes Old Oak Common	31

SOUTH WEST LONDON

Name & Address	Map Ref.	Public Transport	Size (acres)	Opening Hours	Remarks	Page Ref.
Albert Square, SW8	24/U	Stockwell	1	Private keyholders		135
Barnes Cemetery, Off Rocks Lane, SW13	16/U	Barnes	3	Always	Derelict	170
Barnes Common, Rocks Lane/Mill Hill Road, SW13/SW15	16/V	Barnes	70	Always		28
Barnes Green, Station Road, SW13	15/U	Barnes Bridge	5	Always		28
Battersea Park, Queenstown Road/Prince of Wales Drive/Albert Bridge Road, SW11	22/T	Battersea	200	Daylight	Children's Zoo	72
Battersea Cemetery, Bolingbroke Grove, SW11	21/W	Clapham Junction	6	Daylight		166, 170
Biggin Wood, Biggin Hill, SW16	25/AA	Norbury	19	Always		86
Bishops's Park, Fulham Palace Road/Putney Bridge Approach, SW6	18/U	Putney Bridge	37	Daylight		86
Brompton Cemetery, Fulham Road/Old Brompton Road, SW10	19/T	West Brompton	39	Daylight		163
Brompton Square, SW3	21/R	South Kensington	1/2	Private keyholders		133
Bushy Park, Hampton Court Road/Sandy Lane, Teddington	9/AB	Hampton Wick / Hampton Court	1100	Daylight		66, 98
Cannizaro Park, West Side Common, SW19	16/AA	Wimbledon	34	Daylight		28
Carlyle Square, SW3	20/S	South Kensington	1	Private keyholders		133
Chelsea Old Churchyard, Cheyne Row, SW3	21/T	Sloane Square	1/4	Daylight		161
Chelsea Physic Garden, Swan Walk, SW3	21/T	Sloane Square	1	2pm — 5pm Wednesday and Sunday	Admission charge	133
Clapham Common, Clapham Common North Side/South Side, SW4	22/W	Clapham Common	220	Always		26
Eel Brook Common, Kings Road, SW6	19/U	Fulham	14	Always		34
Garrick's Lawn and Tagg's Island, Hampton Court Road, Hampton	8/AB	Hampton	3	Daylight		42

Ham House, Off Petersham Road, Richmond	11/X	⇌ Richmond Bus 65, 71	20	Daylight	Charge for house	106
Hampton Court Park and Palace, Hampton Court Road, Hampton	10/AC	⇌ Hampton Court Bus 111, 131, 216	1000	Daylight	Charge for Palace and Maze	64,98
Holy Trinity Brompton Churchyard, Cottage Place, SW7	21/R	⊖ South Kensington	3	Always		157
Hurlingham Park, Broomhouse Lane/Napier Gardens, SW6	18/V	⊖ Putney Bridge	58	Daylight	Part private club	86
John Innes Park, Watery Lane, SW20	18/AB	⇌ Wimbledon Chase	5	Daylight		86
Kew Gardens, Kew Green/Kew Road, Richmond	12/U	⇌ Kew Gardens	300	10am - 4pm (winter) 8pm (summer)	Small admission charge	140
Kew Green, Richmond	12/T	⇌ Kew Bridge	12	Always		34
King George's Park, Brathway Road/Burr Road, SW18	19/X	⊖ Southfields	49	Daylight		86
Marble Hill House and Park, Richmond Road, Twickenham	11/X	⇌ St Margarets	66	10am - 4pm (winter) 6pm (summer) From 2pm (Sunday)	House free	105
Mitcham Common, Croydon Road/London Road, Mitcham	22/AD	⇌ Mitcham Junction	480	Always		27
Montpelier Square, SW7	21/R	⊖ Knightsbridge	1/4	Private keyholders		133
Morden Hall Park, Morden Hall Road, Merton	20/AC	⊖ Morden	125	Daylight		86
Morden Park, London Road, Morden	18/AD	⊖ Morden ⇌ Morden South	100	Daylight		86
Mortlake Roman Catholic Cemetery, South Worple Way, Mortlake	15/V	⇌ Mortlake	4	Daylight		170
Mostyn Gardens, Martin Way, SW19	19/AC	⇌ South Merton	15	Daylight		86
Natural History Museum Gardens, Cromwell Road, SW7	20/R	⊖ South Kensington	5	Daylight		90
Nonsuch Park, London Road, Ewell	17/AG	⇌ Ewell East	110	Daylight		63
Norbury Park, Norbury Avenue, SW16	24/AB	⇌ Norbury	28	Always		86
Orleans House and Gardens, Orleans Road/Riverside, Twickenham	11/X	⇌ St Margarets	7	Tuesday-Saturday 1pm-4pm Sunday 2pm-4pm		106
Parson's Green, Kings Road, SW6	19/U	⊖ Parson's Green	4	Always		34
Paultons Square, SW3	20/T	⊖ Sloane Square	1	Private keyholders		133
Princes Gardens, SW7	20/R	⊖ South Kensington	3	Daylight		133
Putney Heath, Roehampton Lane/Wildcroft Road, SW15	17/X	⊖ East Putney	50	Always		28
Putney Vale Cemetery, Kingston Road, SW15	16/Y	⇌ Putney Bus 72, 85	35	Daylight		169

Location	Map ref	Station	No.	Access	Notes	Page
Ranelagh Gardens, Chelsea Bridge Road, SW3	22/T	⊖ Sloane Square	13	Daylight		12,83
Richmond Cemetery, Grove Road, Richmond	13/W	⊖ Richmond ⇌ Richmond	37	Daylight	Adjoins new Barnes Cemetery	169
Richmond Green, Green Side, Richmond	11/V	⊖ Richmond ⇌ Richmond	11	Always		34
Richmond Park, Sheen Lane/Priory Lane/Kingston Vale/Queen's Road/ Ham Gate Avenue/Star and Garter Hill, Richmond	14/X	⇌ North Sheen ⇌ Norbiton	2500	Daylight	Includes Isobella Plantation	62
Royal Avenue, SW3	21/S	⊖ Sloane Square	1/2	Always		133
Royal Hospital Chelsea Grounds, Chelsea Embankment SW3	22/T	⊖ Sloane Square	28	Private	Venue for Chelsea Flower Show	83
South Park, Peterborough Road SW6	19/U	⊖ Parson's Green	20	Daylight		86
Streatham Common, Streatham High Road/Streatham Common South, SW16	24/AA	⇌ Streatham	66	Always	Includes The Rookery	27
Streatham Park Cemetery, Rowan Road, SW16	23/AB	⇌ Streatham Common	70	Daylight		169
The Boltons, SW10	20/S	⊖ Gloucester Road	1	Private keyholders		133
Tooting Bec and Graveney Commons, Emmanuel Road, SW12; Bedford Hill, SW16; Tooting Bec Road, SW17	23/Y	⊖ Tooting Bec ⇌ Streatham Hill	200	Always		27
Trevor Square, SW7	21/R	⊖ Knightsbridge	1/4	Daylight		133
Vauxhall Park, Fentiman Road, SW8	24/T	⊖ Vauxhall	8	Daylight		83
Wandsworth Common, Bolingbroke Road, SW11; Trinity Road, SW18	21/W	⇌ Wandsworth Common	183	Always		27
Wandsworth Park, Putney Bridge Road, SW15	18/V	⊖ East Putney ⇌ Putney	20	Daylight		86
Wimbledon Common, Wimbledon Parkside/Kingston Road, SW19	16/Z	⊖ Wimbledon	1100	Always		27
Wimbledon Park, Church Road, SW19	18/Y	⊖ Wimbledon Park	65	Daylight		86
York House Gardens, York Street/Riverside, Twickenham	10/X	⇌ Twickenham	6	Daylight		106

SOUTH EAST LONDON

Name & Address	Map Ref.	Public Transport	Size (acres)	Opening Hours	Remarks	Page Ref.
Addington Hills and Lloyd Park, Coombe Lane, Croydon	28/AG	≈ Coombe Road	244	Always		34
Archbishop's Park, Lambeth Palace Road, SE1	24/R	⊖ Lambeth North	9	Daylight		83
Avery Hill Park, Avery Hill Road, SE9	38/W	≈ New Eltham	86	Daylight	Tropical glass house	89
Blackheath, Shooters Hill/Tranquil Vale, SE3	33/U	≈ Blackheath	270	Always		16
Bostall Heath and Woods, Bostall Hill Road, SE2	40/T	≈ Abbey Wood	160	Always		34
Brockley Cemetery, Brockley Road, SE4	30/W	≈ Crofton Park	21	Daylight		170
Brockwell Park, Dulwich Road/Norwood Road, SE24	25W	≈ Herne Hill	127	Daylight		79
Bromley and Hayes Commons, Bromley Common/Croydon Road, Bromley	34/AE	≈ Hayes ≈ Bromley South	250	Always	Includes Norman Park	34
Burgess Park, Albany Road/Camberwell Road/Old Kent Road, SE5	27/T	⊖ Elephant and Castle	90	Daylight	Still under construction	93
Camberwell Green, SE5	26/U	≈ Denmark Hill	3	Daylight		32
Camberwell New Cemetery, Brenchley Gardens, SE23	29/W	≈ Crofton Park	61	Daylight		170
Camberwell Old Cemetery, Forest Hill Road, SE22	28/W	≈ Honor Oak	29	Daylight		170
Charlton Park and House, Hornfair Road, SE7	35/T	≈ Charlton	43	Daylight	House free	112
Cherry Garden Pier, Bermondsey Wall/Paradise Street, SE16	28/R	⊖ Rotherhithe	8	Always		42
Chislehurst Common, Centre Common Road, Chislehurst	38/AA	≈ Chislehurst	50	Always		31
Cleaver Square, SE11	25/S	⊖ Kennington	1/2	Always		135
Courtenay Square, SE11	25/S	⊖ Kennington	1/4	Always		135
Crystal Palace Cemetery and Beckenham Crematorium, Elmers End Road, SE20	29/AC	≈ Birkbeck	30	Daylight		169
Crystal Palace Park, Crystal Palace Park Road, SE19	28/AA	≈ Penge West ≈ Crystal Palace	105	Daylight	Lakeside Concerts	76
Cutty Sark Gardens, Greenwich Church Street, SE10	32/T	≈ Greenwich	8	Always	Admission charge for Cutty Sark and Gipsy Moth	42
Danson Park, Danson Road/Danson Lane, Welling	41/V	≈ Bexleyheath	185	Daylight		114
Deptford Park, Evelyn Street, SE8	30/S	⊖ Surrey Docks ≈ New Cross	17	Daylight		86
Dulwich Old Graveyard, Dulwich Village/Court Lane, SE21	27/W	≈ North Dulwich	1/2	Daylight		161
Dulwich Park, College Road/Court Lane, SE21	27/X	≈ West Dulwich	72	Daylight	Aviary	76

Elmstead Woods, Elmstead Lane, Chislehurst	35/Z	⇌ Elmstead Woods	61	Always		28
Eltham Common, Shooters Hill/Crookston Road/Rochester Way SE9/ SE18	36/U	⇌ Eltham Park	252	Always	Includes Castle and Jack Woods	28
Eltham Palace, Court Yard, SE9	36/X	⇌ Eltham Well Hall	15	Palace and Grounds open Thursday and Sunday only 11am - 4pm		112
Eltham Park, Glenesk Road, SE9	37/W	⇌ Eltham Park	120	Daylight		28
Forster Memorial Park, Whitefoot Lane/Thornsbeach Road, SE6	32/Y	⇌ Bellingham	43	Daylight		89
Geraldine Harmsworth Park, Lambeth Road, SE1	25/R	⊖ Lambeth	15	Daylight	Surrounds Imperial War Museum	83
Greenwich Cemetery, Well Hall Road, SE9	36/U	⇌ Eltham Well Hall	21	Daylight		170
Greenwich Park, Crooms Hill/King William Walk/Maze Hill/Charlton Way, SE10	32/T	⇌ Maze Hill ⇌ Greenwich	200	Daylight	Includes Flamsteed, Rangers and Queen's Houses	61
Hall Place, Bourne Road, Bexley	44/W	⇌ Bexley	150	Daylight	House free	114
Hillyfields, Adelaide Avenue, SE4	30/V	⇌ Ladywell	46	Always		86
Hither Green Cemetery, Verdant Lane, SE6	33/Y	⇌ Grove Park	65	Daylight		169
Horniman Gardens, London Road, SE23	29/X	⇌ Forest Hill	25	Daylight	Children's Zoo and Horniman Museum	83
Jubilee Gardens, Belvedere Road, SE1	24/Q	⊖ Waterloo ⊖ Embankment (across river)	8	Always		42,95
Kennington Park, Kennington Park Road, SE11	25/T	⊖ Oval	37	Daylight		75
Ladywell Cemetery, Ivy Road, SE4	30/V	⇌ Crofton Park	24	Daylight		170
Ladywell Fields, Ladywell Road/Malyons Road/Ravensbourne Park, SE6 & SE13	31/W	⇌ Ladywell ⇌ Catford	50	Always		86
Lesnes Abbey Park, Abbey Road/New Road/Woolwich Road, SE2	41/S	⇌ Abbey Wood	215	Always	Ruined Abbey	34
Manor House Gardens, Old Road/Taunton Road, SE12	33/W	⇌ Hither Green	14	Daylight		112
Maryon Park, Maryon Road, SE7	35/S	⇌ Woolwich Dockyard	29	Daylight		89
Maryon Wilson Park, Thorntree Road/Little Heath Hill, SE7	35/S	⇌ Charlton	32	Daylight	Children's Zoo	89
Mayow Park, Mayow Road, SE26	29/Z	⇌ Sydenham	20	Daylight		86
Merrick Square, SE1	26/R	⊖ Borough	1/2	Private keyholders		135

Myatt's Fields, Knatchbull Road, SE5	25/U	≽	Loughborough Junction			
		⊖	Stockwell	13	Daylight	83
Nelson Recreation Ground, Kipling Street, SE1	26/R	⊖	Borough	1	Daylight	161
Nelson Square, SE1	25/R	⊖	Lambeth North	1	Daylight	135
Newington Recreation Ground, Harper Road, SE1	26/R	⊖	Elephant and Castle	4	Daylight	86
Norwood (South Metropolitan) Cemetery, Norwood High Street, SE27	26/Y	≽	West Norwood	43	Daylight	162
Norwood Park, Salters Hill, SE27	26/Z	≽	Gipsy Hill	38	Daylight	86
Nunhead Cemetery, Linden Grove, SE15	29/V	≽	Nunhead	52	Daylight	166
One Tree Hill Park, Brenchley Gardens, SE23	29/W	≽	Honor Oak Park	17	Daylight	28
Oxleas Wood, Shooters Hill/Welling Way, SE9	38/V	≽	Falconwood	85	Always	28
Peckham Rye Common, Peckham Rye, SE15	28/V	≽	Nunhead			
		≽	East Dulwich	66	Always	28
Peckham Rye Park, Peckham Rye/Homestall Road, SE22	28/W	≽	Honor Oak			
		≽	Nunhead	49	Daylight	28
Pedlers Park, Vauxhall Walk, SE11	24/S	⊖	Vauxhall	1	Daylight	95
Petts Wood, Orpington Road/Hazelmere Road, Orpington	38/AC	≽	Petts Wood	170	Always	31
Plumstead Cemetery, Wickham Lane, SE2	40/T	≽	Welling	28	Daylight	170
Plumstead Common, The Slade/Plumstead Common Road, SE18	38/T	≽	Plumstead	100	Always	28
Queen's House, (see Greenwich Park, SE10)					Part of National Maritime Museum Admission charge	98
Ranger's House ,(see Greenwich Park, SE10)					Admission free	98
Ruskin Park, Denmark Hill, SE5	26/V	≽	Denmark Hill	36	Daylight	83
St Alphege Churchyard, St Alphege Passage, SE10	32/T	≽	Greenwich	5	Daylight	158
St Paul's Churchyard, Deptford High Street, SE8	31/T	≽	Deptford	3	Daylight	158
Shepherdleas Wood, Rochester Way, SE9	38/V	≽	Falconwood	53	Always	28
Southwark Park, Jamaica Road/Hawkstone Road SE16	28/R	⊖	Surrey Docks	63	Daylight	75
Sutcliffe Park, Eltham Road, SE9	35/W	≽	Kidbrooke	50	Daylight	89
Tabard Gardens, Tabard Street, SE1	26/R	⊖	Borough	6	Daylight	86
Telegraph Hill Park, Drakefell Road/Pepys Road, SE14	29/U	≽	Nunhead	9	Daylight	86
Trinity Church Square, SE1	26/R	⊖	Borough	1/4	Private keyholders	135
West Square, SE11	25/R	⊖	Elephant and Castle	1/2	Daylight	135

Name & Address	Map Ref.	Public Transport	Size (acres)	Opening Hours	Remarks	Page Ref.
William Curtis Park, Off Vine Lane, Tooley Street SE1	27/Q	⊖ London Bridge	3	Daylight	Ecology Park; guides on request	96
Woolwich Old Cemetery, Cemetery Lane, SE7	36/T	⇌ Woolwich Dockyard	15	Daylight		170
Woolwich New Cemetery, Kings Highway, SE18	39/T	⇌ Welling	32	Daylight		170
Woolwich Common, Academy Road, SE18	36/T	⇌ Woolwich Dockyard	80	Always		28

EAST LONDON

Name & Address	Map Ref.	Public Transport	Size (acres)	Opening Hours	Remarks	Page Ref.
Albert Gardens, Commercial Road, E1	29/P	⊖ Shadwell	1/2	Daylight		138
Albion Square, E8	27/M	⇌ Dalston Junction	1/2	Daylight		138
Arbour Square, E1	29/P	⊖ Shadwell	1/2	Daylight		138
Beaumont Square, E1	29/P	⊖ Stepney Green	1/2	Daylight		135
Bedfords Park, Lower Bedfords Road, Romford	46/E	⇌ Gidea Park Bus 175, 247B, 712	214	Daylight		93
Bethnal Green, Cambridge Heath Road, E2	29/O	⊖ Bethnal Green	9	Always		32
Brady Street Cemetery, Brady Street, E1	28/O	⊖ Whitechapel	5	Daylight		166
Central Park, Rainham Road North, Dagenham	43/K	⇌ Dagenham East	135	Daylight		93
Chingford Mount Cemetery, Old Church Road, E4	31/D	⇌ Highams Park	65	Daylight		169
Christchurch Spitalfields Churchyard, Commercial Street, E1	27/P	⊖ Liverpool Street	1/2	Daylight		161
City of London Cemetery, Aldersbrook Road, E12	36/K	⇌ Manor Park	176	Daylight		166
Clapton Common, Clapton Common, E5	28/J	⇌ Stamford Hill	10	Always		31
Dagnam Park, Settle Road, Romford	48/D	⇌ Harold Wood	146	Daylight		93
Epping Forest, Rangers Road, E4; Whipps Cross Road, E11; Woodford New Road, E17; Epping New Road, Epping	34/B	⊖ Snaresbrook ⊖ Loughton ⊖ Epping ⇌ Chingford	6000	Always		21
Ford Square, E1	28/P	⊖ Whitechapel	1/2	Daylight		138
Hackney Downs, Downs Road, E5	28/L	⇌ Hackney Downs	42	Always		32

Place	Map Ref	Transport	Size	Opening	Notes	Page
Hackney Marshes, Homerton Road, E9; Millfields Road, E5	30/K	≷ Lea Bridge / ≷ Hackney Wick / ⊖ Leyton	337	Always	Includes Leyton and Walthamstow Marshes	32
Haggerston Park, Queensbridge Road, E2	28/N	≷ Cambridge Heath	8	Daylight	Not fully completed	95
Hainault Forest, Romford Road, Chigwell	41/D	⊖ Grange Hill	1000	Daylight	Contains public golf course and horse riding	25
Havering Country Park, Wellingtonia Avenue, Havering	44/D	Bus 252, 294, 165, 175,	167	Daylight		93
Havering Green, Orange Tree Hill, Havering	45/D	Bus 175, 247B, 712	2	Always		32
Island Gardens, Saunders Ness Road, E14	32/S	≷ Greenwich Bus 56, 277	3	Daylight	Foot tunnel from Greenwich	42
King Edward V11 Memorial Park, The Highway, E1	29/Q	⊖ Shadwell	8	Daylight		83
Langtons, Hall Road, Upminster	48/K	⊖ Upminster	50	Daylight	House free	112
Lea Valley Park, From Hackney Wick to Waltham Abbey and beyond				20 miles long. Includes numerous playing fields reservoirs and parks		32,96
Lloyd Park and House, Forest Road, E17	31/G	⊖ Walthamstow Central	36	Daylight	House free	112
London Fields, Landsdowne Drive/Richmond Road, E8	28/M	≷ Cambridge Heath	26	Always		32
Lyle Park, Bradfield Road, E16	34/R	≷ Silvertown	9	Daylight		42
Manor Park Cemetery, Ridley Road, E7	35/L	≷ Manor Park	50	Daylight		169
Mayersbrook Park, Lodge Avenue/Longbridge Road, Dagenham	40/M	⊖ Upney	116	Daylight		93
Meath Gardens, Smart Street/Walter Street, E2	29/O	⊖ Bethnal Green	12	Daylight		72
Mile End Park, Grove Road/Burdett Road, E3	30/O	⊖ Mile End	50	Daylight	Under construction	95
Millfields, Lea Bridge Road, E5	29/K	≷ Clapton	57	Always		32
Parsloes Park, Ivyhouse Road/Gale Street, Dagenham	41/L	⊖ Becontree	148	Daylight		93
Rainham Hall, Broadway, Rainham	46/O	≷ Rainham	½	Wednesday and Saturday 2-6pm by written application only		112
Royal Victoria Gardens, Albert Road, E16	37/R	≷ North Woolwich	10	Daylight		42
St Anne Limehouse Churchyard, Commercial Road, E14	30/P	≷ Stepney East	3	Daylight		158
St Dunstan Churchyard, Stepney High Street, E1	29/P	≷ Stepney East	4	Daylight		95
St George-in-the-East Churchyard, The Highway, E1	28/Q	⊖ Shadwell	7	Daylight		158

Location	Map Ref		Station	Area	Open	Notes	Page
St Katharine's Dock, Off East Smithfield, E1	27/Q	⊖	Tower Hill	15	Always	Yacht marina and museum	42
Sephardi Cemetery, Mile End Road, E1	28/P	⊖	Whitechapel	½	Daylight		166
Sidney Square, E1	29/P	⊖	Whitechapel	¼	Daylight		138
Springfield Park, Spring Hill/Springfield, E5	28/J	⇌	Clapton	40	Daylight		93
Stepney Green, Stepney Green, E1	29/P	⊖	Stepney Green	12	Always		95
Tower Hamlets Cemetery, Hamlets Way, E3	30/O	⊖	Mile End	33	Daylight		166
Trafalgar Gardens, White Horse Lane, E1	29/P	⊖	Stepney Green	1	Daylight		135
Tredegar Square, E3	30/N	⊖	Mile End	2	Daylight		135
Valentines Park, Cranbrook Road, Ilford	37/J	⊖	Gants Hill	140	Daylight		93
Victoria Park, Bishops Way/Grove Road/Victoria Park Road, E9	30/M	⇌	Cambridge Heath	220	Daylight	Children's Zoo	68
Wanstead Flats, Centre Road, E7; Aldersbrook Road, E11 & E12	34/K	⇌	Wanstead Park	300	Always		25
Wanstead Park, Warren Road, E11; Northumberland Avenue, E12	35/J	⊖	Redbridge	175	Daylight		25
Wapping Recreation Ground, Green Bank, E1	28/Q	⊖	Wapping	2	Daylight		83
Weavers Fields, Dunbridge Street/Vallance Road, E2	28/O	⊖	Bethnal Green	16	Always	Not fully completed	95
Well Street Common, Gascoyne Road/Victoria Park Road, E9	29/M	⇌	Hackney Central	20	Always		32
West Ham Cemetery, Cemetery Road, E7	33/L	⇌	Forest Gate	39	Daylight		169
West Ham Park, Upton Lane, E7; Portway, E15	34/M	⊖	Plaistow	77	Daylight		80
Woodford Green, High Road, Woodford	34/E	⊖	Woodford	14	Always		32
Woodgrange Cemetery, Romford Road, E7	35/L	⇌	Woodgrange Park	21	Daylight		169
York Square, E14	30/P	⇌	Stepney East	½	Daylight		138

Index

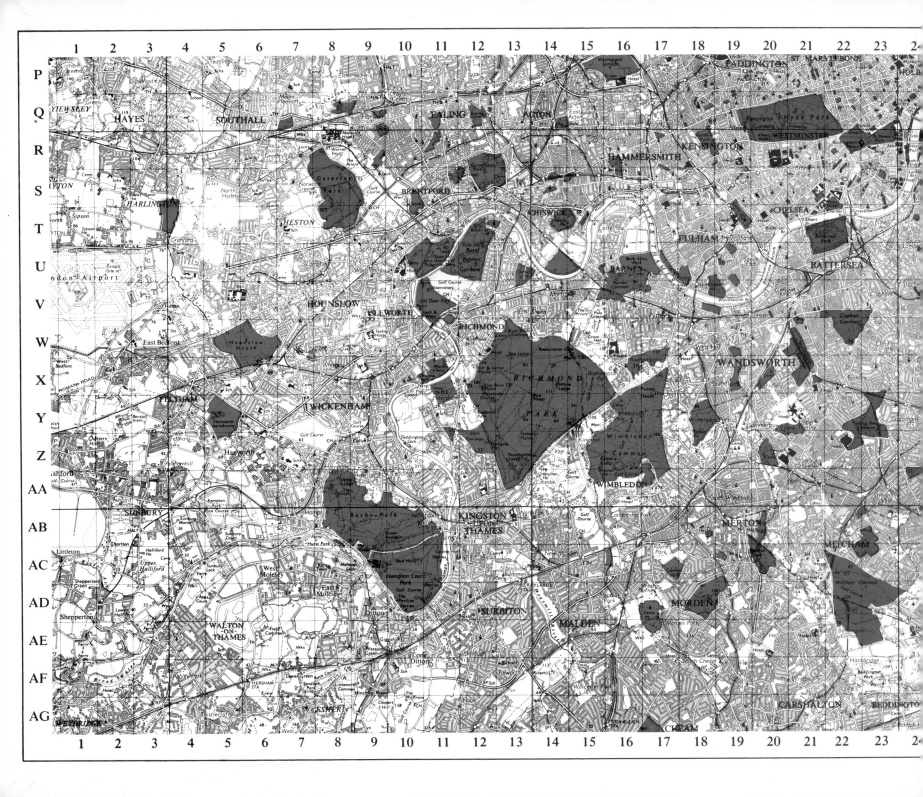